DISABILITY AND AGEING
Towards a Critical Perspective

Ann Leahy

First published in Great Britain in 2021 by

Policy Press, an imprint of
Bristol University Press
University of Bristol
1–9 Old Park Hill
Bristol
BS2 8BB
UK
t: +44 (0)117 954 5940
e: bup-info@bristol.ac.uk

Details of international sales and distribution partners are available at
policy.bristoluniversitypress.co.uk

British Library Cataloguing in Publication Data
A catalogue record for this book is available from the British Library

ISBN 978-1-4473-5715-5 hardcover
ISBN 978-1-4473-5717-9 ePub
ISBN 978-1-4473-5718-6 ePdf

Cover design: David Worth
Image credit: iStock/Svetlanais
Bristol University Press and Policy Press use environmentally responsible
print partners.
Printed and bound in Great Britain by CPI Group (UK) Ltd,
Croydon, CR0 4YY

Contents

Key terms   iv
Acknowledgements   v
Series editors' preface   vi

1   Introduction   1

PART I   The context for disablement in older age
2   Defining disability   17
3   Literature: ageing, disability and lifecourse   29
4   Public policies on ageing and disability   53

PART II   Empirical findings
5   Disabling bodies   75
6   Disabling or enabling contexts   97
7   Responding to challenges   121
8   Comparison: disability with ageing and ageing with disability   143

9   Conclusion   163

Methodological annexe   177
References   189
Index   223

Key terms

DwithA 'disability with ageing', denoting people experiencing disability with ageing having lived relatively disability-free until reaching midlife or late life

AwithD 'ageing with disability', denoting people experiencing ageing having been born with disability, or having first experienced disability in childhood, young adult or adult years (prior to midlife)

See also 'Terminology and abbreviations' in the Introduction, which explains what is meant by disability.

Acknowledgements

I gratefully acknowledge the support of the Irish Research Council by way of a Government of Ireland Postdoctoral Fellowship (GOIPD/2019/472), which enabled me to write this book. The Irish Research Council also supported me to carry out the research that informs it during my PhD studies (EBPPG/2013/58) at Maynooth University's Department of Sociology, where I also gratefully received a John and Pat Hume scholarship.

The research was made possible by the people who agreed to be interviewed and I thank them for their time and the openness with which they engaged in the process. In addition, a range of people working in the fields of ageing and of disability made the study possible by helping me to recruit participants, by giving me advice about how to approach it, or by providing feedback on various drafts. I continue to be grateful to all of you. There are more people who helped me in various ways than I can mention here.

I do wish to acknowledge with thanks the advice and support of Jane Gray, my PhD supervisor. I also mention Patricia Boyd, Delia Ferri, Seán Healy, Maureen Leahy, Eamon O'Shea, Mary Rabbitte, and Catherine Rose to whom I am indebted. My thanks are due too to the staff of Policy Press.

A special thanks to Thomas Scharf for encouragement and ongoing discussion about the book, as well as comments on earlier drafts, which have greatly improved it. All mistakes are mine.

I acknowledge former colleagues from Age & Opportunity, Social Justice Ireland and the All Ireland Institute of Hospice and Palliative Care, and also from the Department of Sociology at Maynooth University, with whom deliberations over time informed my approach to the study and the book.

Finally, my love and thanks to my family members and to a small group of close friends for being there during difficult times, as well as during good times.

Series editors' preface

Chris Phillipson (University of Manchester, UK)
Toni Calasanti (Virginia Tech, USA)
Thomas Scharf (Newcastle University, UK)

Global ageing and the increasing numbers of older people in all world regions raise new issues and concerns for consideration by academics, policy makers and health and social care professionals around the world. Ageing in a Global Context is a book series, published by Policy Press in association with the British Society of Gerontology, that aims to influence and transform debates in what is a fast-moving field in research and policy. The series seeks to achieve this in three main ways. First, the series publishes books which rethink key questions shaping debates in the study of ageing. This has become particularly important given the restructuring of welfare states, especially in the Global North, alongside the complex nature of population change. Each of these elements opens up the need to explore themes which reach beyond traditional perspectives in social gerontology. Second, the series represents a response to the impact of globalisation and related processes, which are contributing to the erosion of the national boundaries that originally framed the study of ageing. This is reflected in the increasing scope and breadth of issues that are explored in contributions to the series, for example: the impact of transnational migration, growing ethnic and cultural diversity, new types of inequality and themes relating to ageing in different environmental contexts. Third, a key concern of the series is to explore interdisciplinary connections in gerontology. Contributions provide a critical assessment of the disciplinary boundaries and territories influencing the study of ageing, creating in the process new perspectives and approaches relevant to the twenty-first century.

In *Disability and Ageing: Towards a Critical Perspective*, Ann Leahy seeks to challenge some of the taken-for-granted assumptions about the connections between the fields of disability studies and social gerontology. With a strong conceptual grounding in critical gerontology, the book considers the ways in which social policies and cultural practices differently shape the lives of people who are ageing with disability and people who develop disabilities in later life. Ann Leahy uses evidence drawn from a fascinating empirical project to question the siloed approaches that have tended to characterise ageing and disability in terms of theorising, activism and policy making. She suggests that as people age, they experience greater disablement in their bodies and in the contexts of their lives. While such processes can challenge individuals' sense of meaning in life, disabled people respond by actively seeking to remake their lives in ways that they understand to be meaningful. In highlighting the need for greater theoretical engagement with disablement processes in later life and their associated cultural meanings, the book makes a much needed contribution to an underdeveloped topic in social gerontology. We anticipate that Ann Leahy's book will be read very widely, becoming a key text for academic researchers, policy makers, activists and a range of professionals who share a passion to study and understand better the multiple ways in which ageing is changing and being changed by a rapidly shifting societal context.

1

Introduction

This book is about how older people experience physical or sensory disability. Its starting point is a belief that the issue of disability is deeply significant for individuals and societies, and that societies must learn from people who experience disability. The basis for the book is an empirical study with two groups rarely considered together in empirical or theoretical work: people first experiencing disability in older age; and people ageing with long-standing disability.

The book takes a critical approach to gerontology, which characteristically explores questions about meaning, asking how older people make sense of their experience and how tacit or explicit cultural ideals shape that experience (Holstein and Minkler, 2007; Twigg and Martin, 2015). Primarily, the book aims to elucidate experiences of disability in older age. To call the experiences considered here 'disability', rather than, say, 'fourth age', is already to take up a position (before discussing what exactly is meant by the word 'disability'), one intended to gesture towards other areas of scholarship. Thus, the book brings disparate areas of scholarship into a critical dialogue, drawing on disability studies, aspects of medical sociology and lifecourse studies, as well as on social gerontology. Disability and ageing are usually approached separately in scholarship. Looking at them together suggests that the subjective experiences of older disabled people are not well understood, with underdeveloped theorising, gaps in empirical evidence and parallel approaches in the fields involved that largely fail to inform each other.

Based on empirical findings, the book argues that older people experience disability and worsening disablement in their bodies and in their contexts. They can be disabled by inaccessible environments and disablist interactions with others. Often experienced in combination with losses of intimates, this can represent a fundamental challenge, amounting to nothing less than a challenge to a sense of value and meaning in life. Older people can also respond dynamically by trying to reinterpret or remake their lives in ways that enable them to perceive value and meaning in life. In other words, older disabled people engage in challenging processes involving interpretation and reinterpretation that are underappreciated in dominant understandings of later life lived with disability as a residual category encompassed in concepts such as the 'fourth age'.

Ultimately, these findings acknowledge suffering and finitude but also signal promise as to older age lived with disability, especially of the potential to seek and generate new meanings that enhance life even when circumstances have changed fundamentally, and often despite challenges that can be personal or socially created. These findings also highlight the need not only for research and scholarship, but also for policy, practice and community interventions that support older disabled people in this endeavour. As Katz (2020: 57) argues in a discussion of cognitive impairment, we need to move away from understandings based on personal decline and terrifying public images that 'separate and isolate old age'.

The potential to make common cause between groups of people otherwise divided informs the book's attempt to engage with different fields of scholarship. This is not so that 'disability' as an identity should be reinforced as an end in itself, but so that – at a time of population ageing and the ageing of disability – we can be better served by realistic, inclusive and collective approaches to the human condition across the lifespan. This is needed because, as Zola (1982: 238) argued, anything that separates and negates disabled people 'will ultimately invalidate not only them but everyone else'.

As this book took shape in 2020, public responses to COVID-19 have echoed the book's attempt to explore links between ageing and disability. With both older people and disabled people or people with chronic or underlying conditions at special risk in relation to the virus, conversations about the two have in many ways become linked (see Leahy, 2020). At times, the COVID-19 crisis has elicited profound sympathy for one another, and it has also highlighted weaknesses in systems of health and social care. It has highlighted human vulnerability in a most stark way. It shows that illness, disability and ultimately death are central to our shared humanity. It would be good if one outcome were that we started to learn from these shared (but frequently denied) aspects of humanity across the lifespan, which have been so forcefully thrust before us. Otherwise, we risk overlooking how disability and, sometimes, vulnerability coexist with creativity, growth and, in a fundamental way, with a desire to be part of society and to live a meaningful life at all of life's stages. This book suggests that we might be better off accepting, accommodating and learning from these fundamental aspects of humanity.

Next, I discuss a series of paradoxes that are central to this book. Then, I introduce the empirical study that informs it, and discuss issues of definition and terminology, before briefly outlining the book's chapters.

Paradox

Paradox is at the heart of this book. Most centrally, paradox exists in how despite concern about ageing populations, social science approaches to ageing are dominated by issues concerning the 'third age', or concerning younger-older people or people not experiencing disability (Grenier, 2012; Phillipson, 2013: 128). Despite how the anticipated economic costs of health and social care dominate responses to population ageing, relatively little is known about subjective experiences of the people most concerned – older people experiencing disability or chronic illness, or who are considered to be in the so-called 'fourth age' (Kelley-Moore et al, 2006; Nicholson et al, 2012; Lloyd et al, 2014). The meaning that older people give to disablement processes is largely overlooked, as biomedical approaches focus attention on identification of objective conditions of 'frailty' (Grenier, 2012: 188) or on the 'management of decline' from the perspective of service providers (Johnson et al, 2020: 2713).

Similarly, lifecourse studies of transitions in older age tend to engage with issues of retirement, focusing less attention on becoming 'frail' or entering the so-called 'fourth age' (Grenier, 2012: 173). Between biomedical constructions of 'decline and decay' (Phillipson, 2013: 132) and the dominant transition of work to retirement portrayed as one of activity and leisure, other later-life transitions – such as experiencing impairment or disability – remain unacknowledged (Grenier, 2012: 182). An implication is that if gerontology is reluctant to engage fully with the difficult issues of impairment, disability and ultimately death, then older people are, as Grenier (2012: 182) says, 'left on their own to negotiate these changes'. Instead, we might be better off preparing for disability rather than 'fleeing from it' (Garland-Thomson, 2016). Denial deprives societies of knowledge and resources that might help everyone to cope with illness and disability as they age (Zola, 1982: 246).

Paradox is also evident in separate approaches to policymaking and activism on disability and ageing, and in how disability is understood and theorised in separate fields. A key distinction is that social processes are emphasised more within approaches to disability generally and medical ones within approaches to ageing. This means that despite impairment often being considered a social norm of ageing, or perhaps because of it, older people with impairments are rarely considered 'disabled' in quite the same way that younger adults might be (Priestley, 2002, 2006). Also, despite how disabled people age, and most people who are ageing will experience disability (Zola, 1989a; Garland-Thomson, 2016), there are no theories addressing both ageing and disability, something that impacts on our ability to conceptualise relationships between the two (Putnam, 2002; Murphy et al, 2007). As Lamb (2015: 314) suggests, while older age and disability have many points of crossover, the desire to claim greater positivity about either category often leads us to reinforce distinctions between them.

Yet, lack of acknowledgement of disability in older age was highlighted decades ago by influential voices associated with ageing (Townsend, 1981a; Walker, 1981a), with disability studies (Abberley, 1987; Wendell, 1996) and with medical sociology (Zola, 1989a, 1989b). For Townsend (1981a: 93, 97), a tendency to categorise 'the elderly' as separate from 'the disabled' meant that the needs of the former were insufficiently acknowledged, and he called for a 'social model of disablement' to focus on the outcome for the individual rather than the cause of disability. Abberley (1987: 15) argued that levels of disability were minimised by overlooking disability associated with ageing, and Wendell (1996: 18–19) argued that reduced opportunities experienced by older disabled people were no more attributable to 'nature' than those experienced by other disabled people. However, others held a different position. Amundson (1992: 115) distinguished between 'age-frailty' and 'disability', arguing against depicting 'handicaps as a natural and expected part of human existence'.

More recently, a range of gerontologists have called for closer links or dialogue with scholarship in disability (Kennedy, 2000; Oldman, 2002; Putnam, 2007; Kelley-Moore, 2010; Grenier et al, 2016; Kahana and Kahana, 2017; McGrath et al, 2017). There are also calls for closer links to scholarship in medical sociology (Higgs and Rees-Jones, 2009). On the disability side, the late Tobin Siebers (2008: 5) asserted that able-bodiedness is a 'temporary identity at best'. He is among the disability scholars who understand disability as an issue across the lifespan (see Priestley, 2003a, 2006; Riddell and Watson, 2003; Shakespeare, 2014a; Garland-Thomson, 2016; Yoshizaki-Gibbons, 2019; Aubrecht et al, 2020). However, others disagree. For Hughes (2009: 402), universalising ideas of impairment would make both the category of disability and its 'exclusion, discrimination and oppression' superfluous. For Meekosha and Shuttleworth (2009: 61), it might 'obscure hierarchies of difference and oppressive social processes and social relations'.

Experts in a range of disciplines internationally advocate for bridges across the fields of disability and ageing in research, policy and practice to address demographic ageing and the longevity of disabled people (Bickenbach et al, 2012; Coyle and Mutchler, 2017). However, these bridges remain limited in practice (Salvador-Carulla et al, 2012). A review of citations suggested that researchers in ageing and disability do not read one another's work (Molton and Ordway, 2019).

In the following sections, I discuss public policies, activism, conceptualisations of disability and theorising on ageing and on disability in more detail to illustrate how 'disability' is approached within separate fields. This highlights assumptions embedded in separate approaches about what it is to experience disability and about what it is to age.

Policy frameworks

Public policies have important consequences in the fields of ageing and disability. They can shape membership categories that affect personal identity and define 'the parameters of legitimate ageing' (Estes et al, 2003: 4; Hendricks, 2010). The very emergence of older people as a distinct category is associated with pension policies. Likewise, disability policies can turn some transitions into 'strongly demarcated events' (Mayer, 1986: 167; see also Marshall and Mueller, 2002).

Separate policy fields operate in many countries on ageing and on disability. Typically, approaches to ageing are based on a medical model, while approaches to disability adopt a social care model influenced by advocacy (Monahan and Wolf, 2014). Thus, public policies can suggest that people are either disabled or older, not both (see Bigby, 2008), and someone who, at age 64 might be considered a disabled person, may be simply categorised as 'old' at age 65 (Kelley-Moore, 2010: 104). Competing ideologies and languages, complexity, and illogicality are associated with these separate administrative categories and with transitions between them (Priestley and Rabiee, 2001; Coyle and Mutchler, 2017; Leahy, 2018). A significant demographic shift is taking place among people ageing with disability (Molton and Ordway, 2019). Policy frameworks are not well developed in many countries for this group (Carter Anand et al, 2012), who may have to negotiate different policy frameworks and can experience difficulty accessing specialised aged services, or, among some, have experiences of premature ageing overlooked (Bigby, 2008; La Plante, 2014).

Arguably, further discordances are introduced by influential 'positive' ageing approaches (in 'successful', 'active', 'healthy' or 'productive' forms) in international policy frameworks on ageing. Based on the medical model, they posit 'successful' ageing as incompatible with ill health or impairment (Estes et al, 2003: 67). They focus on the 'third age' and on delaying disability to improve population health; however, they can construct the experience of disability in older age as a personal failure (McGrath et al, 2016; Kahana and Kahana, 2017). They risk overlooking the role of broader environments (physical, social, cultural and economic) in shaping health outcomes and ability to participate in healthy lifestyles (Pack et al, 2019). They also risk marginalising older disabled people within an active participation policy agenda (Raymond and Grenier, 2013). As Grenier (2012: 87) suggests, critical scholars are left to wonder what happens to older people as they move between the available models of health and decline. This contributes to public policies on ageing that promote little or no understanding of how to 'age well' with disability, whether experienced earlier or later in life.

Political movements

It is a political question, not just a statistical one, as to who is 'disabled' (see Zola, 1989b). Despite sharing concerns about a range of issues, representative groups of older people and disabled people remain separate (Priestley, 2002: 369). Disability activists tend to enter the movement at a young age and issues pursued are often those affecting people of working age or younger (Priestley, 2003a, 2006; Shakespeare, 2006: 75). Even for people ageing with long-standing disability, there is a lack of political voice and community engagement (Westwood and Carey, 2019). Thus, advocacy for disabled people attempts to achieve the rights afforded to adults below retirement age (Jönson and Larsson, 2009).

Disability activism can also be about identity, pride and self-worth. For example, Garland-Thomson (2016) asserts the value of a 'sturdy disability identity', associated with a change in consciousness: 'moving from isolation to community ... from exclusion to access, and from shame to pride'. However, for Kafer (2013: 14), the most difficult group for disability studies and activism to address are people who do not identify with terms like 'disability' or 'crip', among whom she includes 'those with hearing impairments, or low vision, or "bum knees"', while acknowledging that this group may make up most people with impairments.

For their part, representatives of older people often focus on active ageing, and both movements distance themselves from negative imagery of dependency in deep older age (Priestley, 2003a, 2006). In fact, adopting a positive identity of ageing can mean distancing oneself from a disability identity for as long as possible (Priestley, 2006; Pack et al, 2019). To some extent, mutual discrimination is present in the very struggle against ageist and ableist norms (Jönson and Larsson, 2009: 75). Human rights-based approaches used within disability frameworks tend not to be applied to older disabled people or to older people needing long-term care (Larsson and Jönson, 2018; United Nations, 2019). It goes without saying that we have not yet seen a movement relative to disability experienced in older age linked to developing disability identity, pride or empowerment.

Conceptualisations (or models) of disability

Conceptual models define disability, help shape self-identities and determine the professions involved (Smart, 2009). Separate fields employ different models for understanding what disability is. In medical terms, disability in later life is linked to chronic illness, while lifelong disability is linked to congenital or developmental conditions, or injury (Verbrugge and Jette, 1994). Disability in younger people may be independent of illness and we tend to use the terms 'sick' or 'ill' to talk about older people (Kahana and Kahana, 2017: 2, 191). These different aetiologies inform assumptions of difference between experiences of disability across the lifespan. However, medical distinctions help obscure the fact that the very definition of chronic illness involves 'functional impairment or disability' (Department of Health and Children, 2008: 9). In some ways, it is both assumed that disability rates increase with age (see World Health Organization and World Bank, 2011) and underappreciated that older people make up a sizeable and growing proportion of disability populations (Yoshizaki-Gibbons, 2019).

Social models are associated with disability activism and inform understandings of disability generally, positioning it as a social issue, not an individual or medical one (Priestley, 2003a; Titchkosky and Michalko, 2009). In recent decades, the focus within disability studies has been on disability as discursively produced. In other words, 'disability is not a thing-in-the-world', but a 'fluid and shifting' set of meanings involved in the greater question of what it means to be human (Shildrick and Price, 1996: 93; Titchkosky and Michalko, 2009: 6). Interactional or biopsychosocial models attempt to bridge the medical and social, and are linked to human rights frameworks and with attempts to bridge disparate fields (Bickenbach et al, 2012; Naidoo et al, 2012).

While different, sometimes conflicting, definitions of disability are well recognised in disability studies, 'disability' in older age is usually seen as a straightforward inability to perform certain actions (Verbrugge and Jette, 1994; Putnam, 2002). In addition, 'frailty' – usually defined in narrow physical or medical terms – is a powerful construct and even social science literature uses it as a taken-for-granted reference point (Grenier, 2020). The same is true of a range of diagnostic categories, from which even social-gerontological research often starts. This creates silos of scholarship, knowledge and practice within gerontology that, while valid and useful in themselves, may miss opportunities to identify common issues at a broader, societal level and to inform a broader range of interests.

The dominance of the medical model within approaches to ageing can also obscure how health (while foundational) 'is a means and not an end' (Holstein and Minkler, 2007: 16). For older people, striving to preserve health is really about wishing to remain living independently in the community (Kahana and Kahana, 2017: 154). Another consequence is that broader cultural and social-structural influences can be overlooked in explanatory frameworks for disablement in older age (Kelley-Moore, 2010: 107; Larsson and Jönson, 2018). It means too that there is limited engagement with how older disabled people can lead rewarding lives.

Theoretical approaches

Tackling disadvantage is the main theoretical and political aim of disability studies (Vehmas and Watson, 2014). A similar commitment underlies critical gerontology (Phillipson and Walker, 1987; Bernard and Scharf, 2007). However, the two fields have not been 'in regular conversation' (Lamb, 2015: 315). Older age is largely omitted from debates in disability scholarship (Priestley, 2006; Shakespeare, 2014a) and disability activists and scholars have been slow to make connections between forms of discrimination associated with being older and being disabled (Thomas and Milligan, 2018). Something of an exception is represented by an increasing engagement with the issue of dementia as 'disability' (see Thomas and Milligan, 2018; Shakespeare et al, 2019).

For its part, literature on ageing tends to engage with 'disability' as an 'undesirable condition' to be 'limited in scope and compressed in time' (Kahana and Kahana, 2017: 5). The 'third age' is conceived of as a time of freedom to pursue goals and lead a creative, fulfilling life, characterised by health, personal growth and active engagement (Laslett, 1996 [1989]; Lloyd, 2015); the 'fourth age' is seen as a time of decline and disengagement (Laslett, 1996 [1989]). As argued already, we lack understanding of the subjective experiences of older disabled people or of people considered to be 'frail' or in the 'fourth age' (Kelley-Moore et al, 2006; Nicholson et al, 2012; Lloyd et al, 2014).

Critical gerontologists now take issue with over-medicalised or individualised approaches that inform concepts such as 'positive' ageing and 'frailty' (Katz and Calasanti, 2015; Manthorpe and Iliffe, 2015; Grenier et al, 2017). These critiques echo the critiques of the medical model that were a starting point for disability studies (see Oliver, 1990, 1996). However, gerontological critiques are not often framed by reference to similar critiques from disability studies, nor do they usually make identity or pride claims on behalf of older disabled people.

Theorising has taken some similar tracks, with critical scholars in both fields engaging with cultural, discursive and relational issues. For example, Gullette (2004) focuses on social attitudes to the appearance of ageing within postmodern culture, and Twigg (2004, 2006) brings an understanding of both biology and culture to the discussion of older bodies. However, *the* focus of critical disability studies is discourse and the cultural production of the disabled body, or on shifting from the body as the object of scrutiny to the institutional or medical gaze (Snyder and Mitchell, 2001; Titchkosky, 2007; Goodley et al, 2019). The material body is often omitted and the idea of impairment as 'brute fact' is rejected (Feely, 2016: 868). This is associated with taking a liberating approach to disability (Shuttleworth and Meekosha, 2013: 352). However, some dispute the omission of material bodies from scholarship (Shakespeare, 2014a; Vehmas and Watson, 2014). Overall, though, approaches within disability studies make a striking contrast to those within gerontology, which treat disability as a personal characteristic or permanent attribute – something a person has rather than experiences (Putnam, 2002).

Within disability studies, the ageing experience of disabled people was a focus of early empirical work (Zarb and Oliver, 1993). However, that engagement has been limited and there is much less scholarship on ageing with long-standing disability than might be expected (Chivers, 2020). Empirical research that explores that experience is now a growing, if still limited, field of enquiry, and it tends to come from gerontology or from a health perspective (Jeppsson Grassman and Whitaker, 2013; Simcock, 2017; Finkelstein et al, 2020). There are also examples of scholarship that applies concepts from critical disability studies to experiences of later life or to discourses of ageing (Gibbons, 2016; McGrath et al, 2017). However, most critical approaches focus either on disability or on ageing (Grenier et al, 2016).

It may be true that people ageing with disability and people experiencing disability with ageing have too much in common to be served by divided research silos (Molton and Ordway, 2019); however, the discussion thus far signals challenges involved in attempting to open discussions between the disparate fields involved. Conversations across them can be fraught (Lamb, 2015). As Zola (1989a, 1989b) suggested, a more unified agenda will likely need a reorientation in general thinking about disability. Likewise, it may also require a reorientation in thinking about ageing. Thus, critical responses are needed that challenge orthodoxies in both fields. There are also adjacent fields, including aspects of medical sociology and lifecourse perspectives, where the fields of disability and ageing could meet. Key aspects of these perspectives are discussed in Chapter 3, which expands on this brief review of relevant literature.

Finally, limited engagement from disability studies with disability experienced in older age represents a paradoxical omission given that, as Garland-Thomson (2019) suggests, who and what is included and excluded is at the heart of critical disability studies. This indicates that there are some under-acknowledged concerns. One is likely to be that addressing ageing risks re-medicalising sociological understandings of disability or that looking at older age and disability together makes it 'doubly difficult to see beyond the individual-body-as-problem' (Lamb, 2015: 317). Another is that it may risk shifting focus from the rights of people currently considered 'disabled'. If correct, these intuitions reflect understandable and grave issues, as there is no disputing that disabled people in general are a 'highly marginalised and disadvantaged group' (Meekosha et al, 2013: 321). This points to some of the challenges that underlie the effort to enter this arena.

However, the current position also risks leaving older disabled people relatively unsupported – including people who have aged with long-standing disability and with a consequent legacy of disadvantage over time. When theory works well, 'it has the power to capture inequality and articulate hope' (Goodley et al, 2019: 989). This is an argument for attempting to develop less divisive approaches to scholarship. As noted already, this book seeks to contribute to debates out of an empirical study, which is described next.

The empirical study: rationale, key features and findings

The rationale for the empirical study that informs this book can be inferred from the discussion thus far. The study aimed to contribute to elucidating experiences of disability in older age, often cast within social gerontology as studies of the 'fourth age'. Its participants were drawn from two groups usually considered to be categorically different, something constructed by separate approaches to policymaking on ageing and disability, and rarely considered together in research: people ageing with disability (abbreviated as **AwithD**); and people first experiencing disability with ageing (abbreviated as **DwithA**).

A key justification for the study arose from the discussion at the outset as to limited engagement with subjective experiences of the so-called 'fourth age' (see Lloyd et al, 2014) and even more limited engagement with experiences of ageing with disability, especially with physical or sensory disability (Jeppsson Grassman et al, 2012; Westwood and Carey, 2019). Another justification is that it is unclear whether the social (as opposed to the medical) processes of ageing with disability are different from those involved in first experiencing disability in older age (Putnam, 2002; Westwood and Carey, 2019).

The empirical study explored subjective experiences of disability and disablement among older people experiencing disability and the meanings made of those experiences. Being inductive, it did not start with a hypothesis, but rather from the idea that disability in older age involves the two groups mentioned already (AwithD and DwithA groups).

The study was qualitative, with the following research questions:

- How do older people experience disability and processes of disablement, and what meanings do they make of those experiences?
- How do older disabled people respond to the challenges involved in disablement processes?
- In what ways do the social processes (as opposed to the medical processes) of first experiencing disability with ageing differ from those of ageing with disability?

There were 42 participants, whose median age was 72.5, and all but three of whom were aged 65 or over. All were experiencing physical or sensory disability, most typically, issues of mobility or sight. Most were recruited through community centres and organisations of disabled people or older people. Participants were living in their own homes in Ireland in cities, towns, villages and rural areas, and were interviewed between 2015 and 2017. More information about the study's methods is included in Chapter 5 and in the 'Methodological annexe'.

Key findings of the study include that older people experience disability and disablement in their bodies and in their contexts.

Participants could be disabled by factors and barriers that disable people of all ages, such as inaccessible homes and environments, and they could be marginalised in interactions with others and excluded from activities. Experiences of disability onset or worsening were often combined with losses of intimates, which, in combination, could challenge a sense of meaning in life. Participants responded in a dynamic process of trying to remake lives that they perceived as having value and meaning.

Comparing the two groups of participants (DwithA and AwithD) suggests that there were some differences between the two experiences. However, both groups wished for similar outcomes for their lives – connection with others, meaningful engagement and inclusion in the mainstream of life – and both groups of participants engaged in efforts to have lives that they perceived as meaningful. Key differences arise from sociocultural meanings made of impairment at different stages of the lifespan – and this occurs as part of larger societal and cultural processes in which constructions of ageing and of disability, and the social devaluation of each, are intertwined.

Many of the difficulties and barriers faced by the two groups are similar. However, given that people who age with disability do so against a backdrop of disadvantage (Clarke and Latham, 2014; Iezzoni, 2014), they represent a group that especially requires targeted policies, as well as more engagement by activists and researchers to make their experiences better known. The findings of the empirical study are the focus of Part II of this book.

Terminology and abbreviations

The meaning of 'disability' is contentious and it can be argued that it should not be defined. Choice of terminology can distinguish 'allies from enemies', with 'disabled people' signalling a social model approach and 'people with disabilities' signalling a mainstream approach (Shakespeare, 2013: 217). Yet, person-first language ('people with disabilities') tends to be preferred in the US and Australia. In this book, I acknowledge that all terms and definitions are imperfect and contestable, and adopt the term 'disabled people', used (especially in the UK) to shift the focus from the individual to society, or, in other words, to suggest that it is society that turns impairments into disability (Morris, 2001; Priestley, 2003a).

The understanding of disability that informs the book is interactional (or relational or biopsychosocial, as discussed in Chapter 2). It includes, but is broader than, 'impairment', which is defined as problems in body function or alterations in body structure.

This is consistent with the United Nations (UN) Convention on the Rights of Persons with Disabilities, the preamble of which introduces disability as an 'evolving' concept and suggests that disability results from 'the interaction between persons with impairments and attitudinal and environmental barriers that hinders their full and effective participation in society on an equal basis with others' (United Nations General Assembly, 2006). I use the term 'impairment' to exclude social or other external factors but cognisant of how impairment can also be socially constructed. Ideas about impairment are also contested (as discussed in Chapters 2 and 3).

There are some terms introduced already that are important. The first, 'disability with ageing' (DwithA), is used of people who live relatively impairment-free until reaching mid-life or late life and experience age-related conditions (Verbrugge and Yang, 2002). The term 'ageing with disability' (AwithD) is used of people who experience impairment from birth or in childhood or adult years (Verbrugge and Yang, 2002). The terms ageing with 'lifelong' or 'long-standing' disability also refer to this experience. Further elaboration of these categories can be found in the discussion of recruitment of participants in the 'Methodological annexe'. It is also true that these distinctions are somewhat stereotypical since ageing and disability are processes that interleave across the lifecourse (Verbrugge and Yang, 2002: 253). I use the terms **'older disabled person/people'** or **'disability in older age'** when I intend to refer to both groups (consistent with approaches of Priestley and Rabiee (2001) and Priestley (2006)).

Chapter by chapter outline

This book is in two parts: the first provides background and contextualisation; the second presents and discusses the empirical study. Part I contextualises the book and the empirical findings that inform it in different ways. Chapter 2 discusses definitions of disability, clarifying concepts and terms. Chapter 3 expands on the engagement with scholarship started in this introduction, focusing especially on critical studies on ageing and on disability. It also considers other fields that are relevant, namely, lifecourse perspectives and one aspect of theorising within the sociology of health and illness. Chapter 4 outlines facts about disability prevalence and ageing, discusses how public policies traditionally approach disability and ageing, and considers the consequences of the separation between the two for older disabled people (or, as they might more typically be characterised, for older people with care needs).

In Part II, I discuss the empirical findings of the study that informs this book. Chapter 5 briefly outlines the study's methods (see also the 'Methodological annexe'), then discusses how participants experienced disability in the body, considering the physical reality of the body as it impinges on identity. Chapter 6 discusses how a range of contextual factors (like physical environments or disabling social relations) contribute to the experience of disability in older age – factors that can be disabling at any age. It also discusses the issue of disability identity in older age. Chapter 7 discusses ways in which participants responded to the challenges involved in disability and disablement processes, which often occurred simultaneously with, and were partly constituted by, loss of intimates and reduced social circles. Chapter 8 draws out a comparison between the two groups represented in the empirical study, considering how the ageing with disability experience differs from the experience of disability with ageing.

Chapter 9 summarises the study's key findings and the book's key arguments. It finishes by suggesting where there is potential for more links between disparate areas of scholarship and it makes recommendations for social policy.

PART I

The context for disablement
in older age

2

Defining disability

Introduction

Disability is often understood within models that define it, shape self-identities and determine which professions engage (Smart, 2009). With a view to clarifying concepts at the outset, I discuss in this chapter how disability is understood. The chapter expands on one of the paradoxes identified in Chapter 1: how separate models are used to understand what disability is generally and to understand what it is in older age.

First, I consider understandings within approaches to disability generally – involving two key models: social and biopsychosocial – and then definitions that dominate approaches to ageing, which are largely biomedical. Next, I discuss sociological understandings of disability in older age (principally, the 'fourth age'), and one alternative approach to disability from the field of environmental gerontology. This chapter is meant as a bridge to the next, which considers theoretical approaches to disability and to ageing. The two chapters interconnect since definitions are fundamental to theorising and scholarship.

General approaches to defining disability

It is possible to think of what disability is in terms of three main models. The first are medical models, which attribute disability to the person and tend to approach it at the level of the individual. The second are social models, which are associated with disability studies and activism. They attribute disability to the environment and view disability as socially created and, increasingly, as culturally created. The third are biopsychosocial models, which attempt to bridge the social and the medical, and draw on medical sociology. In these models, disability is understood as relational or interactional – linked to the person–environment relationship.

The UK social model and beyond

Until the 1990s, disability was conceived of in terms of medicine, rehabilitation, psychology, special educational needs and social work

(Goodley, 2011). The **UK social model** goes back to a statement from the 1970s on physical disability, which was subsequently broadened to include all impairments (Barnes, 1998): 'it is society which disables physically impaired people. Disability is something imposed on top of our impairment by the way we are unnecessarily isolated and excluded from full participation in society. Disabled people are therefore an oppressed group in society' (UPIAS and The Disability Alliance, 1976: 14). This definition made a crucial distinction between impairment and disability – the latter being a socially constructed experience – and it made a link to oppression. Oliver (1996: 31–2) characterised the medical model as, 'the personal tragedy theory of disability'. Crucially, he argued that 'disablement has nothing to do with the body' (Oliver, 1990: 45). Thus, the social model politicises disability and excludes accounts of the body (Goodley, 2011: 62). Disability thereby became a societal issue that prompted positive identification and mobilisation on the part of disabled people.

Debates often focused on the impairment–disability dichotomy, which feminist and post-structuralist scholars, especially, criticised. They often also remained supportive of social model approaches generally but argued that the impairment–disability dichotomy is not representative of diverse lived experience (Corker, 1999; Corker and French, 1999; Shakespeare and Watson, 2002). For example, Wendell (1996) and Crow (1996) argued that the effects of impairment, such as pain and tiredness, were disabling in their own right. For Hughes and Paterson (1997), a failure to theorise the impaired body hands the body over to medicine.

Thomas (2004: 579) responded by developing a social relational model of disability in which there are 'impairment effects' and social restrictions, arguing that 'once the term "disability" is ring-fenced to mean forms of oppressive social reaction there is no need to deny that impairments and illness cause *some* restrictions of activity – in whole or in part' (emphasis in the original). Despite these tensions and splits within the disability studies community, particularly in Britain (Meekosha and Shuttleworth, 2009), the emancipatory aspect of the social model is acknowledged and even critics acknowledge its practical or political usefulness (Tregaskis, 2002; Meekosha and Shuttleworth, 2009). For Shakespeare (2006: 31), it is 'one of the bravest and most transformative moves in the history of political thought'. For Thomas (2004: 573, 581), disability scholars, whether for or against the social model, are almost always in dialogue with it, and it is 'a powerful organising principle, a rallying cry, and a practical tool'.

Other social models exist. In **North America**, Nagi (1976) pioneered a view of disability where functional limitation is an expression of the failure of environments to accommodate disability. Hahn (1986: 128; 1993: 46–7) expounded a minority group analysis where civil rights concepts were applied to discrimination and segregation on grounds of disability, and disability stemmed from 'failure of a structured social environment to adjust to the needs and aspirations of citizens with disabilities'. Thus, in the US, disability is often seen as a cultural and minority identity (Siebers, 2008: 4). The impairment–disability distinction articulated in the UK social model was not central to the minority politics model (Goodley, 2011). The **Nordic relational model** understands disability as a mismatch caused by individual difference *and* lack of adaptation of the environment (Shakespeare, 2006: 25, citing Tossebro). Thus, North American and Nordic models have not gone as far in redefining disability as 'social oppression', but both attempt to go beyond the medical or individual model (Shakespeare, 2006: 24).

The terms **cultural** or **critical disability studies** are used to signal approaches that move away from the preoccupation with binary understandings, while continuing to employ aspects of social models (Meekosha and Shuttleworth, 2009). Critical disability scholars argue that impairments, as well as disability, are a social construction rather than an essential truth (Feely, 2016: 865). Thus, a basis in nature or physiology tends to be rejected – disability is not 'a thing-in-the-world' (Titchkosky and Michalko, 2009: 6). To be disabled, or to be discursively constructed as disabled, can still be understood as to be subject to social oppression (Thomas, 2007: 4).

These perspectives shift the focus from disability to 'normalcy' or ableism. **Ableism** is defined as a network of beliefs, processes and practices that produces a particular kind of self and body (the corporeal standard) that is projected as the perfect, species-typical and therefore essential and fully human, and that casts disability as 'a diminished state of being human' (Campbell, 2001: 44). In Chapter 3, I discuss theorising within this perspective.

Biopsychosocial models

Interactional or biopsychosocial models attempt to integrate the medical and social. They introduce definitions rooted in medical sociology associated with the view that disability can be caused by impairment at a bodily level *and* by social disadvantage. Prominent among these approaches is the World Health Organization's (WHO's) International

Classification of Functioning, Disability and Health (ICFDH-2) (known as **ICF**) (World Health Organization, 2001; 2002b), which provides an international basis for the definition and measurement of health and disability, aiming to establish a consistent approach across disciplines. It underpins the *World Report on Disability* (World Health Organization and World Bank, 2011). 'Disability', according to the ICF classification, is 'an umbrella term for impairments, activity limitations or participation restrictions' (World Health Organization, 2001: 3). The model is biopsychosocial because disability is said to arise from the *interaction* of individual conditions with contextual factors, which are personal and environmental. Personal factors include, for example, age, gender, social status and life experiences; environmental factors include the natural and built environment, products and technology, support and relationships, attitudes and services, systems and policies (World Health Organization and World Bank 2011: 304, 307). Thus, 'disability' is *relational* – occurring in the *interaction* between the individual and their context; it includes, but is broader than, 'impairment', defined as problems in body function or alterations in body structure (Bickenbach et al, 1999; Bickenbach, 2011: 657).

Advocates for bridging the fields of ageing and disability often associate themselves with these approaches (see Bickenbach et al, 2012; Naidoo et al, 2012). However, the ICF has its critics among disability scholars (see Oliver and Barnes, 2012). For Barnes and Mercer (2010: 39), it provides a detailed taxonomy but 'lacks a coherent theory of social action'. For Goodley (2011: 20), in searching for 'universalism', it risks ignoring the culturally specific foundations on which impairment, disability and disablism are created.

However, it has also somewhat accommodated criticisms by disability scholars of the medical model. For example, Shakespeare (2006: 59–62; 2013: 221; 2014a: 79–80) points to challenges in operationalising it but supports the ICF because it is 'interactional', making it more appropriate than the social model for theorising disability. Similarly, because it balances contributions of personal responses to impairment and barriers imposed by social environments, Hosking (2008: 7) considers it consistent with critical disability theory, summarising its definition of disability as, 'a complex interrelationship between impairment, individual response to impairment, and the social environment'. Shakespeare has also suggested that it needs updating to reflect greater knowledge of determinants and consequences of health conditions, as well as of well-being or quality of life (Mitra and Shakespeare, 2019).

In an earlier study with Irish policymakers, service providers and activists, I (Leahy, 2018) found that participants lacked any concept of disability with ageing, tending to identify older people experiencing impairments as just 'elderly' or 'older people'. Those who did consider that older people experiencing impairment could be encompassed within the category 'disabled' tended to come from the non-governmental (NGO) disability sector and to invoke the UN Convention on the Rights of Persons with Disabilities. Chapter 1 referred to how disability is described in the Convention. Article 1 contains the following definition of who is disabled: 'those who have long-term physical, mental, intellectual or sensory impairments which in interaction with various barriers may hinder their full and effective participation in society on an equal basis with others'. While the social model of disability influenced the Convention, which is sometimes called a 'social model', this definition is interactional or relational (Shakespeare, 2014b; Shakespeare et al, 2019; Lawson and Beckett, 2021). It is also said to embody a 'human rights model' of disability and to be the most influential model in human rights law and policy (Lawson and Beckett, 2021). The UN Convention, the WHO definition of disability and the WHO *World Report on Disability* represent 'decades of activism' by disabled people and allies, and have 'set global standards for access, inclusion, development and empowerment' (Rembis, 2015: 166; Rembis, 2019: xviii).

The Convention contains several references to age or older persons (see, for example, Articles 8, 13, 16, 25 and 28). Although it does not include a specific engagement with challenges at intersections of ageing and disability, it is relevant to disability experienced at any point of the lifespan (Naue and Kroll, 2010; United Nations, 2019). Yet, the Convention is not widely applied to older people, and limited views of what constitutes 'disability' play a role in this (European Network of National Human Rights Institutions, 2016).

Instead, medical definitions and approaches dominate international discussions of ageing, with older people still 'largely perceived as mere beneficiaries of care and welfare' (United Nations, 2019: 7). However, models used internationally, such as the WHO's ICF approach and the human rights approach of the UN Convention on the Rights of Persons with Disabilities, have value for older people because they avoid dichotomous thinking (see Hagestad and Settersten, 2017: 143). Thus, if used within gerontology, these approaches, being broader than the medical model, would represent a step forward as an analytical construct and a political argument (Leahy, 2018).

Approaches to defining disability in older age

I next move to the field of ageing, where medicalised approaches to defining disability dominate. They tell us little about the social construction of ageing in a broad sociopolitical context, but because of their influence, I discuss next how 'disability' and, relatedly, 'frailty' are conceptualised within approaches to ageing. I also consider the concept of the 'fourth age' within sociological perspectives, as well as an interactional definition of disability developed within environmental gerontology.

Biomedical definitions

In biomedical literature, 'disability' in older age is usually seen as a straightforward ability/inability to perform certain actions. Biomedical definitions continue to frame even contributions from social scientists. Traditionally, the terms used include 'functional impairment', level of 'dependency' or 'frailty' (Woodhouse et al, 1988).

The most commonly used measures of 'disability' are self-reports of difficulty in functioning. This tends to be approached as difficulties in basic activities of daily living (ADLs), such as mobility and self-care activities, or as difficulties in instrumental activities of daily living (IADLs) performed to live independently, such as preparing meals, shopping and taking medication (BURDIS, 2004). Critics point to the limitations inherent in this narrow approach (Ryff and Singer, 1998; Lloyd, 2012). Some 'disability' research also recognises the need for a wider focus on environmental factors (BURDIS, 2004).

'Frailty' is a dominant theme in geriatric research, having become a 'powerful and persuasive' construct for research, policy and practice (Grenier, 2012: 170; 2020: 2339). In general terms, 'frailty' refers to risk of death, functional decline, co-morbidities and impairment (Clegg et al, 2013). However, there are many definitions. An international conference of experts failed to agree an operational definition, but they did agree on some aspects; these included that frailty raises vulnerability to stressors and is different from disability (Santiago et al, 2019: 111). Some groups have a higher likelihood of being 'frail' than others (Fried et al, 2001; Caldwell et al, 2019). Lifecourse approaches link frailty with early life experiences (Kuh, 2007). However, there are no widely accepted criteria to identify 'frail' persons, and prevalence estimates differ by definition (Puts et al,

2009; Manthorpe and Iliffe, 2015). Some measures of frailty seek to include the psychological and social as well as the physical but narrow physical/medical definitions predominate (Puts et al, 2005; Gobbens et al, 2010).

One question relevant to the subject of this book is whether biomedical literature distinguishes between 'frailty' and 'disability'. Van Campen (2011) suggests that most frail older persons experience moderate or severe disability. It is a complex issue, however, as some people who are considered 'not frail' are 'disabled' and vice versa. In a much-cited study, Fried et al (2001) consider that frailty is not synonymous with either co-morbidity or disability, but that disability is one possible *outcome* of frailty, others being risk of falling, hospitalisation and death. The *White Book on Frailty* suggests that its aim is to promote preventative interventions against disability (Vellas, 2016: 2). Thus, in the biomedical literature, 'frailty' can be a pathway to disability and is often seen as a distinct but overlapping concept to disability and chronic illness (Daniels et al, 2008).

A critique of the concept of frailty is emerging, especially from critical gerontology (Manthorpe and Iliffe, 2015; Grenier et al, 2017; Grenier, 2020). Kelley-Moore (2010: 103) highlights frailty's social origins, arguing for a social constructionist perspective to describe disabling environments linked with diminished social expectations and exclusionary social structures. Grenier (2020) argues for attention to social, emotional and political aspects of 'frailty'.

As far as subjective accounts go, older people do not always identify (when otherwise classified as such) either as 'disabled' (Kelley-Moore et al, 2006; Darling and Heckert, 2010) or as 'frail' (Grenier, 2006; Nicholson et al, 2012, 2013). People designated as 'frail' discussed frailty and disablement interchangeably, and felt that being considered 'frail' could mean being excluded by others (Warmoth et al, 2016). However, scholarship has not devoted much attention to the psychological effects of the transition to frailty or to gathering the experience of people deemed frail (Fillit and Butler, 2009; Nicholson et al, 2013; Hoeyberghs et al, 2020). Nonetheless, countless articles in social science and humanities use 'frailty' as a classification or reference point (Grenier, 2020).

However useful medicalised concepts are in their own terms, what I challenge is their influence on all aspects of how disability in older age is understood. A point to emphasise is that while disability in older age is usually seen through a medicalised lens, older people tend to want to preserve health so as to remain independent and to go on living in the community (Kahana and Kahana, 2017: 154).

Dominant understanding in sociology: the fourth age

As outlined already, Laslett distinguished between the third and fourth ages, intending that the 'third age' might counter age-based discrimination (Grenier and Phillipson, 2014: 57). The third age was a time when one might pursue goals and lead a creative, fulfilling life (Laslett, 1996 [1989]). Older people were 'demeaned' by being associated with the 'fourth age': an 'afflicted and decrepit minority' in an 'age of decline' and an 'era of final dependence, decrepitude and death', when people become 'passengers or encumbrances' and when it is proper to withdraw from life (Laslett, 1996 [1989]: 3–5, 194). In empirical terms, there are challenges in trying to identify the features that characterise the 'fourth age' (Lloyd et al, 2014; Pirhonen et al, 2016). However, onset of 'serious infirmity' tends to be taken as marking the point of transition between the 'third' and 'fourth' ages (Twigg, 2004: 64; Grenier, 2012).

Furthermore, the fourth age is often linked to frailty and conceptualised as an antonym for 'successful' ageing (Grenier, 2012: 170; Nicholson et al, 2012). It is characterised by the combined effects of ageing, illness and disability, which irreversibly change a customary way of life and call into question one's sense of self (Lloyd et al, 2014). It refers to both an age- or staged-based period and a cultural construct – or 'imaginary' (Grenier et al, 2017). It is not clear how people ageing with disability – people who already experience disability prior to becoming older – fit within these frames.

Its characterisation as a 'social imaginary' (a largely unstructured and inarticulate understanding of social situations) comes from Gilleard and Higgs (2010a: 122–5). For them, it represents not a particular cohort or stage of life, but a kind of terminal destination operating as an 'under-theorized residual social category', a social or cultural 'black hole' (Gilleard and Higgs, 2010a). 'Deep' older age is their model for the fourth age, involving a fear of passing beyond any 'possibility of agency, human intimacy or social exchange' (Gilleard and Higgs, 2010a: 125; see also Higgs and Gilleard, 2015: 19). In addition, in being considered a state that cannot sustain individual agency or individual narratives, this is similar to their discussion of frailty (Gilleard and Higgs, 2010b: 477), representing 'a residual state that remains when other narratives and other identities can no longer be asserted or enacted'.

Characterising the 'fourth age' solely by impairment means that people can be socially and culturally 'othered' from society and within groups of older people (Grenier, 2012: 174). Gender is also relevant – 'deep old age' is predominantly female and misogynistic discourses focus on women's bodies and are amplified in relation to older women

(Twigg, 2004: 65). The concept risks transferring negative evaluations onto the 'oldest old' or onto people who cannot lay claim to 'autonomy, social independence and a youthful outlook' (Irwin, 1999: 695; see also Bury, 2000: 94). Thus, for West and Glynos (2016: 231, 236), the 'fourth age' involves 'powerful othering tendencies' associated with third-age fantasies that seek to indefinitely extend capacities linked to younger, more 'productive' ages, which casts the 'fourth age' necessarily as a 'distant negative horizon that cannot be allowed to intrude upon third age positivity and control'. This means that the potential of engaging wholeheartedly with the concerns of older people experiencing chronic illness and impairment, including issues of death and dying, are thwarted (West and Glynos, 2016).

As argued already, the social sciences have focused limited attention on subjective assessments of late-life disability or the 'fourth age' (Kelley-Moore et al, 2006; Grenier, 2007), and the care of older people is often explored from the perspective of service providers (Johnson et al, 2020: 2713). However, alternative interpretations of the 'fourth age' are emerging that apprehend it as retaining possibilities for expression, communication and agency (Grenier and Phillipson, 2014; Pickard, 2014; Johnson et al, 2020). Lloyd et al (2014) link it with perseverance in maintaining a sense of self and dignity of identity, involving physical, mental and emotional labour. However, as a concept, the 'fourth age' is problematic. Based on the medical model, characterised largely by impairment and 'decline', and tending to 'other' those perceived to be within it, it is obvious why the 'fourth age' lacks traction as an approach to definition within disability scholarship and, indeed, why representative groups of older people do not identify with it.

Definition from environmental gerontology

One sub-field within gerontology – environmental gerontology – specifically addresses issues of disability. This approach is associated with the suggestion from Lawton and Nahemow (1973) that personal competence and environmental characteristics determine the optimal level of functioning. From this perspective, older age is profoundly influenced by physical and social environments (Wahl et al, 2012). The concept of person–environment fit is used to examine environment modifications on disability outcomes in older age (Wahl and Weisman, 2003; Wahl et al, 2009). However, the informing idea that people are more independent of their environments when they have more resources (both socio-personal and socio-spatial) at their disposal holds true for 'basically every age group' (Wanka et al, 2018: 28).

These approaches remain somewhat external to mainstream ageing theorising (Wahl et al, 2012). However, as approaches to disability definition, they can be characterised as interactional or relational, and are more in line with approaches to broader disability definitions than are other approaches within mainstream gerontology, such as 'frailty' or 'fourth age'. Wahl et al (2012: 310) assert that ageing well is maintaining 'autonomy, well-being, and preservation of one's self and identity' as much as possible despite 'competence loss'. Physical environments of home and neighbourhoods are a key focus within this scholarship. Tesch-Römer and Wahl (2017) broaden out to consider use of technologies, which may be unavailable or too expensive for many, bringing in attention to income inequality. Environmental approaches also inform arguments for inclusive urban design based on analysis of environments of disadvantage (see Scharf et al, 2002; Wanka et al, 2018).

To some extent, therefore, there are parallels with approaches to definitions of disability more generally, especially relational, interactional or biopsychosocial models. Indeed, proponents of environmental gerontology make links to the WHO's ICF (discussed already) (Hallgrimsdottir and Ståhl, 2016; Tesch-Römer and Wahl, 2017). The ICF focuses on individual and environmental factors that enable activities and participation, and the environmental gerontology model refers to the capacity to adapt behaviourally to physical-environmental pressure (Tesch-Römer and Wahl, 2017: 314). One contribution to the ICF claimed from this perspective is the potential to differentiate between objective and perceived aspects of environments (Iwarsson et al, 2007). Sometimes, both models are used in combination (Iwarsson et al, 2007; Hallgrimsdottir and Ståhl, 2016).

Environmental gerontology provides useful analyses, often emphasising spatial, not social, environments (Scharf, 2001; Putnam, 2002). By contrast, in the ICF, environmental factors can include not just the natural and built environment and technology, but also support and relationships, attitudes and services, systems, and policies (World Health Organization and World Bank, 2011: 304). However, environmental gerontology has potential to address broader aspects of disabling contexts (see Tesch-Römer and Wahl, 2017: 313). For these reasons, this represents a strand of scholarship that may be able to contribute to linking scholarship on disability and on ageing; indeed, in engaging with biopsychosocial models of disability (such as the ICF), it can be said to be already providing a lead.

Discussion and conclusions

The discussion in this chapter demonstrates that disability is a contested category in scholarship, with different models associated with different understandings of the category 'disability' and of who is encompassed within it. Closer working is impeded by different languages and different understandings. Biomedical definitions in functional terms dominate ideas of disability in older age. Thus, gerontology tends to apprehend disability as largely an individual, medicalised problem, something that informs even social science approaches (often based on concepts such as 'frailty' or the 'fourth age'). Disability in older age is seen largely as a negative condition to be limited as much as possible. A key concern of this book is that this does not do justice to all the issues involved at an individual or societal level. Neither does it provide any basis for collective-identity formation for people first experiencing disability in older age. Social and biopsychosocial definitions are more common within approaches to disability generally. Discursive understandings that reject any basis for disability in the material body are currently influential in disability studies. Everyone operates with some definition of disability, whether we realise it or not (Titchkosky and Michalko, 2009), something that scholarship within gerontology might reckon with more.

The definition of disability used within one field of gerontology – that of environmental gerontology – captures the relational or interactional aspect of disability in older age (albeit usually focusing on physical environments). This approach is sometimes used in combination with the biopsychosocial model of the WHO (the ICF) (World Health Organization, 2001). This is one avenue for opening up conversations towards a more unified agenda. Another is represented by the social relational model of disability from Thomas (2004), which recognises both bodily and contextual aspects of disability – in other words, impairment effects and also socially created restrictions.

However, interactional (or biopsychosocial) approaches have been recognised internationally as useful in attempting to bridge separate fields within scholarship, policies and practice. They inform international approaches to censuses and surveys of disability prevalence, representing supranational, shared definitions that can encompass people of all ages. Their link to human rights frameworks means that they have potential for influencing activism and mobilisation to improve lives.

They represent a broad approach to definition, compatible with many disciplines. This includes critical disability perspectives that have moved beyond binaries associated with the social model of disability (Hosking, 2008), reflecting Shakespeare's (2014a) contention that bodies and society disable people. However, it is also true that these interactional approaches – at least as framed in the ICF – continue to be contested within disability studies. I have already argued that biopsychosocial or interactional approaches are potentially valuable for opening discussions between the fields of ageing and disability (Leahy, 2018; see also Molton and Ordway, 2019). This approach is not accepted by all disability scholars or activists, but one must start somewhere in trying to establish shared concepts where different fields hold radically different views as to what it is to experience disability.

If applied within gerontology, interactional approaches offer the possibility of apprehending disability as more than a personal problem, of revealing experiences in common across individual diagnostic categories and of examining how extrinsic factors (physical, social, economic, cultural and political) contribute to the experience of disability in older age. Crucially, they would avoid a return to an equation between older age and impairment, disability or decline, while also having potential to cease to treat 'disability' merely as an undesirable state. Breaking out of a wholly negative, individual framing of disability could also provide a basis for more attention to what it means to live as fully as possible with disability in older age, and for recognition of the relevance of human rights instruments to impairment experienced in older age. Potentially, it could also contribute to the development of collective identification with 'disability' among older people experiencing impairment.

The issues considered in this chapter shaped how the research questions for the study that informs this book were arrived at (as set out in the Chapter 1). As Part II of this book will show, the experience of disability of participants in the study was broader than the biological processes that dominate understandings of what disability is in older age. People also experienced 'disability' in their contexts, including in physical environments and in interactions with others. It is possible to characterise their experience of disability as interactional or relational. Having said that, I note here too that this book does not use any model of disability to provide a detailed taxonomy, as that is not its aim.

Ultimately, as regards definition, the emphasis that Wendell (1996: 22) placed on identifying the difficulties that disabled people face in surviving and contributing to societies still has much to recommend it. These issues have also yet to be fully explored in gerontology. Chapter 3 considers theoretical approaches within disparate fields.

3

Literature: ageing, disability and lifecourse

Introduction

This chapter expands on the engagement with scholarship started in the previous two chapters. It engages with one of the paradoxes highlighted in Chapter 1: that there are only separate theories on ageing and on disability, impacting on our ability to conceptualise relationships between the two (Murphy et al, 2007). I compare key theoretical perspectives on disability and on ageing, engaging especially with critical or cultural studies, and also consider other areas of scholarship where theorising on disability and ageing could meet. The chapter outlines scholarship that forms a backdrop to, and a rationale for, the empirical study discussed in Part II. It also aims to show how these various fields currently engage, and fail to engage, with the issue of disability in older age, as well as where there may be room for more conversations across them.

I start with social theories of ageing, followed by social theories of disability. I then consider an aspect of the sociology of chronic illness and disabling conditions, and I discuss lifecourse perspectives, before drawing the discussion together. I conclude that critical studies, encompassing a range of perspectives, in both disability and ageing often use similar paradigms to explore ageing and disability but that the two fields largely progress on separate tracks. The review also confirms that gerontologists and some writing within disability studies recognise the need for more exploration of subjective experiences associated with disability in later life.

Scholarship on ageing: social theories

In this section, I introduce social theories of ageing. An informing issue is that despite a 'huge industry' addressing impacts of ageing populations, social science approaches are dominated by issues to do with the third age, that is, issues focused on younger-older people or non-impaired older people (Grenier, 2012; Phillipson, 2013: 128).

While there are many studies of impairment in later life, they usually start from a functionalist perspective (Raymond et al, 2014). Thus, it is arguable that sociological understandings of late older age are at an early stage of development and have been subordinated to a dominant biomedical model (Phillipson, 2013: 128, 134). This review engages mainly with critical or cultural perspectives because of their contemporary relevance. However, I first introduce two early theories – disengagement and activity theories – as they continue to resonate.

Ageing in early theorising: disengagement theory, activity theory and beyond

Disengagement theory viewed older age as an inevitable period of withdrawal from roles and relationships in anticipation of death (Cumming and Henry, 1961). Disengagement was viewed as natural, desirable and universal across cultures (see Estes et al, 2003). It attracted much criticism, including for its lack of concern with structural issues (Baars et al, 2006; Walker, 2006). Disengagement theory is seen as empirically wrong in the degree of its negativity (Walker, 2002). However, themes of loss articulated within disengagement theory continue in decline ideologies of ageing that are still influential (see Gullette, 2004; Baars, 2010).

Activity theory (Havighurst and Albrecht, 1953) aimed at 'denying the onset of old age' and replacing 'those relationships, activities and roles of middle age … with new ones' (Walker, 2002: 122). It treated retirement and widowhood as the key role transitions or losses, which meant that satisfaction had to be found in substituted roles (Ferraro, 2001: 314). Activity theory stimulated the development of several social-psychological theories of ageing, including 'successful' ageing (Rowe and Kahn, 1987; Baltes and Baltes, 1990a).

The empirical link made in activity theory between activity and well-being in older age is considered valid today (Walker, 2002). It is associated with concepts that continue to influence contemporary sociocultural discourses and policymaking trends in 'positive', 'successful', 'active', 'healthy' or 'productive' ageing forms, or in third-age discourse. The terms 'active' or 'healthy' ageing are typically used in public policies aiming to delay disability and chronic illness by, among other things, encouraging healthy lifestyles (World Health Organization, 2002a, 2015). Debates over these approaches continue to be at the heart of ageing studies (Estes et al, 2003: 67).

Rowe and Kahn (1997: 433) defined 'successful' ageing as encompassing avoidance of disease and disability, maintenance of high physical and cognitive function, and sustained engagement in social and productive activities. Many risk factors were considered modifiable by individuals. Widely researched, this definition of successful ageing dominates (Bowling and Dieppe, 2005). Baltes and Baltes (1990b) presented a psychological model, suggesting that older people do the best with the functioning they have and maintain it with adaptation strategies. This involves a model of selective optimisation with compensation, which suggests that older people achieve satisfaction by using strategies to age well when faced with loss.

While these approaches sought to counteract the old 'decline and loss paradigm', and are well intentioned, a range of scholars critique how they have evolved (Katz and Calasanti, 2015). Of most relevance here are critiques challenging the equating of 'successful ageing' with good health, and, by extension, disability or poor health with failure (Holstein and Minkler, 2003, 2007; Phillipson, 2013). For Tesch-Römer and Wahl (2017: 313), 'successful' ageing is based on a misleading assumption that there are two distinct worlds of ageing trajectories, which are instead consecutive segments in the same course of life. A requirement for absence of chronic illness or disability as an indicator of 'successful' ageing is also problematic because it means that people ageing with long-standing disability could not age successfully (Molton and Yorkston, 2017; Molton and Ordway, 2019). 'Successful' ageing has also become linked to notions of individualist personhood, emphasising independence, productivity, self-maintenance and the 'individual self as project' (Lamb, 2014: 41).

Academic views dominate approaches to defining 'successful' ageing (and cognate concepts) (Hung et al, 2010) but research is emerging as to how older people interpret them (Larsson, 2013; Romo et al, 2013; Molton and Yorkston, 2017). People experiencing disability with ageing often felt that they *had* aged successfully (Romo et al, 2013). A study that engaged both with people ageing with disability and people first experiencing disability with ageing suggests that the factors considered important for 'successful' ageing were similar across both groups; avoidance of disability did not predict subjective assessments of 'successful' ageing (Heath, 2018). McGrath et al (2016) sum up the impact of these discourses: while they initially sought to counteract negative stereotypes of 'oldness', the way they have evolved may inadvertently reinforce stigmatising views of disability in later life by framing disability as a matter of failed personal responsibility.

Ageing as a social construction: introducing critical gerontology

Political economy perspectives assumed major significance from the 1980s, and critical gerontology developed from them (Phillipson and Baars, 2007). Critical gerontology involves a value-committed approach to theory and policy, and focuses on both structural inequalities and personal experiences of ageing; it engages with changing the social construction of ageing and going beyond 'everyday appearances and the unreflective acceptance of established positions' (Estes et al, 2003: 3). Bernard and Scharf (2007: 7) characterise it as providing evidence to challenge assumptions and beliefs about ageing, old age and older people, contributing to understanding 'varied dimensions of difference'. It is associated with critiques not only of sociopolitical environments, but also of mainstream gerontology (Holstein and Minkler, 2007: 16–17).

Critical gerontology is constituted by political economy and moral economy approaches. The **political economy approach** drew on Marxist insights to interpret the relationship between ageing and economic structures (Estes, 1979; Townsend, 1981b; Walker, 1981b; Phillipson, 1982). Townsend (1981b) highlighted the 'structured dependency' of later life as a product of forced exclusion from labour markets, passive forms of community care and poverty. Phillipson (2013) suggests that political economy theorists now need to engage more with the social dimensions of health and related changes affecting people in their 70s, 80s and beyond. Moreover, Kelley-Moore (2010) suggests that gerontologists could learn about the social construction of disability from disability scholars.

The **moral economy (including cultural and humanistic) perspective** within critical gerontology has the most relevance to the empirical study that informs this book because of its engagement with subjective meaning-making processes of older people. It is associated with an appreciation of the interplay between culture, structure and agency, and focuses on questions of meaning and experience (Estes et al, 2003). It foregrounds subjectively constructed experience within a wider context, and considers how cultural understandings of age and ageing affect meaning, interpretations, experiences and identities (Moody, 1993; Minkler and Estes, 1999; Grenier, 2012). The term 'cultural gerontology' is now often applied to this scholarship, the most characteristic feature of which is a concern with meaning (Twigg and Martin, 2015).

This is a broad area of scholarship, from which I discuss three areas because of their relevance to the arguments of this book and to the discussion of the empirical findings in Part II. These are: **cultural**

representations, which are relevant to how identities of older people are negotiated, and to how they (and others) interpret age and life stage; **body and identity**, including intersectional approaches; and, finally, how **meaning in life** is approached.

Critical gerontology: cultural representations

In general, critiques of cultural representations of ageing have two separate targets that correspond with the two propositions represented in the early theories discussed already. The first focus for critique is the cultural reduction of older age to a period characterised by decline and inevitable deterioration into a state of frailty and dependency, which limits the identity resources available to older people (Cruikshank, 2003, 2008; Gullette, 2004, 2010; Pickard, 2014). Critiques highlight how these narratives fail to acknowledge diversity and can result in overlooking possibilities for growth and renewal (Cruikshank, 2008: 150). 'Decline' perspectives also reduce the potential for meaning in later life. As Laceulle (2016) argues, 'decline' discourses fail to recognise people's aspirations for self-realisation.

A second critique focuses on cultural perceptions associated with 'successful' ageing (and cognate ideals, outlined already), while sometimes also acknowledging the value of these approaches in challenging some myths of ageing. Critiques contest the implicit suggestion that to age 'successfully', one needs to try and stay young and avert 'decline' for as long as possible, or they take issue with the 'tyrannical' positive ageing culture and the exaltation of the freedom and opportunities of the 'third age' (Katz, 2005: 145; see also Phillipson, 2013). Thus, these critiques often highlight how positive images of ageing risk further stigmatising older people who do not fit the 'active' norm promoted especially by commerce.

Gilleard and Higgs (2013: 372) use a vivid image: 'the brighter the lights of the third age, the darker the shadows they cast over this underbelly of aging – fourth age'. The oldest old – the group most likely to be disabled – may be marginalised by the related cultural emphasis on a consumerist lifestyle, leisure and activity associated with positive discourses (Cohen, 1988; Morell, 2003). A similar critique is made in respect of people ageing with disability, who can continue to see themselves as functioning effectively and having a good quality of life (Minkler and Fadem, 2002: 231). Furthermore, with a strong emphasis on remaining 'youthful', this approach also overlooks the fact that older age may have a value of its own (Laceulle, 2016: 99–101).

There are strands within critical gerontology seeking to move understandings of ageing beyond the binaries within traditional gerontological approaches. Instead, Grenier et al (2017) argue for responses that develop from acknowledgement of fragility and limitations rather than those organised around productivity, success and activity. Others call for the development of alternative narratives that focus on self-realisation or self-development for all older people, not just people in the 'third age' (Cruikshank, 2003: 23; Laceulle and Baars, 2014; Laceulle, 2016).

In addition, critical scholarship now engages with concepts from disability studies to highlight the unhelpful ways that the concepts of 'successful' ageing (and cognate concepts) have developed. This scholarship also sometimes highlights social factors of disablement. This signals potential for more linkages between critical studies in gerontology and disability. For example, for Jönson and Larsson (2009: 75), normalising people by comparison with a prolonged midlife constitutes a form of ableism. Sandberg and Marshall (2017: 8) draw on feminist, queer and crip studies (especially on the work of McRuer and Kafer, discussed later in this chapter) to analyse ableism within 'successful' ageing. They suggest that it depends on the spectre of unsuccessful others, including people who are 'too disabled' or 'too poor' to reap its rewards. McGrath et al (2017) draw on critical disability theory to suggest a focus on interdependence over traditional notions of independence, and to question assumptions pertaining to normalcy. Nonetheless, most critical approaches focus *either* on disability or on ageing.

Theoretical approaches locate ageism at different levels: in cultural values and societal institutions that depreciate or exclude older people; and at the micro level of the individual. In this connection, terror management theory explains ageism on the basis that older adults serve as a constant reminder of mortality and vulnerability (Ayalon and Tesch-Römer, 2018). Indeed, Butler's (1969: 243) original definition of ageism connected it with disability and, in effect, with ableism: 'Ageism reflects a deep-seated uneasiness on the part of the young and the middle-aged – a personal revulsion to and distaste for growing old, disease, disability; and a fear of powerlessness, "uselessness," and death.' Fear is also a factor in keeping in place dichotomous thinking about older age. For example, the 'separating out' of older 'frail' people may be an 'organisational defence against the difficulties and anxieties of dependency and mortality' (Nicholson, 2009: 35). Similarly, for West and Glynos (2016), the more third age independence is socioculturally valorised, the stronger dependency is repudiated and projected onto others. These arguments resemble arguments from disability studies about the othering of disabled people, something considered later in this chapter.

Critical gerontology: the body, identity and intersectionality

Research on the ageing body as social construct has developed slowly within gerontology (Faircloth, 2003). Ageing embodiment is rarely attributed positive meaning but the biological has ceased to be 'the unique reference point in the truth of ageing and old age' (Tulle and Krekula, 2013: 7). Influenced by postmodern and post-structuralist perspectives, scholarship on the body and identity sometimes suggests that identities of older people are less constrained and more open to consumerist choices. Thus, from this perspective, there is the possibility of transcending the ageing body (Featherstone, 1991), or the very idea of 'old age' has been fractured into various 'cultures of ageing' (Gilleard and Higgs, 2000: 22). For Featherstone and Hepworth (1991), a culturally imposed 'mask of ageing' hides a more youthful ageless self.

Feminist critics dispute attempts to draw a radical separation between the body and the sense of self. However, feminist scholarship has been slow to engage with issues of the ageing body, and slower to consider the 'fourth age of frailty and dependence' (Twigg, 2004: 59, 71). Engagement with the body in the 'fourth' age becomes about 'Them, not Us' (Twigg, 2006: 50). Twigg (2004, 2006) brings an understanding of both biology and culture, discussing bathing and caring for older bodies, and arguing for more understanding of the role of the body in deep older age and of how 'frail' older people, especially, experience embodiment. There is also scope, as Chivers (2011: 22) suggests, for more consideration of how an older person's body perceived or read as having a disability is different from an older person's body read as not having a disability.

Hockey and James (2003: 106, 116) argue that the 'chronologised body' continues to 'be a source of constraints', as consumerist practices paradoxically intensify the focus on the role that biology and chronological age play in conceptualisations of ageing. For Calasanti and Slevin (2006: 3), the body is 'central to identity and to aging', and the maintenance of its youthful appearance requires increasing levels of work over time, especially of women. Thus, the role of the body as a marker of social identity is significant – perhaps never more so than at a stage when older age involves onset of impairment. It is also relevant to the empirical findings presented in Part II of this book.

Social constructionist approaches are helpful in showing how identities are not reducible to 'natural' or 'biological' factors but tell us little about the specific character of the body (Shilling, 2012). Holstein and Minkler (2007: 16–18) suggest that traditional approaches within social gerontology often fail to notice the real bodies of older people. Some sociological approaches engage with social attitudes to the appearance of ageing within postmodern culture (Gullette, 2004; Pickard, 2014). However, strong social constructionist approaches may not fully engage with the ageing body (Higgs and Rees-Jones, 2009). I find persuasive arguments that both bodily experiences *and* cultural interpretations are relevant (see Twigg, 2004, 2006; Cruikshank, 2008: 151; Tulle and Krekula, 2013).

Some approaches that focus less on striving to be young than claiming positive old age identities (see Featherstone and Hepworth, 1995; Sandberg, 2013) have parallels with the kind of positive disability identities claimed by younger disabled adults (see Priestley, 2003b: 62). In addition, while the disciplines of feminist disability studies and feminist gerontology have remained disparate fields (Gibbons, 2016), there have been intersections. These include the work of Chivers (2011: 23), who brings an appreciation of cultural disability studies to ageing, arguing that older age and disability are both constructed as 'bodily, threatening, and signalling failure'. They also include Morell's (2003) study, which argues that important needs of older people will be neglected while the 'rejected body' is 'feared and ignored'. In this, Morell draws on Wendell's (1996) notion of the 'rejected body', which is the body associated with weakness, disability and death – feared, despised or rejected in a society and culture. Thus, scholarship in gerontology echoes attempts to reintroduce the body and impairment into scholarship on disability.

Distinguished by a 'dual focus on inequalities and how they are interrelated', scholarship on **intersectionality** indicates the 'simultaneity' of categorical statuses, and focuses on systems of inequalities (Calasanti, 2019: 14–15). Thus, it is argued that a more nuanced picture of ageism can be achieved by looking at several mechanisms creating social inequality together, such as gender and race (Ayalon and Tesch-Römer, 2018). Intersectionality can also be combined with a lifecourse perspective to examine unequal ageing. However, intersectionality remains an uncommon and unclear approach to ageing (Calasanti, 2019), and there is very little intersectional scholarship on ageing and disability. Nevertheless, intersectionality could clearly contribute to making links between the two areas of scholarship.

Critical gerontology: meaning in life

Meaningful orientations prevent the world from being experienced as a 'chaotically unconnected succession of impressions' (Baars and Phillipson, 2014: 11), but relatively little research addresses what it means to lead a meaningful life (Derkx, 2013; Edmondson, 2015). Moody and Sasser (2012) and Holstein (2015) are among the gerontologists highlighting meaning as an important dimension of later life. Yet, Edmondson (2015: 1, 3) suggests that meaning in later life is seldom discussed directly, arguing that exclusionary practices frame meaning for older people (and their meaning to societies) as trivial. Edmondson relates this to a societal view that worthwhile activities are performed largely by people in paid work.

Tornstam (2005) developed the idea of older age as a time of transcendence or gerotranscendence, or as involving a shift from a materialistic, rational view of the world to a more cosmic and transcendent one. This approach can be seen as joining aspects of activity theory and disengagement theory as part of 'success' in ageing (Estes et al, 2003: 77). Some studies explore meaning in life with older people generally (Thompson, 1992) or with people in the third age (Weiss and Bass, 2002), but there is little exploration in the sociological literature specifically of how older people who experience disability, or are considered to be in the 'fourth age', find meaning in life. Yet, from a lifecourse perspective, Settersten (2002: 57) argues that questions about the purpose and meaning of life may become more urgent in the face of finitude and 'age-related declines and losses'. Thus, the need for self-realisation or actualisation may grow with age (Thompson, 1992; Dannefer and Lin, 2014).

Within critical gerontology, Grenier (2012: 175) suggests that the transition to impairment or the 'fourth age' is under-recognised, arguing for more consideration of the fourth age as a process of 'making meaning of continuity and change'. For Holstein (2015), the meaning we give to our lives is affected by illness or impairment that changes our relationship with our bodies, and with family and friends. Kahana and Kahana (2017: 77, 157) connect the issue of 'meaning in old age' to a holistic engagement with illness and disability, which 'can confer great meaning on life'. An empirical study with 'frail' older people found that participants had a sense of meaning in life but could also experience loss of a sense of meaning (Duppen et al, 2019).

Laceulle and Baars (2014) suggest that stereotyping cultural narratives of ageing (decline or age-defying) deprive older people of meaningful frames of reference. Notably, Baars (2017) attributes the lack of perspectives that explore ageing's potential for meaning, beyond 'decline' or 'age-defying' narratives, with a late-modern failure to identify with the fact that vulnerabilities and limitations, *and* creativity and fulfilment, are all part of later life. It is possible that these strands within critical/ cultural gerontology offer some potential for conversations across traditional boundaries in scholarship, emphasising as they do subjective perceptions of meaning and value at all stages of older age, as against more conventional paradigms that characterise good health and absence of impairment as the sine qua non of a good life.

It is worth noting here that meaning in life in older age is a growing area of scholarship in literature on psychology, anthropology, theology and philosophy, and it can be seen as a contributing factor to health, well-being or psychological adaptation (Krause, 2004; Reker and Wong, 2012; Hupkens et al, 2018). Thus, meaning in life can be approached as a contributing component to health or well-being, or as part of ethical debates about a good life (Hupkens et al, 2018). Molton and Yorkston (2017) and Jensen et al (2019) (from a medical or rehabilitation perspective) found that people living with long-term disability valued being able to live lives consistent with personal values.

Addressing the third age, Weiss and Bass (2002: 190) capture a straightforward idea of meaning in life as concerned with having a sense that one still matters, and that life makes sense. Other definitions identify several domains or 'needs'. In Part II, these are discussed in Chapter 7 in relation to a key argument of this book, based on inductive findings from its empirical study: older disabled people respond to perceived losses involved in the onset or worsening of disability by trying to remake or reorient their lives so as to experience them as continuing to have meaning and value.

Disability as social construction: introducing disability studies

In this section, I move to a discussion of approaches to scholarship on disability, considering areas of similarity or overlap with social gerontology. The term 'critical disability studies' describes 'the state of the field' now (Goodley, 2013: 632). Disability studies have developed in close association with activism. However, older disabled people have largely been left out of these debates, which foreground issues of disabled children and adults of working age (Priestley, 2006; Thomas and Milligan, 2018). Thus, research and theorising on experiences both of ageing with disability and of disability with ageing have received relatively little attention.

A key foundational approach to disability studies was materialism – briefly discussed here because of its influence on subsequent approaches, and for its parallels within theorising on ageing. The UK social model of disability was developed within a materialist perspective in which capitalism was perceived to have caused the oppression of disabled people (Finkelstein, 1981, 1998; Oliver, 1990, 1996; Barnes, 1997, 1998). The focus was material exclusion and social marginalisation. Parallels exist with the political economy perspective on ageing, which linked the structural dependency of older age and social policy developments during the 20th century (Townsend, 1981b). Thus, tackling disadvantage has been the main theoretical and political aim of disability studies from its inception (Vehmas and Watson, 2014), something shared with critical gerontology. However, the form it took within disability studies remained heavily materialist, involving 'dogmatic policing of disciplinary, researcher, theoretical and practice boundaries' (Meekosha and Shuttleworth, 2009: 55).

Nevertheless, as argued already, even critics acknowledge the political usefulness of the social model developed within the materialist perspective. The social model has 'almost iconic status' (Thomas, 2004: 573; see also Thomas and Milligan, 2018: 119). This is not least because it turned traditional views of disability upside down (Shakespeare, 2006: 31; 2013), something markedly different to the continued domination of biomedical approaches to ageing. However, the social model is rarely extended to people who first experience disability with ageing, and perhaps not even to people ageing with disability (Lamb, 2015: 314).

Critical or cultural disability studies

What is now termed 'critical' or 'cultural' disability studies arose from contributions by humanities and cultural studies scholars. From this perspective, disability is a social phenomenon that can illuminate culture (Titchkosky, 2003: 3). Attention is reoriented to ableism, that is, to ideas about normativity constructed by those whose bodies and minds are deemed to constitute 'the normal' (Thomas and Milligan, 2018: 121; see also the definition from Campbell (2001) quoted in Chapter 2). Goodley's (2013: 634) review includes a range of perspectives within the term 'critical', suggesting that they all emphasise 'cultural, discursive and relational undergirdings' of the disability experience. This remains a diverse field without consensus on any one way forward (Goodley et al, 2019). Due to their relevance to the arguments of this book and the interpretation of the empirical study that informs it, in the following sections, I discuss: **cultural representation** and **relational issues**; **bodies**; and **identity**, **multidimensionality** and **intersectionality**.

Critical disability studies: cultural representations and relational issues

Scholarship broadened from material and economic bases for discrimination to cultural representations and prejudice in everyday interactions (Riddell and Watson, 2003; Watson, 2003). These approaches emphasised the cultural production and reproduction of disability through the representation and stigmatisation of disabled people as 'other' due to negative media imagery and literature (Shakespeare, 1994). For Snyder and Mitchell (2006), representations of disability and impairment are manufactured by charities, science and popular culture in ways that '*dis*-locate' disabled people. Other contributions stress varied responses to media over time, and ambivalent and contradictory understandings (Wilde, 2010).

A focus on relational issues that cause exclusion or oppression is traced to Hunt (1998 [1966]) and Morris (1991), who highlighted how daily interactions were central to the segregation and oppression experienced by disabled people. Watson (2003) highlighted how disabling social relations (like being ignored or denied agency) make disablism part of disabled people's everyday lives. **Disablism** is 'discriminatory, oppressive or exclusionary behaviour arising from the belief that disabled people are inferior to others' (Miller et al, 2004: 9). Thomas (2007, 2015) developed a social relational approach to disablism, using the term 'psycho–emotional disablism' to refer to disablement that can occur in interactions between people with and without impairment, outlining how it impacts on psychological well-being and results in reduced opportunities to participate in society (see also Reeve, 2012).

Disability scholars argued that non-disabled people project fear of difficult aspects of existence – mortality, frailty and vulnerability – onto disabled people (Morris, 1991; Shakespeare, 1994). Some identified issues common to disabled people and older people. For example, in a ground-breaking essay, Hunt (1998 [1966]) suggested that disabled people and people who are sick or old are a reminder of what is most feared in life, including death. Morris (1991: 85, emphasis in original) argued that isolation and oppression of disabled people and ill or old people come about through fear and denial of 'frailty, vulnerability, mortality and *arbitrariness* of human experience'. For Priestley (2002, 2003a, 2006), cultural distancing of older and disabled people is reinforced by modernist discourses of independence, productivity and youth that devalue older and disabled people as non-adult dependants. Thus, Morris and Priestley point to similarities in the cultural construction of disability and older age, as do others (Irwin, 1999; Twigg, 2006; Chivers, 2011).

In short, similarities in underlying fears lead to cultural distancing from both older people and disabled people (Irwin, 1999), and both disabled and older people are denied full personhood (Luborsky, 1994). Perceived limitations of the bodies of members of 'dependent social categories' preclude the granting of full personhood, in contrast to the positive value placed on independent adulthood (Hockey and James, 1993: 102).

Critical disability studies: bodies

Again, reacting to foundational approaches, and as referred to in Chapter 2, feminist scholars, especially, critiqued the omission of the body from the social model of disability (Crow, 1996; Corker and French, 1999). Morris (1991: 183) argued that 'to deny the personal experience of disability is, in the end, to collude in our oppression'. Famously, Wendell (1996: 66, 85) encouraged identification with the 'rejected body' (associated with weakness, disability and death), arguing that self-acceptance and liberation for disabled people requires accommodating a range of physical conditions. An affirmation model challenged the idea of impairment as a problem, emphasising instead benefits like escaping role restrictions and social expectations, and having empathy with others (Swain and French, 2000). Another approach – phenomenological – characterised impairment as both an experience and a discursive construction (Hughes and Paterson, 1997: 329). Both Twigg (2004), considering ageing bodies, and Hughes and Paterson (1997), considering disabled bodies, argue that there is a danger that macro-level approaches have abandoned the topic of the body to medicine.

Feminist disability theory asserted that disability, like femaleness, is not a 'natural state of corporeal inferiority, inadequacy, excess, or a stroke of misfortune', but a culturally fabricated narrative of the body (Garland-Thomson, 2002: 5). This opened more potential to perceive disability as a political category and to highlight assumptions about disability and disabled bodies that lead to resource inequalities and social discrimination (Kafer, 2013: 14). For Kafer (2013: 3–4), the value of a future that includes disabled people goes unrecognised, as does the fact that illness and disability are part of what makes us human. However, as Gibbons (2016: 73–4) argues, feminist disability studies and feminist gerontology 'are fields on parallel paths' that rarely intersect.

The embodiment focus of critical/cultural theorising is often on meanings that originate in texts (Titchkosky, 2007), or on shifting from the body as the object of scrutiny to the institutional or medical gaze (Snyder and Mitchell, 2001). Feely (2016: 868) concedes that by prioritising discourse, critical disability scholarship may neglect material forces, but resists seeing 'impairment as a brute fact'. On the other hand, some feminist scholars (see Kafer, 2013: 3–6) and scholars in a realist tradition challenge the lack of consideration given to the material and biological. For Vehmas and Watson (2014: 641), seeing 'impairments as acceptable forms of human diversity is not the same as seeing them as neutral or insignificant'. Impairments often have tangible effects on people's well-being, many of which cannot be explained away by deconstruction; abolishing oppression requires 'more than an analysis of their categorisation and their historical genealogy' (Vehmas and Watson, 2014: 643). Siebers (2008: 5) suggests that if the field of disability studies is to advance, it requires accounting for both the negative and positive valences of disability. For Siebers (2008: 180–6), fragility, vulnerability and disability are central to the human condition, and this should inform claims to human rights.

Scholarship in this tradition also sometimes approaches disability as an issue relevant to all human beings. For example, for Shakespeare and Watson (2010: 65), impairment is a universal experience of humanity, and for Siebers (2008: 60), most people do not want to consider that life's passage will lead them from ability to disability as the 'prospect is too frightening, the disabled body too disturbing'. Shakespeare (2014a: 66), arguing from personal experience of two 'painful and disabling impairments', acknowledges the need for approaches that include positive aspects of life with impairment and possibilities for adaptation and flourishing, but also suggests that for most disabled people, impairment *is* a difficulty. For Shakespeare (2014a: 3), 'cultural' disability studies are over-theoretical and offer little practical help in understanding or improving the lives of disabled people, and he calls for more empirical research on how disabled people experience embodiment. Rembis (2015: 166 – emphasis added) asserts the need for 'new theories of disability oppression' that engage with the 'embodied realities of disabled people's lives *and* the materiality of the social relations of disability'.

Overall, the degree of emphasis on discourse and the cultural production of the disabled body within critical disability scholarship is far removed from traditional approaches within gerontology, where the dominant account of 'deep old age' is constructed around the concerns of medicine and policymakers, and is almost entirely one of the body and of decline (Twigg, 2004: 71). Indeed, when it comes to ageing even the social sciences and humanities start from biomedical definitions such as 'frailty' (Grenier, 2020) or the 'fourth age'. These issues highlight how opening dialogue between the two fields is challenging.

Critical disability studies: identity, multidimensionality and intersectionality

Membership of a shared disabled collective is generally viewed positively, its basis sought in shared resistance to oppression (Shakespeare, 2014a). However, approaches to identity linked to activism are challenged on grounds that disability experiences are heterogeneous (Shakespeare, 2014a). Postmodernist or post-structuralist thinking also makes the construction of a shared identity or political vision more challenging (Riddell and Watson, 2003; Feely, 2016). For Siebers (2008: 11), identity is 'out of fashion' as a category in critical or cultural theory. However, Siebers articulates ideas of complex embodiment, associated with the notion of a 'disability' identity based not in biology, but in shared social experiences. I discuss this again in Chapters 5 and 6.

An outcome of feminism and postmodern thought has been a problematisation of singular conceptions of disability, and multidimensionality has become a feature of critical disability theory (Meekosha and Shuttleworth, 2009; Hosking, 2008). A key contribution comes from Campbell (2001, 2009), whose intersectional analysis shifts attention away from the problems of disablism ('the Other') to the problems of ableism ('the same' or 'the dominant'). Critical studies of ableism contend with individualistic, psychological or neoliberal definitions of 'ability', apprehending ableism as 'the exclusion of many people by a cultural imaginary associated with self-sufficiency, autonomy and independence' (Goodley et al, 2019: 986).

Davis (2013b: 12) challenges ideas of normalcy, identifying the 'problem' not in the disabled person, but in how normalcy is constructed, and suggesting the need to reverse the 'hegemony of the normal' and institute alternative ways of thinking about the 'abnormal'. Thus, instead of seeing disability as a problem, studying normalcy reveals what makes disability a form of 'devalued marginality' (Titchkosky and Michalko, 2009: 6).

Another area is the merging of queer and disability studies, an example being the development of crip theory (McRuer, 2006;

Campbell, 2017). McRuer (2006) builds on the idea of compulsory heterosexuality from poet Adrienne Rich to develop the concept of compulsory able-bodiedness, challenging the idea of being able-bodied as an ideal (see also Kafer, 2003, 2013). Through this lens, the disabled body is a queer body with subversive, unruly and enabling aspects of being non-normative (Goodley, 2011: 158–61). It might be interesting to see considerations emerge as to whether disability might 'queer' or 'crip' age, or vice versa.

Critical disability theory also questions concepts of personal independence and interdependence, suggesting that all adults exist in varying states of dependence and independence (Shakespeare, 2000a, 2000b; Hosking, 2008). However, disabled people are also associated with challenges to the concept of care as being inherently unequal and controlling, and as framing them as passive and dependent (Beresford, 2008; Barnes and Mercer, 2010: 139). These arguments are sometimes seen as conflicting with approaches of feminist care researchers (Kelly, 2010, 2016), and feminist care ethics often informs approaches to ageing (see Lloyd, 2004, 2010; Barnes, 2011). Fine and Glendinning (2005) suggest that conflicts between the languages of 'care' and 'dependency' proceed along largely separate lines, with little sense that they are exploring and explaining different aspects of the same phenomenon.

The concept of **intersectionality** is applied to disability, though it is arguable that its application remains limited (Erevelles and Minear, 2010; Bê, 2012; Shaw et al, 2012). Given that intersectionality remains an uncommon approach to ageing (Calasanti, 2019), it is not surprising that this perspective has yet to contribute greatly to exploring intersections of age and disability. According to Gibbons (2016: 71), lack of collaboration between gerontology and disability studies, and their feminist subfields, has 'limited the opportunities for intersectional critiques of successful ageing'. Berghs et al (2019) argue that disability studies must welcome greater diversity and intersectionality of identities across the lifecourse. An intersectional lifecourse perspective is an avenue for greater engagement with experiences of ageing with disability. Thus, intersectionality clearly has potential – yet largely unrealised – to contribute to advancing conversations between scholarship on ageing and disability.

For Kafer (2013: 8), anxiety about ageing can be seen as a symptom of compulsory able-bodiedness/able-mindedness. However, for the most part, disability scholars have not challenged the ableism or compulsory able-bodiedness in the way that successful ageing discourses have evolved (Gibbons, 2016). The work of Gibbons (2016) represents an exception. Basing her discussion on McRuer's concept of compulsory able-bodiedness, she characterises 'successful' ageing approaches as ableist, as well as ageist, constituting what she calls 'compulsory youthfulness', involving ableism and ageism in reinforcing youthfulness and able-bodiedness as ideals.

Even though this section has highlighted scholars in disability and ageing identifying some similar issues, critical disability studies and critical ageing studies remain separate (Grenier et al, 2016), and the main focus in disability studies is on issues concerning young people and adults. There are also scholars who oppose the idea, put forward by Siebers (2008) and others, that able-bodied status is essentially temporary (see Hughes, 2009; Meekosha and Shuttleworth, 2009). However, there are some signs of change. In addition to scholarship in a realist tradition already discussed: Garland-Thomson (2016) argues for a more universal engagement with disability issues across the lifespan; Davis (2013a) asks how older people will define disability as populations age; and Lamb (2015) calls for more conversations across academic boundaries. The call from Yoshizaki-Gibbons (2019) for critical disability studies to engage with ageing is notable, as she suggests that critical disability studies could develop and grow by exploring intersections between ageing and disability.

There is also an emerging engagement within disability studies with dementia as disability (Aubrecht and Keefe, 2016; Shakespeare et al, 2019), as well as evidence that people with dementia experience disablism (Thomas and Milligan, 2018). These approaches can be associated with efforts to make anti-discrimination measures, as well as human rights and other legal protections, available to people with dementia (Thomas and Milligan, 2018), or to afford an enabling identity for self-advocacy (Shakespeare et al, 2019). However, it is also true, I suggest, that those issues are relevant to people experiencing other conditions or impairments in older age.

It is interesting that even though Goodley et al (2019: 980) take issue with realist critiques of critical/cultural disability studies, they also allude to the need to re-centre disabled people and their allies as 'the driving subjects and articulators of theory'. If emancipatory research engaged with experiences of disability in older age (in all their diversity), that could contribute a basis for more links between critical studies on ageing and disability, and, more importantly, for the development of more realistic engagements with human experience across the lifespan.

Aspects of medical sociology

In Chapter 2, I referred to two fields that seek to define what disability is: medical sociology (associated with biopsychosocial or interactional models); and disability studies (associated especially with social models). Debates between the fields of disability studies and the sociology of health and illness are often heated (Thomas, 2007). Although there have been attempts within disability studies to draw a line between chronic illness and disability (Barnes and Mercer, 1996), the importance of chronic illness is recognised in disability studies too (Crow, 1996; Thomas, 2007; Bê, 2016, 2019). For example, Bê (2016) argues that people with chronic conditions are also affected by structural, cultural and external circumstances. Moreover, Grue (2017) argues that disability studies is about the interests not of a narrow minority, but of a diverse and heterogeneous group of people, many of whom do not consider themselves disabled, but may consider themselves ill.

Medical sociologist Bury starts from the perspective that most disabled people experience chronic illness. He understands disability as occurring both in bodies *and* due to social disadvantage, and while reducing barriers to participation is important, he suggests that social model characterisations of disability as social oppression are 'over-socialised' (Bury, 1997: 138). For critics from within disability studies, this perspective insufficiently locates disability in wider economic or political structures (Thomas, 2004, 2007), or it focuses on 'coping' or 'adjusting', not rights (Bê, 2016). However, Shakespeare (2006, 2014a: 79) suggests that his understanding of what disability is aligns with that of Bury. Shakespeare and Watson (2010: 65) also suggest that scholarship from this perspective could do more to examine structural issues faced by disabled people.

An aspect of theorising addresses onset of chronic illness or impairment, seen to interrupt an individual's previous lifecourse assumptions and narratives, forcing renegotiation of biographical identities; this is called 'biographical disruption' and occurs in the context of modern cultures premised on a general expectation of long life and of health (Bury, 1982: 169–70; 1997: 124). Somewhat similar arguments are made by gerontologists who highlight that disability first experienced in older age is a permanent change in the status quo – 'a disruptive force' (Kahana and Kahana, 2017: ix). However, the relationship between age and chronic illness is under-theorised in medical sociology (Higgs and Rees-Jones, 2009: 2–3, 10). In addition, the perspective of people ageing with disability is largely missing (Williams, 2000; Larsson and Jeppsson Grassman, 2012). However,

Williams (2000) suggested that age, timing and context might be important factors – chronic illness might be a biographically *anticipated* event in later life. As regards people ageing with disability, Larsson and Jeppsson Grassman (2012) argue that biographical disruption is relevant to their experience too, and that it can be experienced not as a single or wholly unanticipated 'disruption', but as a series of events.

Overall, despite similar concerns, medical sociology, social gerontology and, for the most part, disability studies proceed separately (Thomas, 2007; Higgs and Rees-Jones, 2009). However, the concept of biographical disruption may be useful in interpreting the meanings that older people make of impairment onset/worsening, and I employed it in interpreting the inductive findings (reported on in Chapters 5 and 6 of Part II). I used it because it resists both postmodernist challenges to a biographically embodied approach, and social constructionist approaches that write the body out of the picture. It allowed engagement with issues that I identified as important to participants, such as impairment, or increasing impairment, at a body level, and extrinsic factors perceived as disabling, including social, cultural, policy and economic contexts, as well as with the consequences of both for a sense of self and identity.

Scholarship on the lifecourse

The final field of scholarship I review in this chapter concerns the lifecourse – the most widely cited theoretical framework in social gerontology (Bengtson et al, 2005: 13). The lifecourse perspective is also recognised as potentially useful in bridging research on ageing and disability (Naidoo et al, 2012; Kahana and Kahana, 2017: 86). For example, Priestley (2001) argues for more research from this perspective on the intersecting pathways of ageing with disability and experiences of disability with ageing.

However, the 'lifecourse perspective' encompasses a vast scholarship and there are different approaches. Associated especially with Elder (1975), the lifecourse perspective in sociology is a 'theoretical orientation' that guides questions, conceptual development and research design, and is associated with five well-recognised general principles: lifespan development, agency, time and place, timing, and linked lives (Elder et al, 2003: 10–13). From this perspective, the lifecourse consists of 'age-graded patterns' 'embedded in social institutions and history' (Elder et al, 2003: 4). This research attempts to explain how ageing is shaped by, among other things, social contexts, cultural meanings and social-structural location (Bengtson et al, 2005: 14).

The lifecourse perspective often presupposes that an institutional pattern shapes lives (Kohli, 1986, 2007: 256). Thus, the lifecourse is often seen as tripartite: preparation for work, working and retirement (Kohli, 1986, 2007; Heinz, 2004). Studies often explore how earlier experiences/resources condition later actions and opportunities (Kohli, 2007). Scholars have examined various types of transitions, often drawing on trends and comparisons of groups and cohorts. Transitions are often anchor points from which to observe social change, such as family type (see Hareven, 1978). Thus, the study of transitions often involves exploring normative structural change.

Applied to the issue of disability generally, the lifecourse perspective provides insights into institutions and assumptions that shape experiences of both disabled people and non-disabled people (Irwin, 2001). Disability can involve life trajectories that position disabled people outside standardised notions of the lifecourse (Grenier et al, 2016). A critical understanding of disability challenges both lifecourse institutions, like policies for employment or pensions, and the cultural rules that define what a 'normal' life means (Priestley, 2000, 2001, 2003a). From this perspective, cultural understandings of what constitutes disability are connected to understandings of time and the idea of a normative lifecourse, which are built on ableist norms (Ljuslinder et al, 2020). However, the construction of the normative lifecourse from a disability (or crip) perspective is under-researched (Ljuslinder et al, 2020).

Within social gerontology, the lifecourse perspective is associated with linking features of early life to outcomes in later life for individuals or populations, and with a shift from understanding ageing as a 'process of organismically governed change' towards recognition of the importance of context and experience over time (Dannefer and Settersten, 2010: 3–7). Later-life impairment, and its prevention, is often placed in the context of earlier stages of life (Walker, 2014: 9; see also Kuh, 2007).

Among lifecourse perspectives are humanistic or interpretive approaches (Holstein and Gubrium, 2000; Hockey and James, 2003). Instead of focusing on predicting relations between 'fixed' variables, this perspective engages with the interpretive dynamics of the world. For Hockey and James (2003: 180), an exclusive focus on macro-level sociohistorical accounts does not always result in insights into embodied experiences of ageing. This approach foregrounds the constructed nature of the lifecourse – examining how people *constitute* the lifecourse through interpretive practice and how experience is made meaningful in relation to the passage of time (Holstein and Gubrium, 2000: 41).

This perspective understands experience as constructed and emergent but also as 'circumstantially shaped' – or constructed under certain circumstances in which individuals draw from distinctive discourses, interpretive resources and structures of normative accountability (Holstein and Gubrium, 2000: 184). This includes engaging with ways that people employ categories and descriptions like 'old age' to make sense of life change, and with terms like 'stage' or 'milestone' used to focus on the *sense* that people have of life having changed (Holstein and Gubrium, 2000: 34–41).

This approach is consistent with critical gerontological approaches, as characterised by Grenier (2012: 12, 19), which emphasise the constructed nature of the lifecourse, question assumptions that inform organisational and institutional practices, and emphasise subjective perceptions of older people as revealed in narratives. Critical gerontology and lifecourse approaches both aim to understand the interplay of structures, history, context and experience (Grenier, 2012: 35). However, while much work in social gerontology claims to ground analysis in the 'lifecourse', what is often meant is that ageing must be conceptualised as a process across the span of a lifetime (Grenier, 2012). Thus, this approach differs from 'the lifecourse perspective' associated with Elder and others (Grenier, 2012).

There are also some limitations with the classic lifecourse perspective as an approach to ageing, especially as an approach to ageing and disability together. Traditionally, the transitions of later life were seen as widowhood and retirement (Ferraro, 2001: 314–15), and they still receive most research interest (see Chambers, 2000; Phillipson, 2002). However, while spousal loss is especially prevalent among the oldest old, who are also more likely to experience disability, there is little dedicated research focusing on their experiences of widowhood (Isherwood et al, 2017). Furthermore, disability or disablement in older age are not always marked institutionally, and the related transitions are not much explored, even in recent lifecourse interpretations (Grenier, 2012; Grenier et al, 2016: 12–13). Overall, scholars still tend to recognise retirement as the dominant transition in older age, paying far less attention to 'frailty' or entering the so-called 'fourth age' (Grenier, 2012: 169–73). Finally, little is known from a lifecourse perspective about the experience of people ageing with disability (Jeppsson Grassman et al, 2012). Kahana and Kahana (2017: 78) summarise what is needed succinctly: 'a lifecourse language and framework that will validate the person living with illness and disability, both in youth and into old age'.

Part of the rationale for the empirical study that informs this book (see Part II) comes from the lack of engagement within the lifecourse perspective with transitions involving impairment in later life and the fact that little is known from a lifecourse perspective about experiences of ageing with long-standing disability. The empirical study used an inductive method, and in interpreting its findings, concepts from the lifecourse perspective (such as linked lives) were sometimes used to help link biographical experiences with wider social contexts. A social constructionist approach to the lifecourse also helped in explicating how people interpreted and made sense of changes over time.

Discussion and conclusions

The review in this chapter of key theoretical approaches within gerontology, disability studies, medical sociology and lifecourse studies supports the contention made in Chapter 1 that there are only separate theories on ageing and on disability. While there is some limited focus within critical disability studies and medical sociology on ageing, and calls for more engagement, these fields remain largely separate from that of gerontology. They also remain separate, for the most part, from each other. In general terms, gerontological approaches to disability in older age insufficiently acknowledge the cultural, social and economic causes and consequences of impairment or disability (Kelley-Moore, 2010; Phillipson, 2013), and tend to engage with the issue of disability largely as an 'undesirable condition' (Kahana and Kahana, 2017: 5).

For its part, disability theorising foregrounds issues affecting children and younger adults, leaving older disabled people out of the picture (Kennedy and Minkler, 1998; Priestley, 2006). Kafer (2013: 14) reflects that it is hard to include, in scholarship and activism, a group that does not wish to be considered 'disabled'. However, discussing disability generally, she argues that the value of a future that includes disability goes unrecognised (Kafer, 2013: 3). This is particularly the case when disability is experienced later in life, in part, because it occurs in the stage of life before death – and death, as Twigg (2006) argues, is something about which modern secular culture tends to be silent.

A key insight of social models of disability and critical disability studies that disability is not just a personal, individual issue, but also socially created, has yet to be applied to any great extent to the experience of disability in older age. Even within social gerontology, scholarship taking its starting point from medicalised approaches (using concepts such as 'frailty' or the 'fourth age') risks acceding to an overwhelmingly negative framing of disability in older age that blots out the potential for seeing the experience in the round. We also lack a comprehensive engagement with subjective experiences of older disabled people (or so-called 'fourth-agers').

There are similarities in the course that theorising has taken within the fields of gerontology and disability studies. Critical gerontology has similar goals, methods and politics to those of disability studies, and focuses on interpretation as much as on materiality (Chivers, 2011: 9). Thus, both engage with cultural, discursive and relational issues. Yet, by focusing almost entirely on discourse rather than lived experience, it is arguable that much scholarship within cultural or critical studies denies the reality of impairment, remaining at a remove from lived experience, and at the greatest remove from the bodies of the oldest older people. Taking a critical realist perspective within disability studies, Shakespeare (2014a) both validates for enrichment of thinking and critiques critical/cultural approaches to disability, highlighting how they do not fully engage with subjective experiences of disabled people's lives or embodiment.

Scholars writing on ageing from a critical/cultural perspective suggest that the issue of meaning in life may become a particularly important factor due to the amount of change involved. Yet, the issue is not often apprehended directly and there are few explorations with older people of meaning in life (Edmondson, 2015). Although it is changing, there has traditionally been almost no specific exploration of meaning in life among older people who are experiencing impairment or disability (or are in the so-called 'fourth-age'). However, arguably, this group experiences the greatest challenge to meaning due to the extent of change and loss involved, and proximity to end of life. 'Disability', as Goodley (2014: xi) says, asks us 'to consider what we value in life'. However, it is under-recognised that this continues to be the case relative to experiences of disability in the last stage of life.

Some lifecourse studies include a focus on experiences of older disabled people or the 'fourth age', or challenge normative depictions of the lifecourse from these perspectives (Priestley, 2003a; Grenier et al, 2016). However, knowledge of disability and ageing is still underdeveloped and the experience of disability in older age, and the transitions it involves, are not well understood, either within the sociological lifecourse perspective (associated with Elder) or within lifecourse studies in gerontology (Grenier, 2012: 169–82; Jeppsson Grassman et al, 2012). Least of all is known about experiences of people ageing with long-standing disability.

Some critical gerontologists suggest that gerontology could learn about the social construction of disability from disability scholars, and some use concepts developed within disability studies to highlight constructions and experiences of late-life disability (see Kelley-Moore, 2010; McGrath et al, 2017; Sandberg and Marshall, 2017). However, insights from critical disability studies about what disability reveals about culture have yet to be applied to any great extent to disability experiences in older age. There is surely much to be explicated from this perspective as to the implications of disability becoming a more widespread phenomenon as populations age. Overall, while scholarship often uses similar paradigms to explore ageing and (separately) disability, the two fields progress largely on parallel tracks. Thus, while critical approaches have capacity to explore disability in older age, most critical approaches focus *either* on disability or on ageing (Grenier et al, 2016). Arguably, neither field engages fully with the subjective experiences involved so as to reveal both what constitutes disability (at micro and macro levels) in older age, and what it means to live a life of value and meaning with disability in later life.

Within disability studies, Siebers (2008), Shakespeare (2014a), Garland-Thomson (2016) and Yoshizaki-Gibbons (2019) are among those perceiving that 'disability' can be first experienced in older age, with Davis (2013a: 272) identifying the need to explore how older people will redefine disability. Correspondingly, within gerontology, Grenier (2012: 188–9) and Lloyd et al (2014) call for more investigation of how the 'fourth age' is defined, of how older people interpret or negotiate it, and of the meaning and significance attributed to the transition to it. These debates and arguments developed throughout this chapter and Chapter 2 informed the research questions for the empirical study that informs this book. They address how older people experience disability and processes of disablement, and how they respond. Thus, the empirical study presented in Part II, in exploring different experiences of disablement and disability in older age, seeks to make an empirical contribution to the debates outlined in this chapter. The disjuncture between scholarship on disability and on ageing that was the subject of this chapter is also found in disparate approaches to public policy, which is the subject of Chapter 4.

4

Public policies on ageing and disability

Introduction

Public policies frame how societies provide care and support in practice, influence a sense of identity, and shape perceptions of what categories we belong to as individuals. They offer a window on how society conceives of disability for younger and older persons (Kahana and Kahana, 2017: 181). In this chapter, I engage with the separation of public policy frameworks on ageing and disability, and the consequences for older people, focusing on social care.

I first introduce how public policies traditionally underscore difference between people with different timings of disability onset. They can operate as if people are disabled or older, not both. This separately constructs 'disability' experienced at different points of the lifespan and makes for an anomalous picture when we consider experiences at the intersections of the two frameworks. The phenomenon of more people ageing with disability highlights the need for connection between the two frameworks. The issues discussed here form part of the rationale for this book's attempt to open more dialogue between scholarship on ageing and on disability, and form a backdrop to the findings of the empirical study discussed in Part II.

To approach public policies in an international context is to engage with a very broad set of issues. Identifying patterns in long-term care is more difficult than in other policy areas (Esping-Andersen, 1990; Glendinning, 2010), as they are often built on existing institutional arrangements. Hill (2006: 42) reminds us that the characteristics of policies require attention to 'constitutional, institutional and cultural factors', and to financing and delivery. In this chapter, I consider key aspects of public policies that are relevant to the arguments in this book, hoping to foster more engagement with the issues involved.

I first discuss disability prevalence linked to increased numbers of older people in populations, and introduce traditional approaches to policies on ageing and on disability. I consider consequences of the traditional separation between these two policy frameworks for people first experiencing disability with ageing and then for people ageing with disability. The chapter goes on to consider attempts to bridge the two fields in practice. I finish by suggesting lessons that can be drawn by those attempting to find a way forward in this area.

Background: disability prevalence

National and supranational estimates of disability prevalence represent one area where older people are usually counted within the category 'disabled'. However, discussion of disability estimates often fails to acknowledge that older disabled people are included (Yoshizaki-Gibbons, 2019). Several studies suggest that rates of disability in older age are declining, but whether disability has been postponed is debated (Bowling and Dieppe, 2005), and there is evidence to the contrary (Freedman et al, 2002; Crimmins and Beltrán-Sánchez, 2010). However, the link between growth in disability and global population ageing, especially among the 'oldest old', is well recognised (World Health Organization and World Bank, 2011; United Nations, 2019: 4).

According to the World Report on Disability, and based on 2010 population estimates and estimates of disability from 2004, there are between 785 million (15.6 per cent) and 975 million (19.4 per cent) disabled people in the world (aged 15 years and over) (World Health Organization and World Bank, 2011). The rate was higher for women than for men. At between 38.1 per cent and 46.1 per cent, the rate was much higher for people aged 60+, of whom, according to one estimate, about 10 per cent experienced severe levels of disability (World Health Organization and World Bank, 2011). Older people are disproportionately represented in disability populations, making up about 35 per cent of disabled people in the US and Australia (aged 65+ in this context) (World Health Organization and World Bank, 2011: 35). More than 250 million people aged 60+ worldwide experience moderate to severe disability (World Health Organization, 2012). Rates are much higher among the oldest old, and people aged 80 to 89 are the fastest-growing age group worldwide (World Health Organization and World Bank, 2011: 35).

In the EU, disability prevalence, based on activity limitations, among people aged 65+ living in private households is about 47.5 per cent, which represents 45.3 million people and makes up 45.9 per cent of all disabled people (that is, people aged 16+ living in private households; data from 2016) (Grammenos, 2018). Approximately 16 million people aged 65+ experience severe levels of disability, with 30 million experiencing moderate levels, and these figures would be higher if people living in residential settings had been included (Grammenos, 2018).

Substantially more women than men experience disability in older age (Fried and Guralnik, 1997; World Health Organization, 2012). The role of socio-economic factors in the construction of disability in older age, and of related concepts such as 'frailty', is evident from many studies (Kuh, 2007; Kelley-Moore, 2010; Yumiko et al, 2012). For example, compared with non-disabled older people, older disabled people in the US are more likely to be female, of a minority ethnicity, to have less than a high school degree, and to live in poverty (Henning-Smith, 2016).

Disability mostly occurs in later life but disabled people are living longer, creating a 'new category of older adults' (Putnam, 2002: 799; see also Verbrugge and Yang, 2002). A demographic shift among this group reflects changes in population ageing, medical advances and disease control (Molton and Ordway, 2019). The precise population numbers of people ageing with disability are unknown due to gaps in the evidence base (Freedman, 2014; La Plante, 2014; Verbrugge et al, 2017). Estimates from the US that isolate age of onset prior to midlife suggest that approximately 33–40 per cent of the disabled adult population experienced onset at or before age 44, based on a functional approach to measurement (Verbrugge and Yang, 2002; La Plante, 2014). Some 12–15 million disabled adults were ageing having experienced onset before age 40 (in 2010) (La Plante, 2014).

This group of people sometimes experiences secondary conditions and more rapid ageing (La Plante, 2014; Verbrugge et al, 2017), often with a legacy of social disadvantage, such as high unemployment, low levels of marriage or cohabiting, and low incomes and educational attainment (see Loprest and Maag, 2007; Iezzoni, 2014; MacDonald et al, 2018). During childhood and at each stage of the lifecourse, disabled people are disproportionately exposed to social factors contributing to health inequalities (Berghs et al, 2016: 1). However, there is a lack of empirical evidence on which to develop approaches designed to support this group (Putnam et al, 2016; Coyle and Mutchler, 2017).

Introducing international policy approaches to ageing and to disability

Historically, both ageing and disability were apprehended as medical problems and institutionalisation was commonplace. However, separate policy fields traditionally operate in many countries (Monahan and Wolf, 2014). The medical model still informs approaches to ageing, aiming to alter the 'trajectory of loss and function', and often involving 'custodial' care (Monahan and Wolf, 2014: S1). Policy frameworks are not well developed across many countries for people ageing with disability (Bigby, 2002; Carter Anand et al, 2012; Raymond et al, 2014). Most literature in this field focuses on experiences among people with intellectual disability (Chicoine et al, 1999), in respect of whom there is growing engagement with policy and other implications of longevity (see McCallion and McCarron, 2015).

A social care model has come to inform approaches to disability (Monahan and Wolf, 2014: S1). Changes from the 1960s are associated with the independent living movement in the US, the self-advocacy movement in Sweden and advocacy by residents of institutions in Britain (Barnes and Mercer, 2010: 71). In practice, though, medicalised approaches, lack of control or inflexibility are still in evidence (Travaglia and Robertson, 2003; Barnes and Mercer, 2010: 127, 154). However, changes in disability policy occurred largely without input of age activism, and people ageing with disability can fear that control and choice will diminish within services for 'older' people (Putnam, 2007, 2017). Concern about the implications of demographic ageing result in surprisingly few linkages with parallel debates over disability rights and policies among policymakers and activists (Priestley, 2002).

Separate policy frameworks tend to categorise people as either disabled or older (Bigby, 2008). Someone considered 'disabled' at age 64 may be categorised, instead, as 'old' at age 65 (Kelley-Moore, 2010: 104). The strong association with illness and death in older age can elide the fact that older people tend to want to maintain their health to stay living in their communities, while the response to them is primarily medical and individualised (Kahana and Kahana, 2017). A key argument of this book is that medicalised distinctions help to obscure commonalities in diverse experiences of disability as a broader socially constructed phenomenon – something that operates in the policy sphere as it does in others.

Advocacy organisations in both ageing and disability now highlight inequities in services in the context of international human rights frameworks. For example, AGE Platform Europe (2017, 2019) catalogues laws and policies imposing age limits in access to disability benefits, mobility allowances or personal assistance. Similarly, the European Network on Independent Living (2018) highlights how supports for independent living are limited to people of working age in several countries. Yet, policies and activism often approach these issues from the perspective either of disability or of ageing. As the UN Special Rapporteur on the Rights of Persons with Disabilities commented: 'The fragmentation of policies for older persons and for persons with disabilities results in the invisibility in law and in practice of experiences of disability in later life' (United Nations, 2019: 5). Human rights violations against older disabled people are often neither monitored nor categorised as such (United Nations, 2019: 10).

Furthermore, changing trends within policies on ageing and disability involving the introduction of a quasi-market in social care and greater consumer direction, at least rhetorically, are now highly influential in bringing issues of 'age' and 'disability' together in practice, sometimes in ways that are arbitrary and contested. Policy decisions can force change on groups traditionally separately categorised, as 'older' or 'disabled', before intellectual understanding and proposed solutions start to have effect (Torres-Gil, 2007). The 'nexus' of ageing and disability, and the 'overlay' of ageing with disability, will become more visible over time (Torres-Gil, 2007: 254). As Putnam (2007: 12) suggests, the phenomenon of ageing with disability brings to the fore questions about lack of integration between ageing and disability fields, as well as the future direction of scholarship, research and practice.

Policies on ageing

Policies on ageing have undergone a 'change of emphasis', from responses to isolated problems, to attempts to prescribe what it is to 'age well and responsibly' (Estes et al, 2003: 4). Two overarching policy principles in health and care are identified in countries with established welfare states (Lloyd, 2012: 1): first, promoting notions such as 'positive' or active ageing so that independence can continue for as long as possible; and, second, keeping a 'tight rein' on care spending to contain costs, associated with the for-profit sector replacing the state and an emphasis on consumerism or individualisation. The terms 'active' or 'healthy' ageing are used within international policies, allied to 'successful', 'productive' or 'ageing well' approaches. As outlined already in Chapter 3, 'active ageing' emphasises maintenance of health, independence and productivity (Walker, 2002; World Health Organization, 2002a: 12). 'Healthy' ageing is defined as 'developing and maintaining the functional ability that enables well-being in older age' (World Health Organization, 2015: 28).

The usefulness of these approaches in supporting some groups of older people to remain active is sometimes acknowledged in the context of critiques (Boudiny, 2013). Again, as outlined already, critical gerontologists take issue with them for their basis in the medical model, characterising 'successful' ageing as incompatible with ill health or impairment (Estes et al, 2003: 67; Holstein and Minkler, 2007: 15). They risk marginalising older disabled people within an active participation policy agenda, and they can construct the experience of disability in older age as a personal failure (Raymond and Grenier, 2013; McGrath et al, 2016). They also risk overlooking the role of broader physical, social and economic environments in shaping health outcomes and ability to participate in healthy lifestyles in later life, and are aligned with key features of neoliberalism (Pack et al, 2019). Lloyd (2012: 84) questions the 'moral pressure' they place on older people given the link between socio-economic disadvantage and poor health or disability.

Another consequence of the dominance of 'active ageing' approaches is that policies promote little understanding of how to age well with disability, whether first experienced early or late in life. Instead, we might be better off moving towards the idea that, with proper supports, life can continue to be rewarding (Torres-Gil, 2007: 256). This reinforces arguments for empirical research with people who have diverse experiences of ageing and disability so that their experiences can influence both societal perceptions and policy prescriptions.

Fundamentally, larger political and economic issues linked to 'active ageing' aim to reduce demand on healthcare, reflecting a preoccupation with economics and the organisation of care, and less concern with the *practices* of care (Lloyd, 2012: 5–9, 81). This focus is almost exclusively on demand, supply and funding of services, not on what care is needed and how it is experienced (Lloyd, 2012). As mentioned, there is a related trend towards privatisation and greater individualisation in home care associated with a rhetoric of 'personalised care' and 'consumer choice' across North America, Europe and East Asia (Higgs and Gilleard, 2015: 38).

Even countries that have traditionally provided universal access to services have seen widespread marketisation of home care. For example, Vamstad (2016) discusses marketisation of home care in Sweden, citing studies suggesting that older people tend to lack access to information to inform decisions. Decisions must often be made in challenging situations (like sudden changes in health), though the choices involved are less of an issue for older people with more income and education (Vamstad, 2016).

This unravelling of the welfare state, in some countries especially, is associated with requiring older people to organise their own social care under the guise of 'individualisation' or 'personalisation' (Phillipson, 2013, 2015, 2020). For Phillipson (2020: 220), these processes have been 'supported' through active ageing policies. Relatedly, austerity measures have resulted in cuts to health and social care in many advanced welfare regimes (Phillipson, 2020: 217–18). Cuts have harmed women more than men, people with fewer resources and people who are oldest (Phillipson, 2020; see Hiam et al, 2017). In some countries, the effects of austerity and neoliberal policies have been highly 'disabling' for some groups of older people (Phillipson, 2020: 220). Drawing on feminist care ethics, Lloyd (2010, 2012: 5) challenges the assumptions that underlie 'the contractual model of relationships' for placing older people experiencing loss of self-reliance and increased dependency 'in a particularly invidious position within markets'. As mentioned in Chapter 3, arguments from this perspective are sometimes seen to conflict with challenges to traditional notions of care from disability studies and activism, considered next.

Policies on disability

The approach to disability has changed over recent decades. As is clear from the discussion thus far, many countries are 'experimenting' with some form of individualised funding or personalised budgets, particularly in long-term care (Gadsby et al, 2013; Pike et al, 2016: 6). The term 'personalised budget' tends to refer to the total amount of money allocated to a service user following assessment. One way in which it can be administered is by way of direct payment. Countries tend to use different personal budget models; a common central idea relates to enabling increased levels of choice and control (Carter Anand et al, 2012).

In the UK, disability activists (Oliver, 1990; Morris, 1993, 2006) argued for a shift to greater choice and control over personal support, as well as for greater user input from a democratic/participatory standpoint (Barnes and Mercer, 2010: 150). The notion of independent living is intended to mean that disabled people have more freedom, with practical assistance 'under the control of disabled individuals' (Barnes and Mercer, 2006: 33; see also Prideaux et al, 2009: 559). Related to this, disability activists challenged traditional notions of 'care' that characterised them as passive and dependent, and campaigned for support in the form of personal assistance (Barnes and Mercer, 2010: 139, 143–4).

Disability activists in some US states, Canada and several European countries are especially associated with campaigns for direct payments (or 'cash-for-care' schemes) (Da Roit and Le Bihan, 2010; Glasby, 2011; Brennan et al, 2016; Kelly, 2016). Studies evidence how direct funding can be liberating by contributing more control, flexibility and freedom in daily life, though approaches vary across countries (Kelly, 2010). However, the 'personalisation' agenda divided stakeholders from the outset and continues to be controversial (Glasby, 2011: 7; Woolham et al, 2017; Carey et al, 2018). As Kelly (2010) argues, the needs of some groups of disabled people are unaccounted for within these types of political demands, which implicitly position rational, independent decision-making as the ultimate 'ability'. Across several countries, studies suggest that people from lower socio-economic groups are less likely to be able to benefit from marketised changes, as are people with conditions like intellectual or neurological impairment (Carey et al, 2018). Responding to some of these issues, Kelly (2010) argues that alongside models that privilege the value of independence, disability activism must advocate for interdependent, community models of care.

In addition, it is arguable that these policies have been reconceived in consumerist terms (Riddell et al, 2006; Beresford, 2008). Carey et al (2018: 29) argue that, in the context of Australia, they have been used to undertake major restructuring of the disability sector in the 'guise of choice and control'. In several countries, implementation of these approaches has coincided with reductions in funding and/or access to support (Brennan et al, 2016; Slasberg and Beresford, 2016, 2020). For example, there have been cuts both to resources and, especially, in the numbers benefiting from social care since 2009/10 in the UK (Slasberg and Beresford, 2020). Although appraisals of personalised approaches continue to be diverse, Slasberg and Beresford (2020: 329) suggest that 'the personal budget strategy has comprehensively failed' in the UK. Their implementation has also coincided in the UK with reductions in building-based services like day centres (Needham, 2014) and with cuts to disability income supports (Cross, 2013; Shakespeare et al, 2017).

While complex and country-specific in implementation, the personalisation agenda can make manifest underlying assumptions inherent in the traditional separation in policy approaches to ageing and to disability. In some countries, 'personalisation' has meant something of a de facto amalgamation of the two sectors. This has resulted in mixed outcomes, something considered later in this chapter. As Lloyd (2010) argues, these concepts advocated for by disability activists have been adopted in response to population ageing to limit state involvement. Thus, the implementation of approaches ostensibly linked with disability activism is underpinned by efforts to contain costs of population ageing.

Issues arising from the separation of policy frameworks

The discussion thus far suggests that ageing and disability policy frameworks traditionally operate as separate categorical systems. Their separation has several fundamental consequences, and these also affect attempts to align or bridge them. As Putnam (2014: S51) suggests, discussing the situation in the US: 'This silo system has produced age-based theories and conceptual frameworks, bifurcated scientific knowledge bases, parallel fields of professional practice and system-specific ideologies, vocabularies and cultures of service delivery.' A growing literature from many countries documents issues associated with the separation of the two fields (Priestley and Rabiee, 2001; Putnam, 2007; Jönson and Larsson, 2009; Leahy, 2018; Molton and Ordway, 2019). Complexity, confusion, illogicality and, sometimes, institutionalised ageism characterise the impact of separate policy approaches to ageing and to disability, and the interface between the two.

Separate policies: consequences for people experiencing disability with ageing

A key issue in respect of people who first experience disability with ageing is that they can sometimes only access a different level, type or range of services than people experiencing disability earlier. Access often seems to be limited not based on evidence of efficacy or outcomes, but to keep a ceiling on spending – and the distinctions can be carried over (explicitly or implicitly) into the implementation of personalised approaches to social care. For example, the United Nations (2019) suggests that people first experiencing disability in later life are often excluded from disability programmes (such as being ineligible for personal assistance or home support), have less access to rehabilitation services and sometimes have no choice other than to live in long-term care facilities.

Age was identified in a review across six countries (Australia, Canada, England, the Netherlands, New Zealand and Scotland) as a key feature in determining eligibility for individualised or personalised budgets (Pike et al, 2016). It was schemes aspiring 'to enhance choice, control and independence' that typically require applicants to be under 65 (Pike et al, 2016: 4, 23). The authors instance schemes from Australia (National Disability Insurance Scheme) and Canada (combined disability support programmes) as only applying to people aged under 65. The European Network on Independent Living (2015) instances several countries where availability of personal assistance is subject to age ceilings. However, the six-country review from Da Roit and Le Bihan (2010), which specifically considered cash-for-care schemes, or direct payments, found that most did *not* impose an age limit on access to the cash-for-care benefit.

In France, there are different schemes depending on whether disability onset occurred before or after age 60, with less generous means-tested care packages for the scheme designed for older people, which – unlike disability benefit – cannot be used to remunerate a spouse or cohabitant (AGE Platform Europe, 2019). Anticipating population ageing, a change in 2016 copper-fastened the boundary but was adopted because it would require 'significant resources' to extend provision for 'disabled' people to 'older people' (Le Bihan, 2016: 2).

In Sweden, a valued system of personal assistance for disabled people excluded people aged 65+ at first, though they were later included *if* impairment had manifested before that age (Jönson and Larsson, 2009). This amounts to institutionalised ageism justified by reference to 'natural' age differences in a way that obstructs the possibility of seeing the situation of younger and older people as comparable (Jönson and Larsson, 2009: 76). People first experiencing disability in older age in Switzerland are not categorised as disabled (Rickli, 2016), with consequences for entitlement to assistance. For example, disability insurance covers a range of assistive technologies, while only basic devices are paid for by the old-age pension. In addition, in the Flanders region of Belgium, a personal assistant can be paid from a 'personal assistance budget' but only for people under age 65 (Van Eenoo et al, 2014).

In Ireland, which has not widely implemented a personalised approach, people working on ageing and on disability characterised services to older people as narrow and medicalised, which some perceived as an inadequate response to the social and emotional needs of older clients (Leahy, 2018). By contrast, the approach to disability generally focused more on self-direction and community involvement – although participants perceived that this was often not achieved in practice. However, a small difference in timing of disability onset around one's 65th birthday may result in experiencing a different service model, which some participants perceived as illogical (Leahy, 2018: 4).

There are also countries in which the age and disability sectors have been brought into closer alignment through 'personalisation'. In the UK, disability services traditionally targeted people aged under 64, with people transferred to older people's services afterwards (Simcock, 2017). People first experiencing disability in older age were offered a narrow range of services, with few receiving rehabilitation services or social support (Bowling et al, 2008). Walker and Walker (1998) illustrated how ageist assumptions and stereotypes built into 'normal' patterns of care for older people operated destructively when applied to people ageing with disability. Transfer from one service category to another due to chronological ageing meant encountering services with a different orientation: 'from supporting independence to reproducing dependence' (Walker and Walker, 1998: 127).

In the UK, a personal budget can be managed by a local authority or third party that commissions services, or it can be given as a direct payment (National Audit Office, 2016: 5). Unlike some other countries where age restrictions mean that people first experiencing care needs after age 65 cannot access individualised approaches, UK government policy requires that anyone with eligible needs be offered a personal budget, preferably as a direct payment, and older people are by far the largest group of social care users in the UK (Woolham et al, 2017). Debates often focus on how well these changes, associated with disability activism, serve older people (Glendinning et al, 2008; Glasby, 2011; Rabiee et al, 2016; Woolham et al, 2017).

Older people have consistently been reluctant to opt for direct payments and are less likely than other groups to report positive outcomes from managed budgets (Rabiee et al, 2016). Direct payments to older people were often found to be insufficient to cover anything other than personal care, and poor uptake can be ascribed to absence of someone with whom to develop a relationship of trust (Woolham et al, 2017: 978). Research with older people using managed personal budgets (not direct payments) found that they did not perceive much control to tailor services to their needs/preferences; instead, low funding levels constrained choices, as did restrictions as to how money could be spent (Rabiee and Glendinning, 2014; see also Rabiee et al, 2016). Resource constraints appear to be the greatest barrier to greater choice and control, as well as inadequate training for staff (Rabiee et al, 2016). A scoping review queried the effectiveness of market delivery for older people, particularly for people with complex needs, for whom inter-agency working and long-term relationships are required (Jasper et al, 2019).

As is implicit in the discussion thus far, the benefits of personalisation do not appear to be available to many older people (Rabiee et al, 2016; Slasberg and Beresford, 2016). Despite a positive narrative about change, it is argued that a two-tier system operates in England, where older service users have experienced little change (Slasberg and Beresford, 2016). Thus, despite the rhetoric of 'personalisation', resources and supports that facilitate 'choice' and 'control' may not be available to older people in practice. Arguably, the narrow, ageist orientation of services for older people identified by Walker and Walker (1998) still underlies care for older people. However, Rabiee et al (2016) identify potential for managed budgets to give older people more control, if, for example, there was more training for support roles.

It is also worth noting that older people are not the only groups to experience problems with personalisation, or with the way it is implemented (Needham, 2014; Graham, 2015; Glasby and Littlechild, 2016). Some similar issues apply across user categories. For example, disabled participants in one study, mostly aged under 65, who were receiving direct payments were frustrated by lack of continuing support and wanted guidance about longer-term consequences of decisions (Rabiee, 2013; see also Lakhani et al, 2018). Lack of emphasis on the interpersonal or relationship aspects of supports purchased using direct payments is considered problematic for (younger) intellectually disabled people (Graham, 2015) *and* older people (Woolham et al, 2017). As suggested already, problems with these approaches are not confined to disabled people in the UK. The review across 11 OECD countries by Gadsby et al (2013: 15) found that while there was increased satisfaction among some budget holders, assumptions that personalised budgets improve choice, leading to greater autonomy and improved outcomes at lower cost, are 'more complex and generally unsupported by evidence' (see also Carey et al, 2018; Lakhani et al, 2018).

It has not been possible here to discuss all issues about implementation of policies, the focus being on how approaches to public policy differ in how they respond to 'disability' experienced at different points of the lifespan. A point to emphasise is that experiences of disability are not uniform – not all disabled people understand one another's experience (Barnes and Mercer, 2006; Shakespeare, 2006). Valid critiques of the inadequacy of 'highly instrumental' personalised approaches to care for older people (Lloyd, 2010: 193) are also applicable to many disabled people. Thus, it is likely that there are people within the service-user categories 'disabled' and 'older' who experience similar issues with the operation of 'personalisation', and with the neglect of collective aspects of care, to which bifurcated approaches to conceptualisation, language, research, evaluation and, indeed, advocacy do not fully do justice.

Separate policies: consequences for people ageing with disability

People ageing with disability can experience a range of issues at the interface of the two policy frameworks. This group requires development of specific, targeted policies to address issues likely to arise due to ageing with a legacy of material and social disadvantage, risks of additional impairment, and accelerated ageing in some cases (though that concept can be contested). However, there are limited empirical studies with this group of people, especially in relation to physical and sensory disability. Specific evidence of their experience, from a social perspective, often comes from quite small-scale studies.

In their review of individualised or personalised approaches in six countries, Pike et al (2016) suggest that people can cease to be eligible for schemes on reaching older age. Examples are instanced from Australia, Scotland and Canada. Thus, under the Australian National Disability Insurance Scheme, eligibility stops on entering a residential service or receiving home care after age 65. In Scotland, direct payments are not permitted for people receiving long-term residential or nursing care, and in Canada, individualised financing is generally only available for people living in the community.

In Ireland, where 'personalisation' is planned but not widely rolled out, I found instances of people ageing with disability staying within mainstream disability services after age 65, which meant that, in some cases, they would benefit from the aims enshrined in general disability approaches (Leahy, 2018). However, there were also instances of people experiencing disruption and diminution of services if transferred to older people's services at age 65 (considered more 'task-based'), a practice that appeared to operate in some regions (Leahy, 2018: 40). Some people experiencing conditions like dementia prior to age 65 could appear to fall between the two systems, having difficulties accessing the appropriate 'older people's' services (Leahy, 2018). An underlying issue here has to do with bifurcated research approaches and professional competencies based on expectations about when in the lifespan conditions tend to be first experienced (see Molton and Ordway, 2019).

Strict divisions in several countries between the ageing and disability policy frameworks may result in people ageing with disability not being able to access specialised aged services, having experiences of premature ageing overlooked or sensing that their conditions are not understood within older people's services (Cooper and Bigby, 2014; La Plante, 2014; Simcock, 2017). Sometimes, this group of people continues to engage with disability services that are not 'geared up' to address ageing issues (Westwood and Carey, 2019: 234). As Coyle and Mutchler (2017: 685) argue, people ageing with disability may have to negotiate 'multiple systems and cultures of support' involving professionals who are not always sufficiently informed to adequately support them.

This is illustrated by a study from Australia with people ageing with physical or sensory disability which found that they perceived that as they had aged, there was a dearth of professionals who understood their impairments (Cooper and Bigby, 2014). Bigby (2002, 2008) illustrates some of the challenges for people ageing with intellectual disability in Australia. The federal government delivers care for people aged 65+, while states/territories do so for people under age 65 (Bigby, 2008). A person ageing with intellectual disability would remain within disability services or move to residential care designed for older people. However, this assumes that residential aged care can replicate and replace disability services, ignoring the lack of expertise on disability within the aged-care sector and vice versa.

How contingent the experience is on the framings of policies is illustrated in a qualitative study from Canada (Bishop and Hobson, 2015). After transitioning to the older people's framework, one participant lost disability benefits, found it difficult to manage costs of disability and had to go without necessary medical equipment. Another had never received disability payments and had no income of her own until she received a pension at retirement age.

Thus, people ageing with disability are likely to have diverse experiences based on a range of personal and contextual factors, and on how local policy frameworks address intersections between the fields of disability and ageing. The discussion here points to the need to develop 'an active interface between respective knowledge and skills' within the two sectors (Cooper and Bigby, 2014: 434). Policymakers also need to learn from experiences in bridging the two frameworks, something considered next.

Bridging between policies on ageing and disability

Implicit in the cases outlined earlier is that artificial distinctions based on chronological age risk overlooking service needs and desires for personal autonomy that bridge age groups (Kennedy and Minkler, 1999). However, bridging the two in practice can be challenging, and applying approaches developed in one sector to the other without scrutiny of all the issues involved can also produce disappointing results. Problems with the way the 'personalisation' agenda has been implemented illustrate this, something also influenced by spending restrictions of recent years. Key challenges and successes of initiatives from the US and Australia that brought supports for ageing and disability together are discussed next.

Traditionally, in the US, disabled adults and older people were viewed as having distinct needs (Putnam, 2011, 2014). Homecare was considered unsuitable for older people experiencing severe impairment, who, it was argued, needed facilities with 24-hour staffing, and the overwhelming majority of public Medicaid funds were allocated to nursing home care (Applebaum and Mahoney, 2016). However, greater integration has resulted from a Supreme Court ruling in 1999 (the Olmstead case), which oriented disability policy towards community living and community-based support (Putnam, 2011). This means that 'rebalancing' or integration and/or linkages between age and disability long-term care programmes have been mandatory under federal grant programmes that seek to maximise community living (Putnam, 2011, 2014). 'Pockets' of action towards convergence have occurred since (Coyle and Mutchler, 2017: 684).

These processes are complex and vary across different US states and agencies. However, Applebaum and Mahoney (2016) suggest that the 'unimaginable' has happened: the numbers of older people accessing home- and community-based services through Medicaid exceed the numbers served through nursing homes in many states. Disability and ageing fields are finding shared goals in supporting community living (Putnam, 2014: S57). However, despite sharing goals at a macro level, competing service philosophies – one stressing consumer control, the other, protection and safety – and imbalances in funding between disability and ageing systems represent significant obstacles (Keefe, 2018).

Challenges experienced across different 'rebalancing' efforts include variations in organisational missions and philosophies, distinctive professional training, unquestioned beliefs about older people and disabled people, limited experience of working with both groups, and competition for programme funding (Putnam and Stoever, 2007; Putnam, 2011, 2014). For example, programmes were negatively affected by assumptions that 'older' people and 'disabled' people needed different services, including information, referral and the spectrum of supports, and by professional investment in age-segmented policies (Putnam, 2011). This meant that staff could emphasise life stages, sometimes reproducing stereotypical notions about what services older people might need – bingo and card games in one case (Putnam, 2011).

Putnam (2011: 338) observes that it is an open question as to whether the 'policy regulations drive professional perceptions or vice versa'. Successful working with unfamiliar client groups required collaboration, professional and organisational training, and ongoing support (Putnam and Stoever, 2007; Putnam, 2011, 2014; Keefe, 2018). Thus, perceptions of people working on ageing or on disability play a key role in successful alignment of disability and older people's programmes, and there has been limited scientific investigation of those perceptions (Putnam, 2011).

A bridging example from Australia involved pilot projects with residents of care homes experiencing long-standing disability (Australian Institute of Health and Welfare, 2006). Participants were predominantly aged 50+, and they had diverse experiences of disability, including intellectual disability. They were assessed as having age-related care needs but were not eligible for services under community care programmes aimed at older people because they were being supported by disability services. According to Bigby (2008), these projects demonstrated improved quality of life and the feasibility of supporting disabled people to age in place largely through additional health planning, access to allied healthcare and daytime community support. Highlighted also was the importance of joint assessment processes by age and disability services (Bigby, 2008). However, the projects were discontinued, partly due to difficulties separating costs of age-related needs from existing disability needs, which is particularly important in Australia as the two services are funded at different levels of government and the costs per capita for disabled people are higher (Bigby, 2008: 81–3).

These examples illustrate challenges involved in aligning traditionally separate policy and practice fields. They also suggest that there can be benefits of doing so. However, there is much to be learned about the issues involved. It is likely that personalisation approaches have implemented a de facto alignment between traditionally separate sectors in several countries, with minimal interrogation of these issues. For example, Carey et al (2018: 28) discuss rushed implementation of the personalisation agenda in Australia, which led to 'a lack of coherence' in policies. More linkages between scholarship in the various fields involved could contribute to more informed choices about how linkages can best be made in practice.

Discussion and conclusions

The issues discussed in this chapter represent complex issues, to which empirical and theoretical weaknesses and a range of underlying historical, sociological and political issues contribute. The traditional separation of disability and ageing policy frameworks creates complexity and illogicality. However, bringing the two closer together is also complex. Different approaches to disability across the lifespan continue to manifest as anomalies in public policies, with consequences for people who need support. The binary of 'disability' and 'ageing' in social care still operates in practice in many countries.

The adoption of 'individualised' or 'personalised' approaches to social care is associated with disability activism but its implementation is informed by the desire to contain costs of care due to population ageing. These approaches have led to a de facto alignment between the two traditionally separate frameworks in social care in some countries, and they have also witnessed the institutionalisation of ageism (with age ceilings applied for some services) or the carrying over of ageist assumptions that older disabled people deserve or require less support than other disabled people. The chapter points to instances of older people being excluded from mainstream disability supports and instances of differences between the approaches towards older people of the same age with different timings of disability onset.

The chapter also discussed how the 'personalisation' of social care can be implemented in ways that raise concerns relative to older people and leave people vulnerable who are least able to negotiate the 'choices' involved. This includes disabled people who are younger, as well as people who are older, especially from groups who are less socio-economically advantaged or associated with certain types of impairments. However, research often approaches these issues either through an 'ageing' or through a 'disability' lens. Commonalities in experience across traditionally separate user groups receive less explicit attention than broad differences between them.

Where a personalised approach to social care is being pursued, common problems identified across studies drawn from 'older' and 'disabled' service users include lack of control experienced in practice related to funding constraints and/or limitations as to what budgets may be spent on, as well as absence of stewardship and support or a trusting, relational element, which is especially important for some among both service user groups. They also include the need for coordination and long-term planning of individual cases. Both groups include people negatively affected by what Barnes (2011: 164) calls the undermining of the value of collective provision. As Kelly (2010) argues, if direct funding is to remain a core advocacy issue for disability movements, it should involve more recognition of aims other than independence and autonomy, and political demands must evolve to challenge oppressive policy regimes.

The experiences of people ageing with disability can be very diverse, and we lack empirical engagement with them. People from this group must often negotiate the boundary between care services for 'disabled' people and 'older' people, with variable experiences depending on how policy frameworks intersect in any given region, as well as on their individual circumstances over the lifespan. This group of people also requires greater linkages between professionals with expertise in ageing and in disability.

Some factors needing to be addressed in attempts to bridge the two service frameworks and some benefits of bridging initiatives were discussed. Barriers to success include lack of resources, limited professional training and experience across different groups, investment of professionals in age-segmented approaches, and unquestioned, stereotypical assumptions about the needs of 'disabled' people and 'older' people. However, the two sectors have common ground in a shared goal of supporting community living (Putnam, 2014: S57). Greater integration also requires defining shared standards of operation (Keefe, 2018).

An issue that is fundamental to the discussion here is that increased disability due to demographic change is taking place against a backdrop of cuts to health and social care. Thus, in many countries, neoliberalism is dominant, the 'social' is in decline and health and social care budgets have been cut (Phillipson, 2020). The rights of disabled people and welfare provision have also been seriously curtailed (Cross, 2013; Roulstone, 2015; Brennan et al, 2016). The way that 'personalisation' has been implemented may have solidified perceptions that the needs of different service-user categories ('older' or 'disabled') are distinct in social care, and cuts in services may exacerbate competition between advocates for different categories of service users. For example, there were fears among people working in social care in Ireland that 'reform' might be attempted to reduce costs and result in lowering standards to the lowest common denominator (Leahy, 2018). These are valid concerns.

Overall, the review presented in this chapter underlines Putnam's (2014) argument that building capacity to conduct bridging research should be a high priority for practitioners, policymakers and scholars working on ageing and disability, as well as Beresford's (2008) suggestion that those involved in social care should subject its underpinning ideas to rigorous review. However, countries are making changes to address demographic change with or without the input of cross-disciplinary research, evaluation or greater linkages in professional practice between the fields of ageing and disability. Increased numbers of people ageing with disability create a growing challenge for the two policy frameworks to learn from each other. Developing greater understanding of similarities as well as differences across traditionally separate service-user groups might help move debates forward.

The discussion here underlines the need for critical responses that seek new ways to 'link the individual to the collective', as well as for collective responses that, as Phillipson (2020: 222–4) suggests, are required to respond to the undermining of social support and to the politics of individualism and associated cuts to the welfare state. If older people do not demand an alternative model to address disability in older age, it is unlikely that policymakers will address their needs for a social model of support to enhance life in their communities (Kahana and Kahana, 2017: 193). Perhaps it is time for the fields of ageing and disability to find areas on which they can respond collectively on these issues.

Human rights frameworks represent one arena where the two advocacy interests have started to meet. The Special Rapporteur on the Rights of Persons with Disabilities has commented that the UN Convention on the Rights of Persons with Disabilities represents 'a unique entry point for dealing with the intersection between ageing and disability from a rights-based perspective' (United Nations, 2019: 7).

Used best, human rights offer a framework of thought and planning that enables society to take a 'fresh, and more hopeful, direction' (Townsend, 2007: 43; see also Phillipson, 2015: 94). Relatedly, and as discussed in Chapter 3, efforts to bring people living with dementia within the category 'disabled' are informed by the possibility of extending legal protections based on human rights to them and to further self-advocacy among them (Thomas and Milligan, 2018; Shakespeare et al, 2019). However, similar arguments can be made in respect of people experiencing other types of impairment in older age.

Public policies need to be informed by the experience of *all* older disabled people – requiring, as argued throughout this book, that people ageing with disability are included within approaches to ageing generally, and that experiences of disability in older age are included within mainstream approaches to disability. People who are ageing with disability could contribute to understandings of people who will experience disability with ageing of what types of policies and services best support them. They may also be able to contribute a more holistic appreciation of what it means to live a fulfilling life with disability in older age, something absent in dominant 'healthy' or 'active' ageing discourse and policies. The experience of people from this group represents a currently overlooked resource. Problems associated with how the personalised social care agenda has been implemented should not operate as a bar to greater interchange between the two fields. On the contrary, these problems underline the need for greater interrogation of the implicit and explicit values, aims and approaches that inform separate policy frameworks and that continue to inform, and sometimes to inhibit, attempted alignments.

Finally, not engaging with the intersections of ageing and disability in the policy sphere risks leaving older disabled people relatively unsupported, including people both inside and outside traditional categorical notions of who is 'disabled'. It risks leaving people with significant needs and rights for support at the mercy of systems that have developed separately, and, in many ways, arbitrarily, with practices that can be informed by unquestioned prejudices and with overarching systems that sometimes institutionalise ageism.

The assumptions that underlie the separation of policy frameworks on disability and on ageing, and their practical consequences as discussed in this chapter, were a further rationale for the empirical study that informs this book. Its findings are discussed in the chapters that follow.

PART II

Empirical findings

5

Disabling bodies

Introduction

I now move to consider the empirical study that informs this book in this and subsequent chapters. This is the first of two chapters in which I address the research question, 'How do older people experience disability and processes of disablement, and what meanings do they make of those experiences?' The context for the study is set out in the previous chapters, which also suggest why this was identified as a key research question. Part of the context involves how disability experienced in older age tends to be understood primarily as impairment or as an individual, medicalised issue. Furthermore, there is a need to understand more about how people interpret and negotiate the changes involved.

In this chapter, I first introduce the empirical study and consider some theoretical concepts by way of background. Then, I discuss the study's findings. The chapter addresses how participants experienced onset of disability, or greater disablement, in their bodies. It shows that this could involve suffering, loss, uncertainty about daily life and the future, and forced abandonment of activities. This could be linked to a sense of finitude and could involve fundamental rethinking about one's self. This was often so even when disablement (and worsening impairment) occurred gradually and at a stage in life when the participants considered it 'normal', 'natural' or 'on time'. This is significant because the normative connection between impairment and older age leads to assumptions that onset of disability in later life might be experienced as anticipated, not disruptive, and that the experience of ageing with disability might be one of continuity, not change.

Also significant is that participants did not define themselves by their bodies or wish to be defined by them. They concentrated on what they could still do and sought ways to perceive a continuous sense of self, as well as meaning and value in their lives. Participants did this in interaction with dominant discourses of ageing, and, indeed, of able-bodiedness, which shape subjective interpretations. Chapter 6 will show that bodily change was not the only thing that contributed to 'disability', which was also experienced in interaction with contexts such as inaccessible physical environments or the disabling reactions of others. That bodies could be perceived as disabling or limiting (or more disabling or limiting for people ageing with disability) is not surprising. Less obvious are subjective meanings made of those experiences and responses to them. How participants actively respond to the challenges involved is signalled here and addressed mainly in Chapter 7.

Introducing the study: research questions and methods

The empirical study that informs this book is based on interviews with older disabled people. Some were experiencing disability with ageing (DwithA); others ageing with disability (AwithD). The study was intended to reveal and compare subjective experiences of these two groups of people, which are rarely considered together in theorising or empirical research. I hoped that it could contribute to understandings of later life lived with disability, and to debates about these issues at a time of demographic ageing which means that older people constitute a greater proportion of disabled populations.

The research questions for the study are set out in Chapter 1, the first of which is relevant to this chapter: 'How do older people experience disability and processes of disablement, and what meanings do they make of those experiences?' 'Disablement process' is used here in a straightforward sense compatible with lay interpretations rather than by reference to any specific model (such as that developed by Verbrugge and Jette (1994)). Here, the idea of 'process' is meant to suggest the dynamics involved in disability onset. 'Process' is relevant not just to people first experiencing disability in older age, but also to experiences of long-standing impairment. These can be thought of in static terms (that is, as approached through a medical lens) but are often instead experienced as dynamic processes (Verbrugge and Jette, 1994; Burchardt, 2000: 4; Simcock, 2017).

Fundamental to the arguments of this book is the fact that because it is such a contested category, a different approach to the concept of 'disability' might have led to a different approach to this study, including as to how its research questions and findings are expressed. Within gerontology, 'disability' might have been approached as functional limitations or through the concept of 'frailty' or the 'fourth age' (see Chapter 2). However, this book is informed by an interactional or relational approach to disability, consistent with the UN Convention on the Rights of Persons with Disabilities and reflected in Shakespeare's (2014a) contention that the social and the biological are always intertwined, and that bodies *and* society disable people (see Chapter 2).

By contrast, a classic social model approach to disability would exclude accounts of bodies or impairment (Oliver, 1990: 45; Goodley, 2011: 62). In Thomas's (2004: 579) social relational model of disability, what this chapter is concerned with would be characterised as 'impairment effects', while the term 'disability' would be reserved for 'forms of oppressive social reaction', which are largely discussed in Chapter 6. Much theorising within critical or cultural disability studies would typically approach impairment, as well as disability, as socially constructed and would not include an engagement with material bodies (Goodley et al, 2019). However, an alternative view from Siebers (2008), also within disability studies, is based on what he termed the notion of 'complex embodiment'. From this perspective, disabling factors deriving from the body are 'no less significant than disabilities caused by the environment', even if they are 'resistant to change' (Siebers, 2008: 25). Within these factors, Siebers includes those associated with ageing.

The **'Methodological annexe'** to this book outlines the approach taken to the study and contains information on recruitment, interviews, participant characteristics and analysis of the interview data. Here, I briefly outline key features of the methods employed. The study was qualitative, involving a biographical narrative approach to interviews, which focused on how participants made sense of events and actions in their lives, aiming to empower participants to co-determine important issues and to illuminate the impact of social structures on them (Chamberlayne et al, 2000: 17; Elliott, 2005).

The study involved a grounded theory method (Strauss and Corbin, 1998; Charmaz, 2014) and took a constructivist approach which assumes that researchers are engaged in an interpretive portrayal of the studied world (Charmaz, 2005, 2014). This involves 'flexible analytic guidelines' for data collection, stages of analysis and conceptual development (Charmaz, 2005: 507; 2014). The process progressed through five steps outlined by Charmaz (2014: 15) as constituting a grounded theory study: data collection and analysis conducted simultaneously and iteratively; analysis of actions and processes; comparative methods; developing conceptual categories from the data; and inducting abstract categories through systematic analysis. Analysis involved identification of categories and relationships between them.

Being inductive, the study started not from a hypothesis, but from the idea that disability in older age involves people first experiencing disability with ageing (DwithA) and people ageing with long-standing disability (AwithD), who are separate categories constructed, in part, by the separate approaches to conceptualisation, theorising and policymaking on ageing and disability discussed in Part I of this book. Participants were living in their own homes in Ireland in cities, towns, villages and rural areas, and were interviewed between 2015 and 2017.

Most participants were recruited through organisations running associations or centres/clubs for, or with, older people or disabled people. Participants all received information about the study in a format that was accessible to them and they gave informed consent. All names used are pseudonyms. To delineate the categorisations for the two groups of participants, I reviewed the literature as to how disability with ageing and ageing with disability are understood (Verbrugge and Yang, 2002; Naidoo et al, 2012), as well as a range of empirical studies (see Methodological annexe).

I then sought participants aged 65+ who were either in the AwithD group, meaning that they first experienced disability between birth and midlife (or age 45) (**Group 1**), or who were in the DwithA group, having begun to experience disability with ageing (from age 45) (**Group 2**). There were 42 participants, of whom, 18 were in the AwithD group and 24 were in the DwithA group. A total of 25 were females and 17 were males. Their age range was 55–90 and the group had a median age of 72.5. All but three were aged 65 or over, though I recruited three people ageing with disability who were aged under 65 for pragmatic reasons. Just over half (22) of the participants self-reported experiencing disability at the most severe level (11 people in both groups). As it is relevant to the study to consider and compare the two experiences, quotations from participants in this and the following chapters identify to which group they belong and I also give their ages.

The study focused on physical and sensory disability but did not otherwise recruit based on type of impairment in order to avoid further separation based on diagnostic categories. I followed a largely unstructured narrative interview format and followed that with disability categorisation questions adapted from the Irish Census of Population, which reflects international approaches to the framing of disability censuses and surveys. I took this approach to situate the data and it reflects how self-identification as 'disabled' was unlikely among the DwithA group of participants (Verbrugge and Yang, 2002; Kelley-Moore et al, 2006; Darling and Heckert, 2010). However, 'disability' is based on a deconstruction of a continuum (Davis, 1995: 11). Attempts at categorisation are somewhat crude given that age and disability are overlapping phenomena occurring throughout the lifespan (Verbrugge and Yang, 2002: 253; Naidoo et al, 2012). Furthermore, I acknowledge that to cultural or critical disability scholars, such efforts may represent attempts to solidify firm definitions based on biology where disability has come to be seen as a discursive category that is fluid and malleable. The Methodological annexe expands on this brief outline of research methods.

Theoretical background

In the spirit of grounded theory, the analysis did not impose preconceived theories on the data collected in interviews. However, the analysis engaged with changes the participants perceived in bodies over time (both the DwithA and AwithD groups) and with the identity questions that could be a key part of how they discussed their experiences. This analysis was informed by an understanding that social identities come into being through their embodiment by individuals (Jenkins, 2008), formed through a triangular relationship between the body, the self and society, and that we come to know that we are ageing through our embodiment (Hockey and James, 2003: 134, 214). It was also informed by the fact that people glean the meaning of the lifecourse and life change through others' definitions (Holstein and Gubrium, 2000: 17; Hendricks, 2010).

Debates about identity in older age have already been touched on (see Chapter 3). It is debated as to whether individual experience is determined by social and economic factors associated with political economy perspectives, or is actively chosen, associated with postmodern perspectives (Estes et al, 2003; Tanner, 2010). Sociocultural framings of ageing – a traditional 'decline' model and 'positive' ageing approaches – represent guiding narratives affecting personal identities (Estes et al, 2003: 33, 67). Of relevance to the arguments of this book is that 'positive' ageing discourses occur within broader idealised notions of independent adulthood and prevailing concepts of autonomy and independence (Baars, 2010; Lamb, 2014; Holstein, 2015). Thus, they fit within an ableist cultural imaginary associated with 'self-sufficiency, autonomy and independence' (Goodley et al, 2019: 986), and form part of what Siebers (2008: 8) terms an 'ideology of ability'.

Changes in self-identity and biographical disruption

Critical gerontologists suggest that the experience of disability in older age is disruptive and that adjusting to changes in one's ability brings corresponding changes to self-identity (Kahana and Kahana, 2017: 201). For Lloyd et al (2014), the 'fourth age' is characterised by irreversible changes to a customary way of life that call into question one's sense of self. In addition, Holstein (2015: 118) suggests that chronic illness 'pushes us further to the margins of the valued self'. Within the sociology of health and illness, the concept of biographical disruption links bodily issues to a sense of self and identity, suggesting that people attempt to maintain a sense of continuity when faced with bodily change (Kelly and Field, 1996; Bury, 1997: 192). As outlined in Chapter 3, disability scholars critique this approach for insufficient focus on wider structures, oppression and rights (Thomas, 2004, 2007; Bê, 2016). However, I found it helpful in interpreting meanings that participants made of impairment onset or worsening because it represents an alternative to approaches that exclude accounts of the body. Shakespeare and Watson (2010: 65) correctly suggest, however, that scholarship from this perspective could do more to examine structural issues faced by disabled people.

Bury (1982: 169–70; 1997: 124) articulated the concept of 'biographical disruption' – when chronic illness interrupts lifecourse assumptions and narratives in the context of healthy adults in modern cultures premised on the expectation of long life and health. Key features are: (1) disruption of taken-for-granted assumptions and behaviours; (2) fundamental rethinking of biography and self-concept; and (3) mobilisation of resources to respond. This can involve changes in relationships, 'disrupting normal rules of reciprocity and mutual support', and growing dependency can be a major issue (Bury, 1982: 189). The chronic illness focus is relevant because the very definition of 'chronic illness' involves impairment. For example, chronic diseases are defined as long-term conditions 'lasting more than six months … involv[ing] some functional impairment or disability' (Department of Health and Children, 2008: 9). In medical terms, chronic illness is also the largest single cause of disability in older age (Verbrugge and Jette, 1994; Bury, 1997).

Bury's (1991: 461) concept of coping refers to processes of learning to tolerate illness, involving 'maintaining a sense of value and meaning in life'. Examples of coping include normalisation and bracketing off the impact so that effects on identity are minimised – like maintaining as many activities as possible and disguising or minimising symptoms. Bury apprehended this experience as occurring once. Charmaz (1983, 1995: 660) uses a similar concept ('loss of self') but emphasises that chronic illness can require frequent adaptation: 'identity questions and identity changes can emerge or reoccur'. From a lifecourse perspective, Williams (2000) theorised that being older could make chronic illness biographically *anticipated*, not disruptive. He suggested that this might be particularly the case for people who were used to hardship or adversity, who might experience chronic illness not as biographical disruption, but rather as a *normal crisis*. Contrariwise, others argued that the experience of disruption and uncertainty is magnified in older age (Becker and Kaufman, 1995; Holstein and Cole, 1996). However, the relationship between age and chronic illness in this literature is under-theorised (Higgs and Rees-Jones, 2009; Lloyd et al, 2020).

Some empirical studies suggest that chronic illness ceases to be out of place in older age, as accumulated life experiences, especially of hardship, mediate interpretations. For example, this was the view of Pound et al (1998), who explored experiences of stroke among predominantly older, working-class people in the East End of London who had also experienced the Second World War. By contrast, other studies found that disruption could apply in older age (Sanders et al, 2002; Meijering et al, 2017; Lloyd et al, 2020). Still others found mixed experiences (Hinojosa et al, 2008; Hubbard et al, 2010). For example, a study with army veterans who experienced stroke (average age of 67) found that the event was disruptive for some but not for others. Among the possible explanations for this were the construction of a strong masculine self and previous experiences of extreme challenge (Hinojosa et al, 2008).

The perspective of people ageing with disability (AwithD group) is largely missing from this literature (Williams, 2000; Larsson and Jeppsson Grassman, 2012). Williams (2000: 49–59) theorised that their experience might be of continuity, not disruption, involving *biographical reinforcement* and a sense that, biographically speaking, nothing had *shifted*. The study from Lloyd et al (2020: 2750) provides some support for this, including an account of having 'incorporated disability and bodily discomfort' into self-identity for many years. Based on a study with people ageing with disability and early-onset chronic illness, Larsson and Jeppsson Grassman (2012) posit an adapted concept of biographical disruption. Their concept is wider than Bury's idea of a single, unanticipated disruptive event. Instead, for Larsson and Jeppsson Grassman (2012), disruptions can occur repeatedly over the lifespan in chronically ill and disabled people. They suggest that changes do not have to be wholly unexpected to be disruptive. This extended concept of 'disruption' proved relevant to the experiences of many participants in the study presented here.

In this analysis, I applied the concept of 'disruption' not just to bodily experiences, but also to disability caused by broader contexts – the latter discussed especially in the Chapter 6. However, this chapter also considers the concept of disruption in light of how participants interpreted discourses of ageing – such as 'success' and 'decline' – and how these interpretations intersect with societal framings of disability and of able-bodiedness. I therefore attempt to engage with both material and social constructions of disability.

Findings: disabling bodies

Most participants felt that their bodies disabled them because they limited, or increasingly limited, what they could do. Some experienced bodies that caused pain, fatigue or balance issues. Among the perceived consequences were ongoing uncertainty and loss of control about day-to-day living and the future. Participants could link impairment onset or worsening with a sense of finitude, and a key consequence was having to let go of activities and opportunities to participate, which could cause loss, suffering and a reduction in social contact. However, participants often emphasised what they could still do and wished not to be defined by what they could not do. They could also interpret the changes involved in light of ideas about 'success' and 'decline'.

Perceiving 'decline' or 'catastrophe'

Participants described not being able (or being partially able) to do things such as lift, walk, see and hear, and/or having an ongoing tendency to fall or to feel pain. Joan (aged 86, DwithA) would like a "new body" and Janice (aged 66, AwithD) interprets fatigue as her body telling her "you can't do it" and was unsure whether to attribute current symptoms to ageing or to progression of her condition. Suffering and sadness were associated with a range of symptoms, especially with pain. For many participants from both groups, bodily experiences were understood as gradual 'decline' relative to earlier functioning. It was 'normal' and irremediable. Others told 'catastrophic' narratives, where disability was related to a single event such as an accident or stroke. There was also overlap, as participants who experienced a 'catastrophic' onset might also employ a 'decline' narrative relative to changes since then.

People experiencing 'decline' were often vague about when changes started, improvements were largely not expected, and they linked the experience to end of life or finitude. This was typical of accounts of the oldest participants from both groups (DwithA and AwithD) who experienced gradual onset of impairment for the first time, worsening of an existing impairment or onset of new impairments. For example, Colin (aged 88, DwithA) used the term "deterioration" to describe gradual changes in his eyesight and perceived this as "natural". Tony (aged 83, AwithD) described changes in his legs making walking more difficult as "just wear and tear". Participants often felt they could expect no improvements. This was summed up in Gloria's (aged 80, DwithA) comment: "But anyhow one can't hope to be any better at this age, one is not going to get any better."

Participants who had experienced sudden or unexpected onset of disability often recalled that event as causing a 'catastrophe' – a major change or turning point involving a strong contrast between life before and after. They did not necessarily make a link to chronological ageing or finitude, though that varied. Onset tended to be experienced as unanticipated, that is, a crisis requiring major adjustment. This was experienced at a range of ages, including among the oldest participants. They used phrases that summed up how defining these events were, such as James's (aged 83, DwithA) phrase "once you get the stroke, the rest is history", about having had a stroke in his 80s. Many recalled the date and time of an event, even if they did not know its full import then. For example, Francis (aged 76, DwithA) recalled a stroke in his late 50s:

> 'I'll never forget it. We were, it happened at night-time around nine o'clock. We were watching television and my foot went to sleep and I went down to the kitchen. We were in the sitting room and I went out to the kitchen and I thought the feeling would come back into it and it did. ... We went to bed and next morning, my foot, I had very little feeling in the leg. [Talks about the trip to hospital and the stay in hospital.] They taught me when I was there, they taught me how to walk which is a bit unusual when you're used to walking all your life.'

At another point, Francis talked about his "past life", saying that life now felt like a totally different life; he said he could not have imagined earlier not being able to do things like farming or DIY. Simultaneously, he was conscious of continuity – describing himself as having had to give up being an "active" farmer – retaining the identity 'farmer'. Thus, he bracketed off the impact and preserved a sense of a valued identity. Similarly, another participant pointed to many things she could not do since having had her legs amputated in her 60s, but said that she did not feel differently about herself – she was still a "decent" person and "still independent – to an extent". Thus, participants exhibited a sense of identity simultaneously continuous with the past and different too because of a 'changed condition' (Holstein, 2015: 118).

Gradual experiences of disablement could, over time, have disruptive consequences challenging a sense of self – even if no one point was identified where this had happened. Sometimes, on top of a 'catastrophic' onset, participants perceived a gradual 'decline' associated with ageing. For example, Francis described a series of problems since his initial stroke, including "mini-strokes", and falls and fractures requiring him to use a wheelchair. He used the term "going downhill" and suggested it might be time to slow down. Francis interpreted his ongoing experiences in terms of 'normal' ageing linked to a sense of decline and finitude.

There could be points of crisis (like a fall) or sudden change in functioning – times when 'decline' really manifested. This could be true of both participant groups (DwithA and AwithD). For example, people with long-term disability (AwithD group) could perceive their functioning as static for years but, over time, there could be gradual or dramatic changes. Alternatively, conditions might always have been experienced as dynamic or fluctuating. Some participants among the AwithD group perceived that conditions associated with ageing (like arthritis) made existing conditions worse or they were not sure whether symptoms were due to age-related conditions or to existing conditions. Thus, for participants from this group, bodily changes were sometimes linked to ageing and also to the progression or worsening of conditions. For most, there was ongoing change, sometimes accelerating with ageing, consistent with findings from empirical studies (Zarb and Oliver, 1993; Jeppsson Grassman et al, 2012; Jeppsson Grassman, 2013).

For this group (AwithD), additional impairments could make life very difficult. For example, Hazel (aged 80, AwithD), visually impaired since her 30s, described getting older as "difficult and not enjoyable", and she associated it with "little pains that you didn't have before". She felt less independent and, in that respect, perceived that her experience resembled that of other older people. However, in recent years, Hazel experienced hearing loss as well, and said: "You can't communicate at all without your hearing. Your eyesight you can manage, but hearing is most important. ... It is so ... you are so alone." Comparing herself with others, Hazel felt more isolated because she could not compensate for hearing loss by lip-reading. Social and family occasions had become difficult, especially since her husband's death, and she sometimes avoided them. Thus, despite many similarities with the DwithA group, there is a sense of a kind of double jeopardy with ageing for some participants ageing with disability (Reyes, 2009; Bishop and Hobson, 2015).

Whichever group they belonged to (AwithD or DwithA) or onset narrative they employed ('decline' or 'catastrophe'), participants could perceive disability onset or worsening as 'on time' in older age. Thus, ideas of finitude and social constructions of age and the lifecourse affected meanings made of disability (Kelley-Moore, 2010). This did not mean that participants defined themselves by their bodies, and, in a seeming paradox, this was also compatible with identifying with aspects of 'positive' ageing, discussed later. It did mean, however, that many could employ a discourse on ageing ('decline') with which to interpret experiences, perceiving them as 'natural' or comprehensible – thus constructing a reasonable level of explanation, which may mitigate the experience of disruption (Bury, 1997: 125).

The search for cause is also a search for its meaning (Bury, 1982). In Bury's (1991: 461) terms, participants learned to cope or to maintain a sense of value and meaning in life. This can be considered as an attempt to impose control on experience in the sense of understanding (or interpretive control or comprehensibility). Thus, in response to change, participants attempted to lead a life that made sense to them or that they perceived as meaningful. This argument is taken up again in Chapter 7.

Having a heightened sense of uncertainty and finitude

A key part of the experience for most participants was a heightened sense of uncertainty, a sense of finitude and a loss of control, and fear of greater dependency. Participants used a range of terms expressing the provisional and dynamic nature of the experience, like 'still', 'as long as' or 'please God', signalling perceptions of contingency. Falls, and fears of falling, were common concerns across interviews, as was the sense that a fall might change everything. When participants talked about the future, it could involve uncertainty about living arrangements associated with anticipated disimprovements in health or functioning. Some participants thought that current living arrangements were unsustainable and dreaded needing more support or admission to a nursing home. For example, Francis (aged 76, DwithA) felt that he would have to move to a nursing home if his wife's functioning changed. Hazel (aged 80, AwithD) said "I often ask myself where will I end up", adding that "on the law of averages" she would become unable to look after herself.

Julie (aged 80, DwithA) talked about fears regarding worsening functioning, her husband's health and what changes in either would mean for her living arrangements. She also likened ageing to "being on a knife's edge", adding: "I never think nothing else is going to happen to me now because it could." All of this suggests that challenges to health and functioning are significant benchmarks for conferring meaning on the process of ageing – because it 'prefigure[s] death and the end of life' (Hockey and James, 2003: 153).

Thinking about the future caused suffering for some, and not every participant found it easy to discuss. James (aged 83, DwithA) wept at the thought that his health might change and he might become a "burden":

> 'Well thank God and his Holy Mother because I dread I should get sick because I would be a huge burden on [daughter] and anybody else. There is nobody else and I am totally dependent on her [weeps] and she is so good. [Pauses.] My health, thank God, is holding up.'

Participants often referred to lack of control over what would happen. Helen (aged 68, AwithD) feared not being able to care for herself (which she distinguished from needing support with self-care and housework at present) or being confined to bed. She hoped that God "won't do that". For Helen and others, talking about death was not as difficult as thinking about greater dependency, something beyond her control: "I think how my health is going to deteriorate and what way it will go. It can't deteriorate much more than it is [little laugh]. Yea, of course it is a big concern. But there is no point, you can't control it." Thus, even though Helen has lived with disability since childhood, and worsening impairment, pain and inconvenience from her late 30s, she was not sanguine about the future. Her reaction illustrates how participants' interpretations fit with Bury's (1982: 169) notion of biographical disruption, involving the prospect of increased dependency. However, as argued already, this experience is broader than the concept as Bury conceived it – as a single, unanticipated event. For participants (both AwithD and DwithA groups), there could be a series of 'disruptive' events that were not always entirely unanticipated. In that respect, participants' experiences were often consistent with how Larsson and Jeppsson Grassman (2012) have expanded the concept of biographical disruption. One difference between the two groups was that for people ageing with disability, a sense of uncertainty or precariousness could have characterised their whole lives; thus, a fear of falling or a sense of being vulnerable could have been part of their experience at any age, discussed again in Chapter 8.

Other participants said that they did not think about the future and some even considered it dangerous to do so in the sense of endangering mental health. Several said they concentrated instead on living in the present. Some felt they had lived to "a good age" (Patricia, aged 90, AwithD) or that they were in the "last stage" of life (Colin, aged 88, DwithA) and wondered when death might come. Several tried to understand the stage they had reached by reference to the health or longevity of parents or antecedents. Arguably, they were trying to make the experience understandable or comprehensible, and in that way to exert 'interpretive control' on events that they could do nothing about (Baumeister, 1991).

Even though participants could interpret chronological age and impairment as signalling the penultimate stage of the lifecourse, it did not mean that they considered their lives over. For example, although Colin considered himself in "the last stage", he was also keen to find ways to continue to engage meaningfully in life (as he put it) (discussed again in Chapter 7). There may be a short event horizon and a strong awareness of finitude, but even among the oldest participants, no one knew when death might come. Participants experienced what Baars (2010: 116) describes as 'the vulnerability inherent in human life [that] radicalises as people get older'. In addition, they continued to be involved in life and in processes of identity negotiation, which are 'inevitably incomplete' (Hockey and James, 2003: 12).

Losing activities and participation opportunities

Another key consequence of a disabling body involved change and loss of everyday activities, opportunities for participation and consequent confinement, mundanity and reduced social networks and roles. Thus, bodies allow us to act, to intervene in and to alter the flow of daily life (Shilling, 2012: 9). However, changes in bodies or functioning may hinder us in doing so. Bodily change was a key reason perceived for these losses, though participants could also experience exclusion due to environmental barriers or disablist social relations (see Chapter 6).

The range of activities and roles that had ceased to be possible included reading, watching TV, holidaying or socialising, volunteering, walking/hiking, sports participation or organising, card playing, and participating in arts/cultural activities – often activities that involved lives linked to others. Several participants contrasted busy, sociable post-retirement phases with quieter, more confined times now. Some people perceived risks to mental health through depression if they did not occupy themselves. All these changes could be associated with sadness, loss and changed social identities and challenges to a sense of a valued self.

For people who could drive, it was often highly valued. As Helen (aged 68, AwithD) described it, her car meant that "life is able to be lived". Correspondingly, discontinuing driving was often a significant point, not always coinciding with initial impairment onset, when participants realised that life had changed. They experienced this as loss of independent functioning or freedom, or in the context of having become more dependent – a blow to a sense of identity as an autonomous person.

However, even where there was alignment with what Gullette (2004: 130) terms a 'decline ideology', this did not mean that participants were fatalistic in how they responded. For example, Gloria (aged 80, DwithA), who linked disability onset with the last stage of life without hope of improvement, continued any activities she could – as a volunteer with meals-on-wheels (sitting down now while working), attending a painting class, looking forward to having grandchildren to stay and so on. Thus, participants responded to the challenges involved and maintained valued activities where they could.

Participants could also make efforts to maintain functioning, though were sometimes ambivalent about what was possible. They often also shifted focus to what could still be done. For example, without a great deal of confidence in its efficacy, Tony (aged 83, AwithD) said: "I do exercises to try and keep yourself kinda right." The ambiguity involved was summed up in Annette's (aged 84, DwithA) comment related to exercises she participates in: "But, please God, it will cure itself and I will get back to normal. But then again, I am getting older, I am 84 now, I was 84 after Christmas, so I can't expect ... [pause]." Thus, a sense of finitude was ongoing, especially for the oldest participants, making the experience ambivalent, that is, balancing attitudes of pragmatism and acceptance with hopes and efforts to maintain or improve functioning. These can be considered efforts to cope with and tolerate impairments by trying to minimise symptoms so that the effects on identity are reduced (Bury, 1991). Fundamentally, all these efforts to cope represent efforts to live lives that are valued – something that participants constructed in interaction with broader societal discourses of ageing and of able-bodiedness, discussed later.

Participants often shifted from describing something they could not do to focusing instead on what they could, and resisted being defined by what they could not do. For example, Stephen (aged 88, DwithA) pointed to how he has had to let go of a leadership role in his local community – something he was proud of. Disablement had been a gradual process but he still felt 'changed', saying, "I am not the [Stephen] that was." However, Stephen perceived continuity through continuing some involvement in a local group, pointing out that people still "respect" him. In addition, Teresa (aged 87, AwithD), who had gradually experienced visual impairment, said she could no longer read (which she loved), adding immediately that she compensates by getting audiobooks.

Thus, by focusing on what could be done, and by seeing 'decline' as inevitable or 'normal', participants sometimes seemed to play down the consequences of disability. While loss and suffering were expressed about changes in functioning and loss of related activities, there was also sometimes a sense that participants wished not to dwell on this. Both were evident in what Tony (aged 83, AwithD) said as he talked about no longer attending football matches:

> 'You haven't got the physical, the physical exercise or walking facilities, running facilities that you had, we'll say, six years ago. And you think about it and it takes you back a bit, but, sure, you are then resigned to it and that is life, life goes on and you have to accept these things [sighs].'

Participants were thus trying to come to terms with challenging issues that were intrinsic to embodiment and to finite lives. However, it is also true that images of the lifecourse can cast some actions as appropriate and inappropriate (Holstein and Gubrium, 2000: 186). Thus, images of the lifecourse, reflected in perceptions that impairment was 'on time', may reinforce the idea that it is appropriate to minimise reactions, and 'coping' or 'managing' implies moral worth in Western culture (Tanner, 2010: 182). Seen through a disability studies lens, participants' reactions can be interpreted as informed by ableism, or, what Siebers (2008: 8, 32) calls, a preference for able-bodiedness or 'the ideology of ability', which demands that disabled people 'present as able-bodied as possible'. Kafer's (2003: 80) suggestion that society's 'compulsory able-bodiedness' requires a constant dialogue on questions of 'cure, loss and disavowal' on the part of disabled people also seems consistent with the types of varied, ambivalent responses that participants expressed. Chapter 7 returns to responses to loss of activities and participation opportunities, discussing further ways in which participants reacted to those losses and exclusions, and arguing that participants were attempting to maintain a sense of value and meaning in life (Bury, 1991: 461).

Negotiating social identities in light of dominant discourses

Participants' accounts were often framed within interpretations of positive sociocultural discourses of ageing. Experiencing disability was no bar to identifying with 'positive' or 'active' ageing approaches – and that was true for both groups of participants. Patricia (aged 90,

AwithD) described the activities of her week as attending Mass and being collected to go to a day-care centre one afternoon per week. Additionally, she occasionally took a taxi to go to a concert. She perceived herself as an active person "do[ing] everything": "I just get out and do everything, go anywhere, go to the concert hall, anything that is going." Patricia's approach aligns with concepts such as the 'third age' or 'positive' ageing – focused on social and leisure participation – not passive or disengaged framings associated with the 'fourth age' (Laslett, 1996 [1989]). As Timonen (2016: 64) argues, even people who 'deviate' from the kind of model behaviour promoted by 'positive' ageing discourses may evince behaviours and attitudes consistent with them. Patricia and others still identified with the imperative to 'age well', and the self-realisation aspects of these discourses continued to resonate.

Participants could identify both with 'decline' and with 'positive' ageing. For example, Annette (aged 84, DwithA) talked about having always had good health until she experienced onset of illness over a period of about a year, resulting in activity limitations in her early 80s. She described this as life changing:

'So, I suppose I had fabulous health up to that Christmas, Christmas of 2014, and then the whole bottom fell out of my world. ... And the shock of that nearly killed me because I was never sick. Still, I suppose it catches up with us all sooner or later. And, like [coordinator of older people's centre] always says, "Age is only a number", and I always had that outlook in life: age is nothing, it is how you view yourself that counts in the end. Oh well, that was it ... I won't let it get me down, I will still continue.'

One of the key consequences or losses for Annette was change in her role in the local older people's centre, where she used to sing and was "the main dancer". Now, she said, "I can't give it my everything." The tensions and ambiguities involved were evident at another point, when Annette said that impairment onset was tantamount to sudden onset of ageing: "I had to give in and admit I am getting old [laughs]."

Annette's interpretation intersects with concepts like 'positive' ageing, describing her pre-illness belief that "age is just a number" and her determination to "still continue". This is typical of the psychological resources associated with these discourses (see Katz and Calasanti, 2015; Timonen, 2016). Annette refers to her investment in these concepts to explain why she experienced shock at her embodied experience of change and limitation. It is as if adherence to 'positive' ageing contributes to perceptions of these changes as almost 'out of time' in terms of the lifecourse, unanticipated in biographical terms and highly disruptive.

Thus, the focus on youthfulness in these discourses and the way they extend middle-aged lifestyles into older age may, for people who invest in them, contribute to making onset of chronic illness or impairment seem biographically disruptive. This is so even in the classic sense in which Bury (1982) defined disruption – as an unexpected event in an otherwise healthy life. These discourses also contribute to a sense in which being older does not make onset of chronic illness biographically anticipated.

Even though the self-realisation aspects of 'positive' ageing resonated, bodily change could require one to 'give in' to being old. These discourses provide few interpretive resources to understand bodily change as anything other than a signal of 'impending old age and failure' (Pack et al, 2019: 2100) and leave little 'space' within which to meaningfully articulate experiences of ageing and disability (Grenier et al, 2016: 18). Relatedly, dominant discourses insufficiently recognise the desire of older disabled people, or so-called 'fourth-agers', to continue to live lives of value, expressed in their desire to engage in activities they enjoy – just like so-called 'third-agers'.

As Kafer (2013: 3–4) suggests, discussing disability generally, the value of a disability-free future is seen as self-evident, while the value of a future that includes disabled people goes unrecognised, as does the fact that illness and disability are part of what makes us human. Participants' accounts highlight the absence of discourses or models of later life that validate living with disability. They underline the need to reframe ideas about disability and ageing to incorporate ideas that, with support, life can continue to be rewarding. We also need to incorporate notions of how disability and, indeed, vulnerability are a normal part of what makes us human.

Heterogeneity in the experience of ageing with disability

The experience of disability in general is heterogeneous, as is the experience of ageing with disability (Sheets, 2005). This was evident among how AwithD participants in the present study discussed their bodily experiences. As argued up to this point, for most AwithD participants, experiences in older age (and sometimes throughout adulthood) involved ongoing bodily changes and challenges, which could mean inability to control things and fears of fundamental change in social lives consistent with a sense of ongoing disruptive events.

Having coped with many challenges throughout life meant that participants from the AwithD group were resilient, but they could also be significantly challenged and fearful about the challenges faced now, such as new impairments on top of existing ones, and, especially, the prospect of greater dependence on others. However, bodily experiences were heterogeneous among the AwithD group of participants. For a small number, bodies had so far caused no difficulty or minimal difficulty, setting them apart from all the other participants. These heterogeneous experiences are discussed in Chapter 8.

Discussion and conclusions

This chapter discussed how participants experienced disablement through bodies that limited activities or caused pain, fatigue or balance issues – or did so to a greater extent than previously. Justification for this engagement with material aspects of the body is found especially in critical gerontology, such as the argument from Holstein and Minkler (2007: 16) of the need to engage with the 'real bodies' of older people, and Gilleard's (2018) call to document suffering by older people. As Twigg (2004: 63) puts it, ageing forces engagement with physiology, 'not least because of the ultimate undeniability of death'. However, by discussing how material issues were interpreted by participants in light of dominant societal discourses of ageing, I also sought to engage with social constructions and interpretations of disability.

For most participants, the impaired body, or the more impaired body, was a key way in which they experienced disability or disablement processes. This is hardly surprising given the dominance of the body in biomedical accounts of ageing. Less well recognised, however, are subjective reactions and interpretations that interact with broader societal discourses and ideologies. Even when disablement occurred at a stage in life considered – by the people concerned – as 'normal' or 'on time', it could create a sense of disorder, requiring efforts in response. Thus, disability and greater disablement tended to be experienced as 'a disruptive force', redefining the person and their family life, relationships and social networks (Kahana and Kahana, 2017: ix; Bury, 1982, 1997). This challenges the assumption that the normative connection between impairment and older age might make onset of chronic illness *anticipated*, not disruptive (Williams, 2000).

However, even where there was an identification with 'decline' and a consciousness of finitude, participants did not define themselves by their bodies, and they did not treat their lives as over. Rather, they focused on what they could still do and often made efforts to both improve functioning and to maintain connections and activities. They tended to maintain a sense of identity different from, but also continuous with, the past.

Narratives of 'catastrophic' onset of disability, whenever it occurred, clearly evoked Bury's (1982) original concept of biographical disruption of that which was taken for granted, followed by the mobilisation of resources to respond. However, gradual onset had similar consequences over time. In addition, with the passage of time, 'catastrophic' narratives could mingle with narratives of 'decline'. Further challenges and cycles of adaptation could follow. This is why the most relevant concept of biographical disruption is the expanded version from Larsson and Jeppsson Grassman (2012) – that biographical disruptions may occur repeatedly, and that changes do not have to be wholly unexpected to be experienced as disruptive.

These findings are consistent with some condition-specific empirical studies with older people. For example, people with arthritis could view symptoms as 'normal' and inevitable, and also experience disruption (Sanders et al, 2002). Older people as well as younger people who had strokes could experience biographical disruption (Meijering et al, 2017). A study by Lloyd et al (2020) suggests that older people could experience 'frailty' as both disruptive and anticipated. Again, consistent with the findings of Larsson and Jeppsson Grassman (2012), disruption could be experienced by the AwithD group of participants (as well as the DwithA group), as lifelong activities might be curtailed by further, or worsening, conditions, creating fears of greater dependence on others or a sense of greater isolation. For the AwithD group, experiences of disruption could happen repeatedly across the lifespan, often worsening as time passed. This led to the repeated need for adaptation and raised ongoing identity questions (Charmaz, 1995). While this group of participants was diverse and had had to be resilient in facing challenges over time, additional or worsening impairment with ageing could represent a kind of double jeopardy. By this, I mean that it could compound difficulties in functioning with existing conditions. I resume a discussion of the embodied experiences of this group in Chapter 8.

Participants, from both groups, used dominant discourses of ageing to interpret their experiences, namely, master narratives of 'success' and 'decline' that shape ageing identities (Laceulle and Baars, 2014). Participants typically invoked ideas of 'decline' with age, using it as a resource to 'impose meaning on threatening and seemingly arbitrary events', helping to mitigate disruption by providing a level of explanation (Bury, 1982: 175; 1997: 125). Thus, being older could 'buffer' self-concept as disablement occurred (Kelley-Moore, 2010: 105). In this, participants were trying to interpret their lives in their contexts in ways that enabled them to understand events, to cope and to maintain a sense of value and meaning in life.

In a seeming paradox, participants could link impairment onset or worsening with being 'old', with 'decline' or with a sense of finitude *and* still identify with 'positive' ageing discourses. They communicated tensions between seeing impairment, or worsening impairment, as a signal of death, on the one hand, and, on the other, as a time to commit to regaining functioning or to resist the effects of age. However, 'positive' ageing provided little help with meaningfully articulating experiences of ageing and disability, providing few interpretive resources to understand bodily change, which was typically seen as a signal of decline and, sometimes, as a time to 'give in' or withdraw. For some, adherence to positive ageing principles, like 'age is just a number', contributed to the sense that disability onset was disruptive in the classical sense in which Bury articulated it, that is, as a single event in an otherwise healthy existence.

Furthermore, the emphasis on activity and self-realisation enshrined in 'positive' ageing models resonated more than is generally imagined for people who might be considered in the 'fourth age'. Thus, people's engagement with life and with processes of social identity formation continued to be incomplete (Hockey and James, 2003: 12). This highlights the need for development of more holistic discourses of disability and ageing that model how life lived with adequate support can continue to be experienced as meaningful and rewarding, and that also enable integration of more difficult aspects of the experience. Without wishing to deny the challenges involved, including existential ones, there is scope to learn from disability studies that different ways of being in the world can be sources of knowledge, creativity and happiness (see Chivers, 2011: 9).

'Decline' discourses may also have contributed to playing down difficulties – wishing to be perceived as behaving in a way that was 'culturally appropriate' for older age (Sanders et al, 2002: 246). However, there can be a cost associated with identification with a 'decline ideology' (Gullette, 2004: 134). It may de-emphasise sociocultural contributions (Laceulle and Baars, 2014), and cause problems and suffering to be accepted with equanimity (Kane and Kane, 2005; Jönson and Larsson, 2009). Pretending that disability does not increase with ageing (as reinforced by ideologies of 'positive' ageing), or that it is the same thing as ageing and therefore 'normal' and to be accepted (as reinforced by a decline ideology), both have the effect of eliding bodily experiences.

It also means that participants find themselves negotiating ageing identities in tension with binary discourses that are ableist. This is because discourses of 'positive' ageing occur within broader idealised notions of independent adulthood, prevailing concepts of autonomy and independence, and fears of human vulnerability (Baars, 2010; Lamb, 2014; Holstein, 2015). Through a disability studies lens, participants' reactions are typical reactions to ableism – which can involve distancing from other disabled people and emulation of ableist norms (Campbell, 2008; Loja et al, 2013: 191). As Campbell (2009) says, ableist ideologies promote atomistic, solitary forms of personhood. Thus, a 'preference for able-bodiedness' is a powerful overarching societal ideology (Siebers, 2008: 8), and 'disavowal' of disability can be part of the reaction of disabled people generally (Kafer, 2003: 80).

Therefore, a final point to reinforce here is that these experiences are not unique to older disabled people. Participants' accounts echo personal accounts of denial of bodily experiences by disabled people generally (Morris, 1991; Zola, 1991; Luborsky, 1994). For example, it was only when Zola (1991) encountered disability activism that he could acknowledge bodily discomfort and realise that some of his experience was socially constructed. Paradoxically, it was only through the political that he could acknowledge the bodily.

Thus, influential discourses intersect and largely promote individual-level interpretations and disavowal of the experience of disability. Intersecting cultural concepts mean that both older people and disabled people are 'easily devalued' or marginalised (Priestley, 2001: 246; Gibbons, 2016: 77). This suggests that there is value in approaches to scholarship and activism that address the lived experience of disabled people across the lifespan, and that challenge societal discourses that 'other' disabled people of all ages. The attempt of this book is to include the bodily *and* the contextual. As Kafer (2013: 6) argues, both impairment and disability are social, stating: 'I want to make space for people to acknowledge – even mourn – a change in form or function while also acknowledging that such changes cannot be understood apart from the context in which they occur.' Although individual-level or bodily experiences have been the focus of this chapter, participants also experienced disability in broader contexts, which is the focus of Chapter 6.

6

Disabling or enabling contexts

Introduction

This is the second chapter addressing the research question, 'How do older people experience disability and processes of disablement, and what meanings do they make of those experiences?' It discusses how participants in the present study experienced disability and disablement in interactions with their contexts – social, economic, physical, cultural and political. The chapter starts by returning to the issue of a 'disability' identity introduced in Chapter 3 by way of background. I then discuss findings which suggest that participants perceived themselves as more or less disabled due to a range of contextual factors: social/familial factors; support and care; physical environments; and sociocultural meanings in everyday interactions. Participants could be disabled by factors that disable people of all ages, such as inaccessible homes and environments, and through being marginalised or excluded in interactions with others.

Experiencing disability with ageing (DwithA) could be perceived as entering a socially discredited or devalued category – a transition, therefore, experienced not just at a bodily level, but also at a social, cultural and political level. An inverse process meant improvements in aspects of life for some participants ageing with disability (AwithD), even if life was challenging in many ways and often because earlier life had been marked by a sense of exclusion or confinement. The chapter then discusses how participants related to a disability identity and how some people were in the process of negotiating a disability identity in response to perceptions of being discriminated against or excluded, and some were developing a new sense of belonging with other disabled people.

Theoretical background: disability identity

Disability identity was originally associated with membership of a shared collective, understood as a somewhat fixed or stable phenomenon (Watson, 2002: 513). Oliver (1996: 5) suggested there were three elements to a disability identity: presence of impairment; experiencing externally imposed restrictions; and self-identification.

Disability is now recognised as involving a variety of intersectional experiences, and many people experiencing impairment do not identify as 'disabled' or engage with activism (Riddell and Watson, 2003; Ridolfo, 2010). Studies with younger disabled people suggest that most did not incorporate disability within their identity; instead, they sought to be part of the mainstream (Priestley et al, 1999; Watson, 2002). Thus, disabled people often emphasise what they have in common with non-disabled people, seeking inclusion and equal status, not separation (Shakespeare, 2014a).

Postmodernist thinking makes the construction of a shared political vision more challenging (Davis, 2013a). From this perspective, identity is constructed in relations of discourse and power, and ideas of disabled and non-disabled identity only strengthen essentialist arguments. Thus, identity is 'out of fashion' as a category in critical or cultural theory (Siebers, 2008: 11). However, identity may be most important when you belong to a minority group whose selfhood is challenged by the actions of a majority group (Tregaskis, 2004: 93). Having a group identified as 'disabled' provides a basis to mobilise politically (Vehmas and Watson, 2014), and, even for Davis (2013a: 263), 'there is a strategic kind of identity politics'. Crucially, Siebers (2008: 11) suggests that claiming 'disability' is both a political act and a practice that improves quality of life. For Siebers (2017 [2013]: 119), disability identity is based in shared knowledge as to what it is to be 'disabled' – or shared social experiences that are both negative and positive. Thus, it is based in shared experiences of oppression, discrimination and medicalisation, as well as (more positively) shared knowledge of survival strategies, healthcare policy and environmental conditions.

People first experiencing disability in later life (the DwithA group) are thought not to identify with a disability identity. This is because of a lifetime's identification as non-disabled and due to perceptions of their functioning as normal for their age (McGrath et al, 2017). While the findings discussed in Chapter 5 might be said to support this, those discussed in this chapter show that resistance to a disability identity is only one part of the picture. Instead, dominant discourses of ageing, a societal tendency to cast disability as a diminished state and separate policy framings and approaches to activism help construct (or not) a 'disability' identity in older age.

Experiences of disability in interaction with contexts

Participants experienced disability in interaction with their contexts. The categories I identified through inductive analysis concerned social/familial factors, support and care, physical environments, and sociocultural meanings in everyday interactions. These categories were interlinked, and class and access to financial resources could mediate experiences. It is expensive to experience disability in older age (Cullinan et al, 2013; Morciano et al, 2014) and life could be very difficult for materially disadvantaged participants.

Part of the background to the findings presented here is the earlier discussion of social care policies on ageing and on disability, showing how approaches to ageing are typically narrower and more medicalised, with less emphasis on the social (Monahan and Wolf, 2014). As suggested by the National Council on Ageing and Older People and National Disability Authority (2006) and borne out more recently (Leahy, 2018), these distinctions operate in social care services in Ireland. As Chapter 4 illustrated, they are also reflected in traditional approaches in other countries too.

Experiencing social and familial factors as enabling or disabling

The lifecourse concept of linked lives highlights how people live with others and how changes in others' lives affect them (Elder et al, 2003). Participants often understood their functioning not as individuals, but in conjunction with support received from others. Thus, lives were linked in ways that influenced how disability was understood and experienced. Participants' accounts of relationships reflected both the deeper meaning made of impairment for identity and its practical consequences.

Others reducing perception of disability

Participants enjoyed time spent with family and friends, and exchanges of love and support were very important. Others also facilitated functioning. Environments could be experienced as less disabling and participants could perceive themselves as less 'disabled' due to the way they functioned with others. Spouses, adult children (especially daughters), siblings, nieces and nephews, neighbours, and friends helped with tasks like personal care, shopping, housework and transport.

These supports could affect how participants understood activities and participation, and how they related to 'disability'. In other words, 'disability' was often understood as part of a relational or social unit rather than in an individual way. This was particularly true of spouses. Thus, a participant might describe their functioning as impaired in one dimension, understanding it in an individual or bodily sense, and as not at all impaired in another due to functioning with a spouse – typically, in relation to getting out of the home. For example, William (aged 70, DwithA) described how his wife helps him:

> 'She puts the clothes on me in the morning anyway and when we're out together, if I get a steak ... I couldn't cut up a steak with one hand, so I do get salmon or some meat I can manage myself or she cuts it for me. ... There is a lot of stuff you can't do with one hand.'

However, talking about getting out of home *alone*, William did so in terms of how he functioned with his wife as a unit: "I can manage that all right, fairly well. She [wife] brings me, like, she brings me wherever I have to go." Thus, William's wife's driving was crucial to how he understood disability. Others had similar understandings. Desmond (aged 72, AwithD) felt that visual impairment caused him no difficulty. He did not think of being blind as a "disability" – it was just how things had always been. However, since he retired, his wife goes everywhere with him and Desmond considered that they functioned as "one".

Perceptions of not being disabled due to the presence of a spouse were associated especially with men. It is a likely factor here that caring roles are more easily taken for granted in women (Arber and Ginn, 1995: 26), along with male perceptions of relative power in society (Cancian and Oliker, 2000). Women too relied on spouses and family members. However, if some seemed to take functioning jointly with their spouse for granted, others were reflexive about it or resisted it. Some, including men, understood their functioning in a more individual way. Participants often said they wished not to be a 'burden' on family members, reflecting a wish for independence or autonomy. These findings support arguments that people find it easier to rely on spouses than on others like adult children (Warner and Adams, 2016).

Lack of intimates (or impairment among them) increasing disability

Conversely, *not* having someone who was willing and able to facilitate functioning was linked to the experience of disablement or greater disability. Losing a spouse, or a change in their health or functioning, could mean finding it harder to leave home or to function in social situations. For example, Simon (aged 66, AwithD), who was visually impaired, said that he and his wife had been "joined at the hip". Her death meant that "everything has changed" and he went out little, saying he had no "confidence" outside without her. Stephen (aged

88, DwithA) felt that his mobility had declined since his wife's death, as he was less active.

Precariousness about intimates as their health or functioning changed was linked to fears about maintaining one's own functioning. For example, Julie (aged 80, DwithA) felt that current living arrangements were contingent on her husband's health. In addition, of course, not everyone had a spouse/partner or adult children. Francis (aged 76, DwithA) perceived lack of adult children as a "handicap", as he explained that he is now largely confined to home due to a condition that his wife had developed, which meant that neither he nor she could stow his wheelchair in the car.

Not all relationships were supportive. A small number of participants related impairment to grudging support or changes in relationships over time that resulted in less support and greater disability. These experiences tended to be reported in the context of long-term disability, pointing to disadvantages associated with experiencing disability for a long time (Verbrugge et al, 2017). People with the smallest family circles or supportive networks experienced disability maximally, consistent with evidence that less socially integrated older people perceive greater disability, independent of functional status (Kelley-Moore et al, 2006).

It is relevant to the experience of the AwithD group of participants that disabled people generally are less likely than others to have been married or have cohabited (Loprest and Maag, 2007; MacDonald et al, 2018), so are less likely to have supportive intimates in older age. Thus, there are differences between groups. In a broad sense, however, loss of intimates and reduced social networks is characteristic of older age (Settersten, 2005, 2006; Baars, 2010), and an implication is that community participation of older disabled people cannot be left entirely to families and friends (Litwin and Levinson, 2018: 1787). This requires collective societal and community responses. It highlights the paradox of public services aimed at older people de-emphasising social aspects, as discussed in Chapter 4. Approaching it through the lens of disability may help frame this as a social issue rather than an individual failure.

Experiencing support and care as enabling or disabling

The way that support and care were experienced could be perceived as disabling or enabling. Participants perceived less disability if individual resources, public services and aids/appliances were available, and more disability if they lacked access to them, or if they were provided in inflexible ways. Participants with financial resources bought support, care, therapies and appliances. Others relied on what they sometimes perceived as limited or inflexible public provision of care and experienced more difficulty functioning as a result. However, there were also positive experiences of public support and care, including warm relations with people providing home care.

Something to acknowledge at the outset was that there were anomalies and inconsistencies in the provision of support and care. For example, some participants from the AwithD group benefitted from a disability model of support because they had remained within disability services after age 65. Other participants from the AwithD group experienced levels of support more typical of older people's services, for example, not having access to personal assistance. This is consistent with the anomalies identified in an exploration of policy frameworks in Ireland (Leahy, 2018).

The situations of Gloria (aged 80, DwithA) and Hazel (aged 80, AwithD), though atypical, illustrate how financial resources could facilitate functioning and participation. Both benefitted from live-in carers. For example, Gloria had a live-in carer who accompanied her shopping and helped with cooking and housekeeping. Hazel, visually impaired since her 30s, said that her husband left her well off. She paid for a range of supports, including for a 'family' of migrants who lived with her and alternated the role of keeping her company. Thus, Hazel lived independently but with company overnight, and was supported to engage in activities like shopping for clothes or meeting friends for lunch. This resembles the role of the personal assistant, a key advocacy focus for the disabled people's movement. Hazel's resources enabled her to live securely, to make decisions and to engage in social activities – fulfilling the kind of ideal for services advocated for disabled people generally (see Chapter 4).

However, Hazel's and Gloria's situations were very different to other participants in terms of ability to purchase support. Experiences that were in some respects comparable involved two participants from the AwithD group who lived in supported-living complexes run by disability services, illustrating how public policies can contribute to minimising the experience of disability and maximising participation.

One was Babs (aged 67, AwithD). Born with cerebral palsy, the course of her life was strongly marked by the experience of impairment because it was of a type seen as needing to be 'safely wall[ed] off' (Davis, 1995: 7). Babs spent childhood in hospitals or care settings, and spent adulthood mainly in her family home. When she was 50, her mother became ill and Babs moved to a care home. She subsequently moved to a supported-living apartment at age 60, and she continued within disability services after age 65. Thus, Babs benefitted from a commitment to decongregation of residential settings within Irish disability policy (Health Service Executive Working Group on Congregated Settings, 2011) and from service norms set by reference to the adult disabled population. She enjoyed independent but also supported living and had a personal assistant, who helped her to do things like going swimming. Babs described her carers as supportive and encouraging of her taking on new challenges and making choices. She was delighted with her living arrangements: "Oh, I LOVE it. And I'm able to go over to [supermarket] on my own and I'm able to go up to the town on my own … the best thing is you're your own person. There's no one telling you what to do. You are the boss." Several times, Babs identified being "the boss" – making her own decisions – as the most positive aspect of life nowadays.

Babs benefitted from approaches to disability policies discussed in Chapter 4, involving more freedom and control (Barnes and Mercer, 2006, 2010). Her living arrangements also provided high levels of security and support, with carers on call 24/7. Babs described how she did her own shopping: her carers make a list of what she wants, which she needs to show to shop assistants in case she cannot reach from her wheelchair and they cannot understand her speech. Yet, Babs experienced an autonomous sense of self. She benefitted, perhaps for the first time, from feeling validated by dominant discourses, or by a 'cultural imaginary' associated with independence (Goodley et al, 2019: 986). Thus, the level and nature of available supports fundamentally affected her functioning, the extent to which she experienced disability and her sense of self.

However, few participants from either group lived with the degree of support that Babs had. Several lived in their homes with support from family members or public services in the form of home help. They did not have personal assistants. Sometimes, support to live at home was perceived as inflexible. Within older people's services, Carmel (age 69, DwithA), a wheelchair user, experienced disability first at age 65. She rejected the advice of a medical consultant that she would have to go into a nursing home, characteristic of the custodial care emphasised within aged-care models. Carmel returned to her rural home once adaptations were made with a local authority grant. However, Carmel did not have a personal assistant and regretted that she could not leave home on her own. She felt "restricted" as a result and said: "I am not independent at all in that respect." She did not have support on call despite several occasions when she fell and needed help.

Carmel also lacked income that would enable her to use a wheelchair-accessible taxi. She lacked supports that enabled others (like Gloria, Babs or Hazel) to experience life as independent and self-directed, and also secure. However, it is also true that several people from both groups, including Carmel, reported warm, supportive relationships with people providing care. For example, Carmel instanced her home help popping in, outside allotted hours, to light a fire so that the house would be warm for Carmel's return. Participants, including Carmel, also called on carers like home helps in times of trouble.

Participants' experiences of support and care are shaped by class and income. They are also shaped by the level and type of public services available and the respective public policy models and practices that operate in disability and older people's services in Ireland at present. Variations in experiences illustrate anomalies inherent in the aims and approaches embedded in the separate policy frameworks on ageing and on disability. Some participants who would be considered to have the most severe impairment also experienced great satisfaction with life nowadays – and the least 'disability' – mediated not only by perceptions of having lived very restricted lives in the past, but also by a supportive public service model.

This points to the possibility of more older disabled people living fulfilling lives with appropriate support, and for the development of positive models of life with impairment in older age to inform policies and discourses more broadly. Aspects of the model currently applied to social care for disabled people in Ireland (albeit inconsistently), including self-direction and personal assistance, could enhance the lives of other older disabled people. Interpersonal aspects of care were also important. The importance of collective aspects of care is discussed again in Chapter 7.

Experiencing physical environments as enabling or disabling

Participants understood 'disability' in terms of how homes and environments facilitated functioning. If homes or available transport were accessible, then perceptions of being disabled simply did not arise in certain domains – again underlining how meanings made of disability were broader than is encompassed by purely biomedical approaches to ageing.

Homes

Most obviously, a home without stairs and with an accessible bathroom could be experienced as enabling by people with physical impairments.

Some participants had made adaptations to homes, paying the cost themselves or getting help from local authorities. Others waited for grants or for adaptations to be made to local authority housing. Waiting for adaptations meant being more disabled in the meantime. It could mean, for example, only having access to a commode, not a toilet.

Liz (aged 55, AwithD) lived on disability payments since she had to give up supermarket work when she experienced sudden onset of disability, aged 42. With her savings depleted, she experienced disability maximally. For example, Liz had a mobility scooter but did not use it much because her house lacked a suitable ramp and the scooter had to be kept in a shed outside. Liz described a very inconvenient and lengthy process of accessing her shed to use the scooter as she waited for a local authority grant to fit a ramp. Thinking about what would make life better, she said a ramp, a wet room and a seat in the shower.

By contrast, participants with more financial resources minimised experiences of disability. For example, Josephine (aged 78, DwithA) had her house adapted with ramps and rails to facilitate functioning to the maximum extent possible. She also described being unable to hang out clothes on her clothesline but felt that she had enough income to be able to use the tumble-dryer without worrying about the cost.

Therefore, the accessibility of homes could support functioning and reduce perceptions of disability. Having or not having financial resources directly affected this, as did access to public grants for adaptations.

External physical environments

Participants perceived their ability to function as limited by external environments, and identified barriers in accessing public transport and using footpaths, toilets and buildings like shops and restaurants. These issues tended to be raised by participants who were using wheelchairs, walkers/rollators or mobility scooters. Hearing-impaired participants also experienced environmental barriers in public places.

For people who lived on limited income, getting out of home could be difficult. For several participants from both groups, public transport, where it was available, had to be negotiated with difficulty because taxis were relatively expensive. For Liz (aged 55, AwithD), it meant even getting access to physiotherapy was almost impossible as it required paying for taxis or negotiating several buses to get to the hospital. Without physiotherapy, Liz felt that her mobility was worsening over time, and she found this very frustrating: "Trying to get physio, that is the most frustrating part, big time."

By contrast, some participants did not have to think about the cost of taking taxis. For example, as Kathleen (aged 85, DwithA) perceived and experienced it, she had no difficulty leaving the house alone: "taxis all the time". Thus, in this respect, she was not 'disabled'. In short, life could be especially difficult, limited and confined to home for materially disadvantaged participants, who lived with greater disability as a result.

Among rural dwellers, several regretted the paucity of public transport or the inaccessibility of available buses. City dwellers, like Phil (aged 74, DwithA), a wheelchair user following amputation of his legs in his 60s, was frustrated by inaccessible footpaths, buses and the urban train (the DART) – by virtue of which he felt he was classed as a "second-class citizen". Others too were frustrated by public transport. Paul (aged 69, DwithA), whose balance was affected after a stroke, had given up using city buses. Using a rollator, Paul used to try to get seated before the busses moved but that meant depending on "the courtesy of drivers".

For participants with hearing impairment, barriers were often within families and social groups. They could also experience environmental barriers. Seamus (aged 78, DwithA) wanted greater accommodation of the needs of deaf people: "I want more subtitling on TV, I want subtitling on the cinema." He had joined the committee of his local film club to try and get subtitling on screenings. However, other members rejected his request, as "they found it distracting". Thus, despite his actions, Seamus is disabled because the members of the film club are not prepared to make adjustments to include him.

If anything, people in the DwithA group emphasised physical barriers more – probably, as this experience was a more recent one for them. The AwithD group of participants might have become used to living with barriers to participation, or working around them, over a longer period, though they continued to be significant barriers that they could perceive as unjust and that had influenced their lives for decades. Experiencing environments as inaccessible could be interpreted as exclusion and positioning as a 'second-class citizen' or as a member of a discredited social category – experiences of oppression in a classical social model sense (Brisenden, 1998 [1986]). Thus, feeling excluded, discredited and discriminated against could form part of the meanings made of the experience of disability, and another way in which experiences of disablement were disruptive of biography and self-concept (see Bury, 1988, 1991, 1997).

Experiencing sociocultural meanings made of disability in everyday interactions

The final heading under which I discuss disabling or enabling environments relates to everyday interactions with others. Here, differences were notable between the two groups of participants. People in the DwithA group could perceive rejection and exclusion in everyday interactions, associated with disability onset. Thus, meanings made by others of disability (as discrediting) construct ageing and the lifecourse (Kelley-Moore, 2010). A different – inverse – process was experienced by some among the AwithD group. Against the backdrop of exclusion over decades or over their lifetimes, some people perceived positives associated with ageing, as meanings made of ageing and the lifecourse constructed disability as less stigmatising at their life stage.

Disability with ageing: experiencing exclusion

Participants from the DwithA group could associate impairment onset, or starting to use aids or appliances, with the embarrassment of others or with being excluded by others. This is something of a surprising finding given how impairment is often considered a social norm of ageing (Priestley, 2006). Despite not being considered 'disabled' in general perceptions and often in their own accounts, participants suffered disablement as 'the outcome of the withholding of social and cultural recognition' (Watson, 2003: 50).

For example, Joan (aged 86, DwithA), who experienced gradual onset of mobility issues, described an incident where she brought a walking stick to a relative's house, intending to lend it temporarily to a family member who was recovering from illness. Joan described another family member's reaction as "a cannuption of 'oh no, no, no, no, no'". Joan said:

> 'And I was *shocked*. Because at that stage, I'd got quite used, 'twas just a part of me but *a part*. It [walking stick] wasn't *me*. But she saw it as *me*. I was deeply hurt and I was enraged more than anything else. ... Like that *I* was *other*, *but* her mother [pauses]. ... It was ... was seeing me as just an old woman with a stick.'

Joan experienced this reaction as rejection and social devaluation – as having been placed in a category below the 'normal'. Joan added that one of the biggest changes of recent years was her consciousness of others' perceptions of her, "as an old disabled person". She added: "I feel conscious, very conscious, of that."

Thus, a big change of recent years was how others consigned her to a different, discredited category – "as an old disabled person". Joan's account suggests that she found herself at the intersection of ageism and ableism, or at the effect of 'compulsory youthfulness' (Gibbons, 2016). This again illustrates how perceptions of being othered or excluded can be disruptive of biography and self-concept (see Bury, 1982, 1997).

Exclusion could be experienced within a community of older people. For example, Carmel (aged 69, DwithA), a wheelchair user, felt excluded from outings by an active older group *because* she was impaired, and attributed it to an unspoken prejudice on the part of those who run the organisation:

'There are times that I certainly feel disabled, like when you can't go on the bus when there is a group going to a shopping centre and you can't go. ... That does make me feel bad. ... It is not a problem with the bus; it is only a problem with the organisers. They think I am disabled. ... It is not said in so many words, but there is no other reason why I can't go.'

Even if the impaired body was not central to Carmel's concept of identity, it resulted in exclusion from a group of age peers. She "feel[s] disabled" on these occasions – in other words, being disabled is not so much a fixed condition of impairment, but something she experiences *when she is excluded*. As is the experience of disabled people generally, Carmel's identity merges with her wheelchair in the public mind and disability limits her participation because others 'do not welcome her presence sufficiently' (Siebers, 2017 [2013]: 118). Carmel had challenged the organisers of the outings, arguing that she could wheel herself. She could be said to be developing a disability consciousness. Raymond et al (2014) found that people ageing with disability (AwithD group) can experience barriers to participation in places targeting seniors. Experiences like Carmel's illustrate how exclusion can also apply to people experiencing disability first with ageing (DwithA group).

Another example illustrates how perceived lifecourse norms – such as images of events being 'on time' or 'off time' – can be used to constrain behaviour (Holstein and Gubrium, 2000). George (aged 76, DwithA) explained that friends and family were "embarrassed" when he visited using a rollator from his late 50s, and that they would put his rollator out of sight once he sat down leaving him "stranded". George felt that a close family member was also embarrassed by his use of a rollator or a wheelchair, and that she did not like to attend Mass with him as a result: "I suppose she thought it was a slight on her." Although conscious of this person's embarrassment, George minimised its impact. He said it did not bother him "to an awful extent", even though it meant not attending Mass, and even though he regretted that his days were confined to home. At another point, George said: "There are things that I'd like to do but at 76, you might as well start slowing down."

By referring to his age, George may be invoking what Gullette (2004: 135) terms a 'decline ideology' to help deal with the suffering associated with the reactions of others. From a disability studies perspective, it is possible to understand the reaction of George and other participants in terms of reactions to ableism or as internalised oppression or internalised ableism – internalising prejudice or negative stereotypes of what it means to have an impairment, thereby invalidating and restricting oneself (Reeve, 2012). This is to experience 'psycho-emotional disablism' (Thomas, 2007, 2015; Reeve, 2012).

Thus, participants sometimes invoked a decline ideology to buffer self-concept when faced with disablism – something that *actively* limits them – but they could also resist perceptions of othering, and both could coexist in the account of one person. Identifying these experiences as resulting from disablism clarifies that the problem lies in the attitudes and behaviours of others and in society.

Ageing with disability: experiencing greater inclusion

Participants who were ageing with disability (AwithD group) could describe an inverse process, sometimes perceiving that with ageing, lives now resembled the lives of others more closely in some respects, as meanings they and others made of ageing and the lifecourse constructed disability as less stigmatising. This takes place in the context of societal institutions and cultural ideas, based on an able-bodied ideal, that define what a 'normal' life means. Discussion here of a 'normal' life or references to 'normalisation' do not signal an uncritical acceptance of these concepts, as the lifecourse is culturally embedded and socially contingent (see Chapter 3). Living with disability involves encounters with barriers over which one has no control, and disability activism seeks a redefinition of both disability and the 'normal' lifecourse (Priestley, 2000).

Some accounts suggested that daily interactions continued to be challenging, as, say, a progressive condition still had to be explained to others and the reactions of others managed, as is the experience of disabled people generally (Reeve, 2012: 81). However, for some AwithD participants, having input of carers meant that their lives resembled those of their age peers more. For Eileen (aged 66, AwithD), "It's time I should be looked after." For several other participants, there had been an improvement over time in how others reacted to them or in how they responded. These experiences are consistent with those of some participants in empirical studies with this group (Jeppsson Grassman, 2013; Bishop and Hobson, 2015). The present study also illustrates how normative understandings of lifecourse transitions are open to challenge and disruption based on experiences of disabled people over their lifespans.

Helen's (aged 68, AwithD) account illustrates how improvements could be experienced in tandem with increasing disablement. Childhood scoliosis was followed by ill health in her 30s, and, more recently, Helen needed to carry an oxygen tank at all times and was experiencing near-constant pain. Yet, life had improved in some ways:

> 'Well, I am at the stage in my life I suppose ... when you have scoliosis, and mine is quite visible, you get used to people looking at it, and I am at the stage where I am not too worried about the fact that, well, I have to wear it [oxygen tank], but I am worried about the fact that it is such a nuisance for me to carry it around. ... I suppose I got used to that, maybe it was more of a problem when I was younger and going to dances and things because you can see where you would run into problems there. But now, it is not such an issue. That is the beauty in some ways of getting old, some things are less of an issue and other things become an issue. But no, it doesn't bother me, now I don't care less, it is more your problem than mine.'

Helen articulated how she had been subject to others' gaze all her life because of a body that did not match cultural standards (Garland-Thomson, 2002). Changes in her body with ageing made life increasingly difficult. However, reactions to Helen's perceived impairment were more problematic when she was "going to dances" – so the exclusion that it caused as a young person was less of an issue with ageing. Thus, ageing constructs the meaning of impairment by making a visible impairment less visible or noteworthy. It also helped Helen to resist others' judgements and to assert her own sense of self-worth and of living a life of value.

Still others experienced a new sense of engagement with ageing – which could be experienced along with ongoing challenges in bodies. This was most marked among participants, discussed earlier in this chapter, who had moved to supported-living complexes run by disability services later in life and whose appraisals of life nowadays were very positive. However, others also reported positive experiences with ageing associated with joining older people's groups. This experience will be discussed again especially in Chapter 8. It is worth stressing that public services and inclusive community organisations were central to positive perceptions of life nowadays, and that such perceptions were informed by experiences of confinement or exclusion for decades, and were compatible with increasing health or impairment challenges.

Identifying as disabled?

The discussion so far raises the issue of whether meanings made of experiences of disability and disablement encompassed ideas of a disability identity. I found that there was quite a fluid and complex picture. People ageing with disability (AwithD group) often used terms like 'disabled' or 'disability' of themselves. They could also understand 'disability' as consistent with disability activism based on a social model. For example, April (aged 65, AwithD) valued participating in disability activism over the years and said: "It is society that disables you." Some participants from the AwithD group could both talk of themselves as 'disabled' and say that they had not felt 'disabled' – by which they meant that impairment had not stopped them doing things that they valued. However, several participants valued contact with other disabled people and several also enjoyed volunteering through disability organisations, which connected them with others. Thus, 'disability' had provided, and continued to provide, a valued outlet.

Participants from the AwithD group could also resist identification with a collective of disabled people. April did not completely identify with the category 'disabled' because she did not wish to be treated as different: "I don't want people to see me as disabled because I don't see me as disabled." And while Janice (aged 66, AwithD) said she had made more friendships since having "this disability" than before through involvement in disability organisations, she said "no" when asked if she thought of herself as disabled: "No, not in my head, no."

Thus, most participants from the AwithD group did not stress their 'disability' identities. Rather they stressed that their experiences were ordinary and 'normal'. At the same time, the concept of disability could be useful, particularly by providing empowering analyses and through contact with other disabled people that they found supportive, and it could represent a cause to which they could contribute. In other empirical studies, participants ageing with disability emphasised the need to maintain a disability identity with ageing (Jeppsson Grassman et al, 2012: 102; Holme, 2013; Cooper and Bigby, 2014). The findings of the present study are more consistent with a study in which people ageing with disability perceived disability as one characteristic among many and stressed that they had lived an 'ordinary' life (Raymond et al, 2014). For participants, impairment was not dismissed, but difference was not internalised, consistent with Watson's (2002) study with disabled people generally. However, the ageing with disability experience is heterogeneous.

For their part, people who first experienced disability in older age (DwithA group) did not readily use terms like 'disabled' and could resist use of that term about them. For example, Paul (aged 69, DwithA) said that to describe himself as "disabled" would be "pigeonholing" and he stressed, instead, how he had adapted and continued with activities. Participants from this group sometimes said they resisted using mobility and other appliances to begin with, explained as reluctance to be seen as 'old' – impairments and appliances made one 'old' (see Morell, 2003: 73). Stephen (aged 88, DwithA) said that using a rollator hurts people's "pride" – "They don't want to admit that they are old." Their experiences are consistent with suggestions that people experiencing disability onset in (earlier) adulthood may resist a disability identity due to previous negative socialisation towards disability as 'personal tragedy' (Hutchinson et al, 2018). As discussed in Chapter 5, for older people, there might also be other factors at play – participants might also perceive impairment onset as signalling unwelcome change, such as increasing dependency or the inevitability of finitude.

Other participants said they feared being 'left out' when they started to use hearing aids or other appliances. Now, they knew that using appliances, or attending care centres, meant that there was a gap between how they saw themselves and how others saw them. For example, Joan (aged 86, DwithA) attributed her initial reluctance to using a rollator to 'vanity' and characterised using it as becoming "other": "I know that it [rollator] differentiates me from other people. Because I remember going on a pilgrimage to Lourdes one time and there was one lady with a walker. And I saw her as 'other'. And now I am the 'other' myself." She added: "It gradually began to feel quite natural, though initially I hated having to use it [rollator]. ... And it's great, a great help and I can walk as fast as anyone else when I have it – almost." For Joan, it had become "natural" to use a rollator and it meant she functioned like "anyone else". At another point, she said she did not wish to be labelled either as "old" or "disabled" and her initial reluctance to using a rollator is consistent with an awareness of a change in social status – crossing boundaries of identity (Grenier et al, 2016: 14). This experience is shaped by overarching policies and othering discourses in which disability is understood as a diminished state or as 'deficit' (Campbell, 2001; Loja et al, 2013: 198). As discussed already (in Chapter 5), participants negotiate these changes in interaction with dominant discourses and policies of ageing that reflect ableist norms and provide little by way of useful interpretive resource.

However, Joan and other DwithA participants moved beyond these initial negative reactions to appliances. A few participants said they enjoyed using mobility scooters because that made it possible to get out alone. Thus, initial resistance could be followed by acceptance, even enjoyment, because appliances enabled participants to act in the world and conferred a sense of independence. Like bodies and impairment, appliances did not ultimately define them. Participants had had to confront ideas of disability as deficit, and they ultimately resisted ableist norms by adapting, even enjoying, using appliances, and, indeed, attending care centres, which marked them as disabled or discredited in the eyes of others.

Participants' responses to disablism included hurt, anger or resistance (voiced or unvoiced), resembling the resistance of disabled people generally, which can be indirect or unspoken (Watson, 2003; Loja et al, 2013). For example, George (aged 76, DwithA) explained that he felt "case-hardened", which he explained meant that people must take him as he is: "They can take me as I am or forget about me. ... Yes. Here I am. That's it." In some ways, participants adjust to a disabled identity (though typically not using the term), involving accepting the reality, though not the justice, of stigma, a process described by Wendell (1996: 26).

However, as is implicit in the discussion in earlier parts of this chapter, there were some among the DwithA group of participants who *did* identify with disability activism – even if not always couched exactly in those terms. Carmel (aged 69, DwithA), talking about not being able to get out of her house without help, said: "But that doesn't really have anything to do with my age. It has to do with my disability or immobility or call it what you like." She attributed being restricted to home as "disability" not age, positioning herself within the category 'disabled' rather than a chronological categorisation as 'older'. Thus, experiences of Carmel, Seamus or Phil, already discussed, suggest that in responding to disablism, they expressed resistance and were in the process of negotiating a disability identity, something consistent with experiences among disabled people generally (Ridolfo, 2010).

For some, identification with disability activism may have arisen through engagement with mainstream disability organisations, which could also confer a sense of belonging with other disabled people. Phil (aged 74, DwithA), a wheelchair user since his late 60s, attends a centre run by a mainstream disability organisation that – unusually in an Irish context – admits members first experiencing disability after age 65. Phil identified his greatest challenges in terms of environmental barriers, which he associated with changes in political processes and cutbacks that reduce disabled people to "second-class citizens". Talking about not being able to access his local train, he said:

> 'I'd go into town. ... Something I'm doing for years I can't do it anymore, you know. I can't go there. And it's the trains that are at fault, you know. As I've said, the CIE [train company] class us as second-class citizens, they do yea. Like, they won't put a man there. ... It's just that that hurt me, you know, not to be able to go over and get the DART [train] you know. That hurt me. ... I'm not allowed to go into town to see my family. That's the way I look at it.'

The experience was hurtful, and he engaged in lobbying with other people who attend his disability centre to try to address it. Phil located disability squarely within the political – meaning it is 'implicated in relations of power' – as disability scholars and activists do (Kafer, 2013: 9). Phil also demonstrated a disability consciousness, as articulated within the classic social model (Oliver, 1996).

Some participants from the DwithA group also had a sense of belonging through engaging with mainstream disability organisations. For participants experiencing hearing impairment, for example, a lip-reading class could be a supportive community. Timmy (aged 78, DwithA) described his lip-reading class as "my new social circle", adding: "They understand me like I understand them." June (aged 82, DwithA) joined a disability centre that admits people aged 65+ two years previously. She described coming to the centre as like coming "home". She also engaged in activism in relation to cars illegally parking at her local shopping centre that blocked her from accessing the dipped section of the footpath on her mobility scooter.

Overall, these DwithA participants had much in common with participants from the AwithD group in how they related to a disability identity – valuing contact with and support from other disabled people and identifying with and engaging in disability activism at times. No participants wished to be defined by their bodies, impairments, aids or appliances. Both groups resisted labels and wanted to be part of the perceived mainstream, and they resisted ageism, exclusion and ableism. They can be said to reject the idea of an exclusive normalcy, which it is argued is the experience of disabled people generally (Davis, 1995: 10; Watson, 2002; Shakespeare, 2014a: 99).

However, as argued throughout this book, policy environments shape membership categories that affect identities, as do dominant discourses of ageing. Both asserting and resisting collective identification is 'definitively political' (Jenkins, 2008: 43). Policies and services can reinforce a disability identity (Grenier et al, 2016). These findings evidence how a disability identity can be adopted even if oppression or exclusion is first experienced later in life and even if 'disability' approaches to policy and services are only encountered in later life. This points to the possibility of more common cause being made between older disabled people and disabled people more generally.

A final point to reinforce here is that contact with other disabled people could improve lives and be empowering of participants, as it can be for disabled people generally (Siebers, 2008; Shakespeare, 2014a: 82). It can highlight alternatives to the equation of disability with loss and lack (Reeve, 2012: 85). However, participants experiencing disability with ageing did not typically have contact with disability activists and (presumably) encountered a medical model within older age policies/services. Confined within medicalised approaches, they experienced prejudice and exclusion due to disablism without, for the most part, the sense of support or solidarity from identifying or connecting with other disabled people. They also do not have access to the empowering interpretations or models of disability that other disabled people might have.

Discussion and conclusions

The discussion in this chapter demonstrates some key points about how disability and processes of disablement are experienced and interpreted in terms of interactions with contexts – social, economic, physical, cultural and political. This is the second of two chapters that together evidence that participants experienced disability in their bodies and in their contexts. Thus, participants were dealing with existential challenges that were the inevitable results of senescence and finitude, *and* contingent challenges of social origin that can be alleviated (Settersten and Trauten, 2009). This challenges purely biomedical explanations of disability in older age, which omit significant aspects of the subjective experience – aspects that are amenable to change. These experiences are also consistent with an interactional (or biopsychosocial) model of disability.

Disability was experienced within lives linked (or, increasingly, not linked) to others. Participants perceived themselves as not 'disabled' in some domains and experienced less 'disability' if a spouse or other family supported their functioning and participation. Given that increased likelihood of bereavement and reduced social networks distinguish older people from others, this is a systemic issue that should inform collective policy and community responses, and should be reflected in more emphasis on social aspects of public services for older people. Public services that facilitated choice and engagement, and that provided supportive relationships and security, reduced perceptions of 'disability' and contributed to positive appraisals of life and of selfhood, even for people with severe levels of impairment.

Participants could experience homes and physical environments as disabling. People from the DwithA group often emphasised environmental barriers – partially accessible homes and public transport – presumably, as they had encountered them as barriers relatively recently. In certain domains (like homes or ability to leave home), participants were not 'disabled', either in terms of how they thought about themselves or in practical terms, but people who had least access to financial resources had least scope to compensate for the barriers encountered. The findings illustrate how social inequalities play out in experiences of disability in older age and signal the need for attention to experiences of long-standing disability where people age with a legacy of disadvantage. They also confirm the importance of practical measures in various environments that help people to experience less disability and to continue to engage (Wahl et al, 2012; Hallgrimsdottir and Ståhl, 2016).

Disablement first experienced in later life could involve transition not just at a physical or bodily level, but also at a social and cultural level. Accounts of suffering from being excluded from community group outings (for using a wheelchair) or treated like a 'second-class citizen' in public transport show how disability experienced for the first time in older age could be disabling and oppressive in the classical sense in which it was articulated within the social model of disability. Participants could also be aware of the power imbalances involved. Of course, these barriers could also continue to exclude people from the AwithD group from participation opportunities over the long term.

Social interaction with others was another area where people first experiencing disability with ageing could start to experience the exclusion that the AwithD group of participants had always experienced (or had experienced over decades). This was often linked to starting to use appliances such as rollators or wheelchairs. Thus, the social construction of disability (as discredited) could construct ageing and the lifecourse, and participants encountered intersecting ideologies of ageism and ableism. What participants often described, though no one used the term, was disablism – discriminatory or exclusionary behaviour related to beliefs about disabled people (Miller et al, 2004). This included being ignored or discredited, having agency denied, or experiencing embarrassment or fear on the part of non-disabled people, just as (younger) disabled people do (Watson, 2003; Reeve, 2012).

Thus, a societal tendency not to consider older people as 'disabled' does not protect them from disablism or overarching ableist norms. An implication is that disablism, and, indeed, resistance to it, is likely to be a more widely experienced phenomenon than is generally appreciated, not confined to any one diagnostic category or to any age group. Another is that gerontological studies that start from biomedical categorisations, often treated as totally separate from each other, may miss broader relevance of the experiences concerned, which an engagement with concepts such as ableism or disablism could help explicate.

Chapter 5 showed how participants often associated their stage of life with 'decline', which could buffer self-concept as disablement occurred (Kelley-Moore, 2010: 105). For disabled people generally, self-imposed restrictions can be understood as flowing from internalised ableism (Reeve, 2012). The findings presented in this chapter enable the additional argument to be made that the phenomenon of withdrawal in the 'fourth age' can be interpretively achieved in societies through environmental barriers and disablism in everyday interactions. Thus, participants may start to identify with 'decline' and use withdrawal as a strategy to buffer self-concept when faced with not just impairment of the body, but also disablist exclusion experienced in their contexts.

There were some differences between the experiences of the two groups of participants. If people first experiencing disability with ageing (DwithA group) could experience it as entering a socially discredited category, for some participants ageing with disability (AwithD), there could, by contrast, be a sense of having re-entered the standardised lifecourse. A critical understanding of disability challenges lifecourse and cultural rules that define what a 'normal' life means (Priestley, 2001, 2003a; Grenier et al, 2016). However, it is also true that participants perceived that their lives had begun to resemble the lives of other older people within their contexts. Positive perceptions were informed by exclusion over decades, which highlights exclusions inherent in normalising society. Life for this group of participants (AwithD) could simultaneously be very difficult in many respects. However, experiences within this group – a few of whom had severe levels of impairment but also expressed a lot of satisfaction with life nowadays – also provide models of how, with the right support, being disabled and older is no bar to living a fulfilling life.

I discussed the extent to which a disability identity featured in the meanings that participants made of disability or increasing disablement. The picture that emerged is complex, suggesting considerable fluidity between the categories 'older' and 'disabled'. Typically, the AwithD group of participants had analytical or political approaches informed by disability activism, and they valued collective experiences over their lifetimes with other disabled people. In those ways, the concept of 'disability' was useful to them. Simultaneously, they perceived their experiences as 'ordinary' or 'normal', and resisted being thought of primarily in terms of bodies or impairment.

The DwithA group of participants predominantly did not want to identify with a 'disability' label, which is not surprising given that ableist societies cast disability 'as a diminished state of being human' (Campbell, 2001: 44). However, they could resist prejudice and disablism in similar ways to voices represented in disability studies literature. They had to confront ideas of disability as deficit (in their own minds or in the perceptions of others) when they started to use appliances, and they ultimately adapted to using them and sometimes enjoyed doing so. They learned to resist or ignore ableist norms without articulating things in those terms. However, typically, they experienced disablism without the sense of support or solidarity from identifying or connecting with other disabled people. For the most part, they do not have models to move from 'shame to pride' (Garland-Thomson, 2016). As argued already (see Chapter 5), they negotiate bodily change in light of, and often in tension with, 'positive' ageing discourses (embedded also in policy prescriptions), which provide little by way of interpretive resource for disability onset, other than as a signal of decline and a time to 'give in' to old age.

However, some participants from the DwithA group engaged in activism to address accessibility issues, and exhibited what might be considered a disability identity (see Oliver, 1996). Participants who were involved with mainstream disability or condition-specific organisations also communicated a sense of belonging and identification with other disabled people. This suggests that non-identification with a 'disability' identity among the DwithA group in general is associated with the schism between policy frameworks and activism on disability and ageing, which therefore points to the possibility of disability providing an enabling identity for people experiencing impairment in older age. As outlined earlier in this chapter, Siebers (2017 [2013]: 119) suggests that a disability identity is constituted through a shared encounter with oppression and also positive experiences, such as shared knowledge of survival strategies. Both these encounters featured in how some participants (including people from the DwithA group) experienced 'disability'. This illustrates how there is scope for engagement in disability activism across the lifespan. The findings also suggest some of the challenges that would be involved in terms of reframing societal knowledge of, and attitudes to, disability in general.

Finally, referring to Bury's concept of biographical disruption, this chapter argued that experiencing disablism – feeling excluded and othered by unsupportive models of support, inaccessible environments and discrediting encounters with others (the last particularly reported by the DwithA group as a recent experience for them) – was another way in which experiences of disability in older age could be 'disruptive' for participants. Again, for many participants (DwithA and AwithD groups), the experience was consistent with Larsson and Jeppsson Grassman's (2012) expanded version of the concept of biographical disruption as a series of disruptions, not always entirely unexpected. If Chapter 5 discussed intrinsic experiences that caused a sense of biographical disruption, this one showed how a range of contextual factors could contribute to the experience, and how many of those factors are shaped by ableist societal norms. As Shakespeare and Watson (2010: 65) suggest, these extrinsic and structural aspects of the experience of disruption also deserve more attention in the 'disruption' literature.

The key implication of the discussion in this chapter is that while disability in older age tends to be largely subject to medical analysis and individual framing, a range of contextual factors actively disable and limit the potential of older disabled people, as they do all disabled people, which is something that deserves greater recognition in research, policy and activism. Chapter 7 addresses the issue of how participants responded.

7

Responding to challenges

Introduction

Previous chapters showed how participants lived with ongoing uncertainty, how activities ceased to be possible or accessible, and ways in which they could experience disablism in being excluded from opportunities for engagement or confined to home by environmental barriers. I argued that efforts to cope with disablement processes (both at the level of the body and in broader contexts) amounted to attempts to maintain a sense of value and meaning in life, something constructed in interaction with broader societal discourses of ageing and of able-bodiedness. The focus of this chapter is on responses to the changes involved. I discuss findings relative to the third research question: 'How do older disabled people respond to the challenges involved in disablement processes?' As I do throughout this book, I use the term 'older disabled people' here to include both participant groups – people ageing with disability (AwithD group) and people first experiencing disability with ageing (DwithA group).

In this chapter, by way of background, I first return to the issue of meaning, raised already in Chapter 3, and address what is understood by 'meaning in life'. I then discuss how loss of intimates is intertwined with experiences of disablement. In combination, these, I suggest, amount to threats to perceptions of life as meaningful. In the main part of this chapter, I discuss how, in response, participants tried to reinterpret and remake their lives to perceive them as meaningful. They did this by investing everyday activities with new meaning and by continuing to maintain activities, participation and connections, sometimes achieving this with the help of community organising and public responses, including care centres. This could involve new opportunities for connection and self-realisation. Participants identified with goals of self-development, activity and social connectedness more typically associated with the 'third age'. This process is essentially a meaning-making one, as there is an intrinsic connection between self-realisation and a search for meaning.

Theoretical context: meaning in life

First, what is understood by 'meaning'? 'Meaning' is a way to make sense of one's existence (Stillman et al, 2009). Perceiving that one is living a meaningful life is associated with a range of positive outcomes like satisfaction with life, happiness, physical health, well-being or living longer (Krause, 2004, 2009; Stillman et al, 2009; Shao et al, 2014). Indeed, happiness may be impossible if life is perceived as meaningless (Baumeister, 1991; Derkx, 2013).

Scholars distinguish between finding meaning *in* life and the meaning *of* life, the latter understood in a metaphysical sense (Laceulle and Baars, 2014: 35; Edmondson, 2015). For example, Edmondson (2015) frames this as a distinction between taking positions about the meaning of life and practising activities that give one satisfaction, also recognising that the two overlap. Similarly, Holstein (2015: 119) distinguishes between meaning in a cosmic sense and the abiding importance of meaning to all human life in everyday terms. The concern here is with the latter – or how people form a sense of meaning with what society and culture offer in a process that is context-specific (Baumeister, 1991: 9; Baars and Phillipson, 2014).

Despite the unstable, socially defined nature of the self in late modernity, there is a deep-rooted need for a sense of 'coherence and integration of one's identity' (Laceulle, 2014: 103). Late-modern striving towards a life of one's own indicates the continuing appeal of self-realisation as a moral ideal (Laceulle and Baars, 2014: 40). However, as Baumeister (1991: 77) argues, the modern dilemma of selfhood is linked to meaning, and concerns with identity are often about wanting life to make sense 'in some acceptable fashion'. As seen in Chapter 5, Bury (1991: 461) makes a similar point, suggesting that learning to cope with the biographical disruption caused by chronic illness onset is about trying to maintain a sense of value and meaning in life.

As mentioned in Chapter 3, definitions of meaning in life often identify domains or needs. For Dannefer and Lin (2014), a three-dimensional formulation of human needs and interests is common across disciplines, which, they suggest, applies irrespective of age. The three are: competence, associated with ideas of efficacy or confidence; autonomy, associated with ideas of choice and control; and relatedness, associated with ideas of connection, affirmation and solidarity. Baumeister (1991, 2005) identified four overlapping 'needs' for meaning sought by individuals to satisfy a meaningful expression of self:

1. **Purpose**: the need to experience that one's life is meaningfully connected with some positive future goal, or inner fulfilment

based on developing a personal talent. It can be one thing or many simultaneously.

2. **Value or moral worth or justification**: that the way one lives can be morally justified, being right, good and legitimate, and having positive value.

3. **Self-worth**: that one positively values oneself and is respected by others, especially for what one does or can do better than others. This can be acquired through membership in a collective such as a nation, religion, employment or lifestyle.

4. **Efficacy**, competence or perceived control: the experience that one has some control over one's life, encompassing **interpretive control** – merely understanding something lends a sense of control even if one can do nothing about it.

Someone who is not satisfied relative to these needs will be inclined to restructure life through changes in behaviour (Baumeister, 1991: 32). Baumeister did not include 'belonging' or 'connection' among the four needs, but characterises belonging as a most basic human need and a motive for meaning making (Baumeister, 2005; Stillman and Baumeister, 2009; Baumeister et al, 2017).

Others argue that a dimension of connection or interdependence needs to be added to Baumeister's framework (Derkx, 2013; Baars and Phillipson, 2014). As Derkx (2013) argues, Baumeister's four needs could be compressed or expanded. Taking a humanist perspective, which he explains as involving 'meaning frames' that people use in the daily practice of their lives, Derkx (2013: 42) expands on the four needs. He articulates seven in total (Derkx, 2013, 2016; Derkx et al, 2020), adding the following additional 'needs':

5. **Connectedness**: which can be connection to other people or to 'the impersonal other', or it can be realised in citizenship or in trying to create a more humane society.

6. **Comprehensibility** (or **coherence**): the need for control, in the sense of **interpretive control** (which he links to Baumeister's fourth need), or the need to understand the world and explain what happens to us – to 'replace chaos with order'.

7. **Excitement**: something that breaks the monotony of routines, and sparks curiosity, wonder or interest.

Taken together, the needs for moral worth, connectedness and excitement can be seen to constitute an overarching need for something that may be called *transcendence*: the experience of being connected to a larger whole (Derkx et al, 2020). These 'needs' illustrate that meaning in life encompasses a moral judgement, based on personal and societal values (Hupkens et al, 2018).

Meaning in later life

Chapter 3 introduced approaches to meaning in later life within critical or cultural gerontology. As Edmondson (2015) argues, meaning in older age is seldom addressed directly. Associated with death, the last stage of life can be perceived in culture as empty of meaning (Twigg, 2006: 51). Similarly, for Baars (2017), an emphasis on 'hectic adulthood' can suggest that life becomes less meaningful and residual in older age. Cultural narratives of ageing (decline or age-defying) deprive older people of meaningful frames of reference (Laceulle and Baars, 2014). However, this is somewhat paradoxical given that older age is seen as a time of 'constant reconstruction' (Thompson, 1992: 39). What constitutes a meaningful life may change as people age (Krause, 2012: 412) and traumatic events may trigger a renewed search for meaning (Reker and Wong, 2012: 448, 453; Shao et al, 2014). Thus, the challenge of self-realisation or actualisation is likely to grow with age (Dittman-Kohli, 1990; Settersten, 2002; Dannefer and Lin, 2014).

Baars and Phillipson (2014: 17) consider Baumeister's needs in light of ageing – when the 'time horizon of life' is gradually changing. They suggest that ageing may have several implications for Baumeister's 'needs'. Ageing may cause the need for a sense of purpose to become more urgent, or, alternatively, further achievements might not matter. An awareness of finitude might mean appreciating some people or situations more deeply, or it might confer a sense of being part of larger processes continuing after death. Issues such as moral worth and self-worth may become more problematic if older people are considered a burden to society (Baars and Phillipson, 2014). A study with 'frail' older people exploring the seven needs for meaning (as Derkx articulated them) found that challenges were experienced in three of them: purpose, coherence and connectedness (Duppen et al, 2019: 72). However, participants compensated by 'satisfying' at least one other need for meaning.

While psychological literature engages with meaning in later life and includes many scales that seek to measure meaning, if not scales specifically for older people (Krause, 2012), there are few empirical studies exploring meaning with older people from a sociological perspective. This is especially the case as regards older disabled people – or people considered 'frail' or in the 'fourth age'. One study with people ageing with disability (AwithD) suggests that social participation conferred a sense of 'life meaning', associated with having a sense of purpose, often by helping others (Couture et al, 2020). Other research with this group (AwithD) found that participants valued being able to live lives consistent with personal values (Molton and Yorkston, 2017; Jensen et al, 2019).

A review of the literature found that meaning in older age comes from various sources, including activities that express who one is, and suggested that relationships were the key source of meaning (Hupkens et al, 2018). Thompson (1992) suggested that the spheres of activity in which older people (that is, older people generally) find meaning are work/occupation, leisure and relationships. For Thompson, the greatest threat to meaning faced in older age is loss of purpose and boredom. Addressing the 'third age', Weiss and Bass (2002: 5–9, 190) identify these same areas (engagement and relationships) as important, and suggest that meaning in life is 'to do with feeling that one still matters, to oneself at least, and that what one does makes sense. It has to do with the conviction that one's life is about something more than simply surviving.' This straightforward definition, while discussing the 'third age', suggests both the ordinariness of the endeavour and the profound and human nature of the challenge.

Meaning associated with experiences of disability

Riddell and Watson (2003: 3) argue of disability generally that cultural constructions fail to present disabled people as 'ordinary people trying to carve out meaningful lives, like everybody else'. There are personal accounts linking disability onset with finding or re-finding a sense of meaning in life (see Murphy, 1987). However, as discussed in earlier chapters, *the* focus of disability studies involves challenging discursive and relational constructions of disability and oppression. This can be associated with calls to move beyond 'personal narratives' lest they invite reactions of pity and sympathy, and distract from social and political issues (Mitchell and Snyder, 1997: 11; see also Siebers, 2008: 47).

Typically, an engagement with meaning in life is found within psychological literature on disability, where it is thought to facilitate adaptation to chronic illness and disability onset (Psarra and Kleftaras, 2013: 80). Having a sense of meaning or purpose in life can be a means to (and a measure of) adjustment to spinal cord injury (Thompson et al, 2003). Empirical research with people experiencing physical disability suggested that the greatest sources of meaning were relationships and 'service', understood as helping and educating others (Arvig, 2006). Thus, in this literature, there are echoes of several of the seven 'needs' for meaning discussed already (associated with Baumeister and Derkx), such as purpose, moral worth and connection.

Meaning and this study

As the study that informs this book was inductive, I identified the issue of meaning in life as important from analysing participants' accounts. No 'meaning' framework was imposed on the analysis. To discuss participants' accounts, I employ here the seven domains of meaning from Baumeister (1991) as expanded by Derkx (2013, 2016; Derkx et al, 2020). I refer to them hereafter as 'Derkx's seven needs for meaning'. Taken in their totality, they 'facilitate an important reflection on what makes life meaningful' (Derkx et al, 2020). Also relevant is the overarching idea that a meaningful life involves having a life that makes sense (Weiss and Bass, 2002). Occupations and relationships were identified as key areas of challenge to meaning in life for participants in this study, which is consistent with arguments relative to the 'third age' (Weiss and Bass, 2002).

To an extent, arguments made throughout this book meet in the issue of meaning in later life. I have argued that (for different reasons) neither gerontology nor disability studies engages as comprehensively as they might with subjective experiences of disability in older age so as to reveal both what constitutes disability and what is entailed in living a life of value and meaning. I also challenge discourse and policies of ageing organised around an axis of able-bodiedness. Instead, I argue for more engagement with the issue of disability in older age such that 'disability' may cease to be viewed as an individual, medicalised problem, and so that societies learn from what is a profoundly important stage of life.

As Baars (2010: 108) suggests, 'positive and negative stylisation' of ageing result from not looking at an uncertain future of ageing 'in the eye', leading to negative aspects being denied the 'dignity and careful attention they deserve'. In addition, as Jensen et al (2019: 196S) argue, a more realistic aim than reduction or elimination of disability is that older people can live consistently with personally meaningful values and goals, because 'if successful aging always requires maintenance of health ... and avoiding disability, then ultimately few, if anyone, will age successfully'. An overwhelming focus on health as a measure of success reduces the cultural space to address critical existential questions and risks devaluing people who flourish despite impairment (Holstein and Minkler, 2007: 16). By contrast, if older disabled people were understood to be engaged in processes of asserting a sense of meaning in life, that could challenge assumptions that lack of impairment, self-sufficiency and independence are core to defining lifecourse aims (see Moulaert and Biggs, 2012; Edmondson, 2015: 197).

Challenges to meaning

In this section, I briefly recap and expand on findings presented in the previous two chapters to illustrate how participants faced challenges to their sense of meaning in life. I then discuss how they responded. Participants' experiences of relationships were important to them. However, processes of disablement could mean having fewer connections to communities. Simultaneously, participants often experienced death of a spouse or family members, or illness/impairment among them. These losses could be part of a cycle of further reducing opportunities for participation and connection with others. Compensating for changes could be challenging, especially without significant supports and resources. Thompson (1992) suggests that loss of intimates represents a significant challenge in later life. However, this has greater consequences when later life involves disability – threats to meaning can be more significant and responding can be more challenging.

Several participants discussed with sadness the loss of spouses or other intimates like siblings. Loss of intimates, especially a spouse, could also be experienced as disabling (as shown in Chapter 6). One consequence was that for many participants, days were more confined, mundane and boring, and, in some cases, solitary or lonely. Participants were often unable to get out of their houses alone or, if they did, had few places to go. Other narratives did not suggest that participants were lonely, though they sometimes felt they lacked the company of friends and things to do.

Josephine (aged 78, DwithA) talked of the combined effects of the death of her husband and onset of visual impairment:

> 'I was widowed three years ago … so I am there in the house on my own most days. Now five years ago, I developed glaucoma, sight impairment, so I couldn't get a [driving] licence, so I am confined more or less to the house unless I do something about it.'

Like other participants, Josephine was experiencing changes in her body and in her family, and challenges to participation in her community – she experienced the effects in combination – resulting in being "confined". Her phrase "unless I do something about it" also signals how Josephine responded, which was to join a local older people's centre that provided accessible transport. Sheila (aged 61, AwithD) was widowed in her 40s, and subsequently had a good friend with whom she used to socialise and have great fun. She said: "About three years ago, she died, and I really miss that, not having somebody." Sheila used to spend time out with her friend ("Herself and myself would go into town"). Instead, she was now often alone at home. Increasing impairment meant she could also be frustrated trying to do things on her own.

Describing his days, James (aged 83, DwithA) said: "There is a possibility somebody might call but it is very rarely." As well as grieving for his wife, he missed the life they had together, involving membership of a bridge club. James still played bridge when his brother took him to the club but he was anxious about the possible loss of his brother, whose health concerned him. Thus, life no longer linked to intimates could involve not only sadness and uncertainty, but also having fewer outlets for social participation.

As argued already, worsening impairment with ageing could have similar consequences for people ageing with disability (AwithD) as for people experiencing disability with ageing (DwithA). Obviously, both groups could experience deaths or illness among intimates. However, members of the AwithD group are less likely to have married than non-disabled people and are affected by the ageing of their informal care networks (see MacDonald et al, 2018; Westwood and Carey, 2019). Participants from that group (AwithD) could experience the loss of a key advocate or champion. For example, Teresa (aged 87, AwithD) said, "My sisters made life good for me", but now, "there is not really anyone". That said, Teresa also identified the local older person's centre as having improved her life – again signalling the important role played by community centres and networks.

As argued in Chapter 5, changes participants experienced involved disruptions of that which is taken for granted and fundamental rethinking of biography, involving potentially damaging losses of control and altered social relationships. The experience was also shaped by ableist societal norms, which could mean feeling excluded and othered by unsupportive models of support, inaccessible environments and discrediting encounters with others. These experiences could also be 'disruptive', as discussed in Chapter 6. As Bury (1991: 461) suggests, attempts to learn to cope with chronic illness are about trying to maintain a sense of value and meaning in life. Furthermore, social exclusion reduces perceptions of life as meaningful (Stillman et al, 2009: 692).

That participants were experiencing threats to a sense of meaning in life is evident when these findings are considered in light of Derkx's seven needs for meaning. The changes experienced meant challenges to fill time or to find something purposeful to do. There were fewer opportunities to exercise a sense of efficacy and consequently to do things conferring a sense of self- or moral worth or excitement. Additionally, for many participants, the simultaneous loss of intimates caused grief as well as a cycle of further reducing connections and participation opportunities. Participants lived with fears of ever-greater dependency, involving challenges to a sense of efficacy and comprehensibility or control. For the DwithA group of participants, these processes could also be experienced simultaneously with a sense of crossing a boundary into a discredited social category because ableism constructs disability as a diminished state (Campbell, 2001: 44). For the AwithD group of participants, it could mean coming to terms with new or additional impairments, and consequently with a new set of barriers to negotiate. All of this could involve additional threats to a sense of efficacy, of self- or moral worth or connection. Together, these processes amounted to challenges to perception of life as meaningful and forced change in how participants gave meaning to their lives.

It is also true that participants' accounts of relationships were not all of loss. Even if spousal or other losses caused suffering, participants often had other positive relationships – with family, neighbours and friends, and, especially, with adult children. Some participants felt connected to others through religious practice or had an ongoing sense of connection with God. Some had long-standing supportive relationships with carers. All these connections supported a sense that participants' lives mattered, which is consistent with findings that relationships are a key source of meaning for older people (Hupkens et al, 2018). That is why the loss of intimates, which was a common experience for participants, is also a key challenge to a sense of life as meaningful.

Responding to challenges

Perceptions of disability onset or worsening, othering and exclusion, and losses of intimates could exist in parallel with efforts that were broader than trying to maintain and improve functioning, or to maintain activities of daily living. Participants also sought to participate in activities they considered worthwhile and to maintain or make connections with others. Losses of either activities or relationships might mean seeking to compensate in the other area (Litwin and Levinson, 2018: 1786). The effort involved in any task could be striking. As discussed in Chapter 6, difficulties could be compounded if people were without social or financial resources to compensate, or if they did not have access to facilitative public/community services.

Seeking something 'meaningful'

Chapter 6 showed how participants from the DwithA group often asserted a sense of their worth in response to being consigned to a discredited category by others. Joan (aged 86, DwithA), who perceived that she was now 'other', responded by characterising herself as full of life:

> 'Don't define me by my disability or don't define me by age. There's a lot more to me than all of that. I'm still brimming with ideas all the time. Absolutely brimming. I'm coming up in my head with themes for poems. ... I think about having parties ... I want to gather them all. I love ... there's nothing I like better than the whole family being here around and just having the craic.'

Thus, Joan's account of herself focused on personal goals (writing poems) and plans for parties and "craic" (or fun). Her account is far from the stereotype of a passive older person, experiencing 'decline' in her 'fourth age', acted upon but not acting and only needing unchallenging activities that pass the time.

Other participants were reflexive about the impact of losses of activities or social participation. They talked about opportunities they still sought and could see them in terms of conferring meaning in life. For example, Sheila (aged 61, AwithD) made a distinction between services that "keep you alive" and those that "made you feel like you were living". The latter were ones that included fun and changes of routine – or excitement in terms of Derkx's seven needs for meaning. Sheila also perceived that there were fewer of those opportunities available to her now due to cutbacks in disability services, and, given the death of a good friend, she lacked communal activities.

Colin (aged 88, DwithA) sought to do things that he considered "meaningful", characterising this as something "worth doing and which would leave a trace of some sort". Experiencing visual impairment in recent years, he had stopped reading, going to art exhibitions and using his computer: "All the things that I used to do are gone and, therefore,

I have to find new things." Colin used initiative and wanted to make decisions about activities – he said that others doing everything for him, like washing up, was not "the solution". Colin came back several times to the difficulty of finding something "meaningful":

> 'It shouldn't be something that you're just doing … the trouble is to find meaningful activity. When you can't see, it's very challenging. And that's why … apart from the radio, the television and the computer [pointing to the iPad], I don't know what I'd do. But even that is difficult because my eyes get worse.'

Colin said he is "inventing things to do" and demonstrated that it was important to have a sense of coherence and control as he described how he "practises" for being totally blind:

> 'I try to do as many things as I can by touch. For example, every day, I eat a banana, which I slice up. And I slice it without looking at it. And that's a good exercise. Doing things like that. Well, it helps you deal with the world around you. … But I am doing really well all the time I'm dealing with things. I'm keeping up.'

Thus, Colin described meeting a dynamic bodily situation, and reduced opportunities for activity and participation, with attempts to maintain a sense of purpose, efficacy and coherence. This is somewhat similar to how other participants engaged with the anticipated necessity of moving to a nursing home, though they could not control when or how it would happen. Thus, life change was dynamic and complex. Participants were constantly interpreting and reinterpreting their experience within their contexts.

However, despite his ingenuity, Colin's worsening sight meant being challenged to find things he wanted to do – he longed, without finding it, for something "significant" to do and said: "But there's nothing to look forward to, that's the problem. It's just how do you diminish the grimness of just sitting there doing nothing." Colin perceived as "meaningful" activities that were not just about filling time, but that engaged him fully or left a "trace". Writing about how people in the 'third age' can be challenged to find things that make them feel 'fully engaged', Weiss and Bass (2002: 6) describe one man as wanting engagement to which he could give himself wholeheartedly, that others would recognise as valuable and that might 'even make a difference for them as well as for himself'. This characterisation of someone in the 'third age' is also precisely how Colin and others described their needs for purpose, coherence and self- and moral worth. It is also present, for example, in how Annette (aged 84, DwithA) regretted that she was no longer the "main dancer" in her local group and could no longer give her "everything" to her beloved activity of dancing. It is also reflected in the emphasis Sheila (aged 61, AwithD) placed on activities that made you "feel like you were living".

This, I suggest, is a challenge of the so-called 'fourth age' (as well as the 'third'), or for later life lived with disability, when it also becomes harder to meet. Heikkinen (2000: 474) suggests that bodily changes can be profound enough to thwart ability to find meaning in life. Colin and other participants showed an imaginative and dynamic engagement with that event horizon, not as passengers on the journey, but by being reflexively engaged in anticipating and preparing for it. Their accounts displayed vulnerabilities and limitations, *and* creativity, strength and determination.

However, contextual factors are also relevant. Not every participant had the resources or interests that Colin had. For example, Colin's access to an iPad provided an outlet. On the other hand, in other ways, Colin may be disadvantaged relative to others. Despite liking to use technology, he no longer used a computer and did not use assistive technology to help with sight loss. While it was not true that all the AwithD group had access to assistive technology, some visually impaired participants used screen-reading software on computers and phones extensively. Other participants from the AwithD group did not seem to have any assistive technology to address visual impairment. For example, Teresa (aged 87, AwithD), who had lived with a physical impairment since birth, and now also experienced visual impairment, did not use a computer, though she had loved to read. This suggests the need for access to technologies and training to become more widespread. A prerequisite for this is more recognition that things that improve the lives of disabled people in general can do likewise for older disabled people, as well as more recognition of the impacts of additional impairments in later life on people ageing with long-standing disability.

Investing everyday activities with new meaning

Activities associated with daily living like housekeeping, cooking or shopping often presented barriers that participants creatively worked around. Daily activities took on new significance – maintaining a sense of connection to former routines and identity, helping to structure time, representing a goal, being an opportunity to exercise efficacy, or creating connection with others. Everyday tasks were often a meaningful goal in the day, requiring planning and effort. Tony (aged 83, AwithD) described getting in and out of his car with his rollator as increasingly difficult and time-consuming. Yet, he attended daily Mass, which he valued for its sociability and for how it structured the day: "It is a goal you have and it gets you up in the mornings and I kind of use it for exercise if you know what I mean." Participants who would not accept help with tasks like housework described wanting instead to have a sense of efficacy and control. Some everyday activities connected participants to others. Joan (aged 86, DwithA) used her rollator to carry shopping bags in "instalments" from her car, a process she found exhausting, but shopping is, "a very pleasurable part of my week". Family would do it for her but it provided purpose and was sociable: "the people you meet in the supermarket, you've people to chat to". Similarly, William (aged 70, DwithA) described a daily walk to a local shop: "People are very nice … always talk. I enjoy that too."

Even seemingly minor tasks like washing up or sorting medicines could be imbued with significance. Francis (aged 76, DwithA) regretted that there were many things he could not do. However, what he could still do took on greater significance, such as sorting his medicines, which he did "to keep my mind a bit active" and to feel "still capable of doing something". Thus, he understood this task as about efficacy and control, with a future-oriented sense of purpose in maintaining functioning by keeping the mind active.

Participants maintained a sense of continuity with the past through ordinary routines: 'the mundane and comforting sameness of repetitive activities ... give structure and logic to people's lives' (Becker, 1997: 4). Relationships did not have to be deep to be experienced as supportive (Duppen et al, 2019: 66). Everyday activities took on new significance as they became threatened (Reed et al, 2010). Participants demonstrated determination and creativity in meeting these challenges, and they helped fulfil several of Derkx's seven needs for meaning.

Participating and engaging

Participants often maintained activities they loved or sought opportunities for participation and connection. Some described participating in activities to have a focus or goal, or to connect with others. Just as with maintenance of daily activities, this required effort. Joan (aged 86, DwithA) described the effort she made to continue with several activities, including singing with a church choir. As she described it, accessing the choir gallery was slow, painful and risky. She strategised, arriving early to climb the stairs without delaying others. Then, she left her rollator downstairs and used both hands to pull herself up the 22 steps ("Oh to think of those steps"), while another choir member carried her stick. She weighed this effort against the enjoyment:

> 'Like, the last thing you want to do, say, is go out to choir practice. But coming home, you're glad you did. It makes you happier. The singing makes you happy. The interaction with others – the friends you've made there … that makes you happier. So, all these things are the good sides of it and worth making the effort and worth going through, you know, putting up with the downsides of it.'

Singing continued long-standing routines, connections and fun, and Joan balanced its challenge with its contribution to her life.

Several participants engaged in learning or creative activities, and, again, valued these outlets for sociability and for a sense of purpose, efficacy and self-worth. For example, Alice (aged 72, AwithD) described how she felt about learning to paint/make art at a disability centre that she had started attending in recent years. Communicating a sense of self-worth and of purpose, Alice said:

> 'One great achievement for me is art, doing the painting, because I never knew in my heart or soul that I could do anything like that or be good at it. I remember the first picture I painted. … My family cannot believe it; I can't believe it myself to be honest.'

For a few participants, having reached a certain age was a spur to action. Julie (aged 80, DwithA) said of reaching 80: "Putting things on the long finger … is probably not a very good idea." She used that as a spur to self-publish short stories to raise funds for charity.

Some accounts of change outlined decreasing involvement in informal, community organisations. For example, Stephen (aged 88, DwithA) talked about continuing in a reduced role on the committee of his local community centre:

> 'Before, if you like to say, I was the brains. I am not the brains now, but I am one of the committee. Before, I was able to get my way … speak my mind. But they still respect me like that and they rang me to make sure I'd be there.'

Stephen's continued participation connected him with others and conferred a sense of purpose and efficacy (an area where he could improve things), and self-worth and moral worth (doing something he considered valuable, where others "respect" him). The losses that Stephen experienced included the death of his wife, which caused him great sadness. He also had to give up a range of activities, including membership of a walking group, which he missed terribly. However, Stephen's ongoing community role helped him perceive continuity and coherence, in short, that his life is still valuable and has meaning – he still matters.

Participants often contributed to the lives of family members financially and in other ways, and often sought to contribute more broadly. They explained their motivations as both wishing to express caring or connectedness, and considering it worthwhile to do. This conferred a sense of purpose, connection or self- or moral worth. Some, like June (aged 82, DwithA), raised funds for charities; others contributed to the work of NGOs. For example, April (aged 65, AwithD) volunteered with a telephone helpline for people affected by polio. In terms of Derkx's seven needs for meaning, these actions could confer a sense of purpose and efficacy, of self- or moral worth, and a sense of connection to others.

Joining community groups

Implicit in some accounts discussed already is that participants perceived positive changes in their activities and in their sense of connection through joining a local centre or club. Participants attended various types of clubs, centres or organisations targeting older people or disabled people. Most were day centres; others focused on leisure activities. Most provided accessible transport.

There were anomalies in attendance at disability and older people's centres as between the two participant groups (DwithA and AwithD). This is not surprising given the backdrop of anomalies and inconsistencies created by separate service frameworks for ageing and disability in many countries, and given how the boundary between the two frameworks creates inconsistencies in practice in Ireland (Leahy, 2018). Specifically, while people categorised as in the DwithA group typically attended older people's centres/clubs, there were others attending centres run by mainstream disability organisations. Similarly, while many people I categorised as in the AwithD group attended centres run by disability organisations, others attended centres/clubs for older people.

Centres addressing losses of activities and people

Many participants talked not only about lack of company and boredom as having motivated them to start attending a centre, but also about looking forward to going, meeting new people and learning new things. Several spoke enthusiastically about changes in their lives since they started attending a local centre. For example, Peggy (aged 83, AwithD) talked of starting to attend a disability centre, which she did some 16 years previously, as "a big change, the company that is here", and about enjoying crafts-based activities there, consistent with her sense of self as someone who, throughout her life, had been "blessed with two great hands".

June (aged 82, DwithA) described a life that had become largely confined to home until she joined her local disability centre two years previously. She enjoyed the centre's activities and evening outings for films and meals: "And it has changed my whole life. That's what, two years ago. I come in that door and I am home. I live for it a few times a week. ... I wouldn't miss a day unless I really have to."

Trips away organised by centres were sometimes recalled as highlights. Attending a day centre might be the only time a participant left home in the week – facilitated by accessible transport provided by the centres. Thus, Francis (aged 76, DwithA) relied on a disability centre bus to get out. He used the words "monotony" and "dull" of days at home: "If I don't come here [disability centre], I go nowhere." He also described how attending had confounded his expectations – he valued having learned to use a computer, had started using one at home and reckoned that better Internet access at home was the thing that could most improve his life. In terms of learning and challenge, it is possible that Francis might have benefitted from attending a disability centre (one not just designed to cater for older people), with its service model and menu of activities thus influenced by what is considered appropriate for adults under retirement age.

As noted in Chapter 6, participants from the AwithD group could take up activities in their communities as they got older – like joining groups of older people. Thus, positive perceptions of joining centres occurred among the DwithA and AwithD groups. What was different was the perspective of people among the AwithD group who had lived lives they perceived as confined or isolated. These experiences could be their first time, or their first time in decades, of engaging in communal activities with their age peers. Teresa (aged 87, AwithD), who perceived that her adulthood had been very confined, talked with delight about starting to attend her local older people's centre the first time in her 50s, which had "opened up a new life".

However, there appears to have been an element of (what we might call) 'normalisation' for some of the DwithA group on joining a disability centre or condition-specific organisation, associated with a sense of belonging and shared experiences with other disabled people. This can be seen in the case of June, quoted earlier. Rory (aged 68, DwithA) praised the staff of the disability centre he attended, saying: "I mean they let you believe there's nothing you can do wrong. And it's a great feeling." Implicit here is a sense that being disabled, even when older, can feel like doing something 'wrong' in some situations. Thus, participants – from both groups (DwithA and AwithD) – could have positive experiences through contact with others having similar experiences or with centres where disability is not treated as exceptional. Participants' accounts echo Wendell's (1996: 27) description of no longer 'struggling alone' when she connected with other disabled people. The satisfaction expressed may be associated with the relative difficulty of negotiating life generally with impairment or with perceptions of prejudice or othering. It may also be associated with a paucity of opportunities for any communal experience if experiencing disability, particularly if not well networked due to loss of family members and friends.

While participants appreciated what disability and older people's centres or clubs offered, they could also be critical. For example, the staff and volunteers might be praised, while the activities were experienced as passing time rather than being worthwhile or meaningful. Thus, while Rory praised the staff of his centre, he critiqued the quality of activities. Hazel (aged 80, AwithD) enjoyed socialising and activities at the centre she attended but critiqued one she used to attend for not having much "going on". Peggy (aged 83, AwithD) talked about loving activities – art and pottery – but critiqued the standard of teaching as uneven.

Thus, there is little sense that participants were passive recipients of support in the centres they attended. Rather, they were clear-sighted about strengths and weaknesses. Connection with others and fun, and opportunities for a sense of purpose, self-realisation or efficacy, were what they identified as most valuable. Some participants had discovered, or rediscovered, a sense of connection and community. Attendance helped reconstruct a sense of a valued self and meet several of Derkx's needs for meaning, especially for connection but also purpose and efficacy.

As discussed in Chapter 5, even where participants' main outlet was attending a day-care centre, several framed their approach in ways suggesting identification with 'positive' ageing (or cognate concepts), talking about needing, for example, to 'keep yourself active'. Even though participants might not meet the conventional criteria for 'successful' ageing (and cognate concepts), one reason for evincing attitudes consistent with these discourses is that participants identified with the goals they promote. This includes goals of self-development, remaining active and staying socially connected (see Laceulle, 2016). These discourses continued to resonate because participants did not define themselves by bodies or impairments, and wanted lives they valued. This may also, of course, have helped participants to fulfil the prescription to 'age well and responsibly' embedded within these discourses and the policies that reflect them (Estes et al, 2003: 4).

Experiencing centres as opportunities to contribute

Being of service to others is identified as a key source of meaning among disabled people generally (Arvig, 2006). It is also identified as such among people in the 'third age' (Weiss and Bass, 2002). One study with older disabled people found that they perceived opportunities to volunteer as meaningful in that they facilitated contributing to and connecting with others (Sellon, 2018). Contributing is also encompassed within Baumeister's need for moral worth and Derkx's idea of connection.

Care centres (and other groups of which participants were members) sometimes provided opportunities for contributing. By being more connected to others, participants could express support for others in their actions. They could also communicate a dual sense of their attendance, both as a member or client and as a contributor. Several participants helped provide entertainment or contributed in other ways. For example, Tony (aged 83, AwithD) described a dual role at a day centre: "I go there to play music but I am part of them myself, you know." Kathleen (aged 85, DwithA) joined an older people's club when she was asked to come to sing. She felt that others enjoyed her singing and said: "That does keep you going." Tony and Kathleen asserted a status and identity – as active contributors – while also being recipients of support and care. They may also have been resisting societal framings of older people as burdensome. As argued throughout this book, all of this suggests the need for models of how to live well with disability in older age and for societies to learn from experiences of older disabled people.

Discussion and conclusions

This chapter drew on the empirical study that informs this book to show that older disabled people are engaged in dynamic processes of trying to make sense of their lives through redefining and recreating a sense of meaning in life. Finding meaning in life could become at once more important and more challenging following experiences of changed bodies, activities and participation outlets, and, in some cases, perceptions of having crossed a boundary into a discredited social category due to ableist norms. These processes often occurred simultaneously with loss of intimates and reduced social circles, creating a cycle of ever-fewer participation outlets and connections. This could challenge a sense of self and perceptions of meaning in life.

The focus on meaning in this context is consistent with challenges from critical gerontology to the overwhelming focus on health and lack of impairment as a measure of 'success' in older age, or to ideas of self-sufficiency or independence as defining lifecourse aims (Holstein and Minkler, 2007; Edmondson, 2015: 197; Baars, 2017). Participants' accounts suggest limitations and vulnerabilities caused by individual and contextual factors, on the one hand, and resourcefulness, creativity and determination to have a life that makes sense, on the other. Thus, participants were constantly reinterpreting their experience within their contexts (Holstein and Gubrium, 2000: 83). They sought to restore order following disruption, 'reworking understandings of the self and the world' (Becker, 1997: 4).

I considered participants' accounts in light of seven needs for meaning from Baumeister (1991) and Derkx (2013, 2016; Derkx et al, 2020). This involved a search for purpose or inner fulfilment – maintaining routines that created a 'goal' in the day, seeking activities that challenged or left a 'trace'. It involved a sense of efficacy – continuing everyday activities and making one's own decisions. It meant having a sense of self-worth or moral worth – doing things that contributed to others or that others would value. Connection with others and fun or excitement were also important to participants, and they valued the social side of attending a centre or club, as well as of everyday activities, like shopping. Thus, maintaining activities and finding new participation opportunities were associated with experiencing a sense of a continuous self and with perceptions of lives as meaningful.

A sense of purpose is understood as being connected to some future goal and to gaining a sense of inner fulfilment (Baumeister, 1991, 2005). That might be different for older people, especially the oldest people, when the time horizon of life is shortening (Baars and Phillipson, 2014). However, even the oldest participants wanted a sense of purpose and had a future orientation. For some, a shortening event horizon was a spur to fulfil an ambition. Contributing to others might also have conferred a sense of connection to the future, consistent with the argument that older people gain a sense of purpose by embracing goals that go beyond one's own life (Baars and Phillipson, 2014).

However, these were not the only future orientations. Participants did not know how much time was left – they still had a future orientation. This was implicit in many actions, such as joining new groups and engaging in new activities, where they were available, and in many frustrations – not being able to find anything 'significant' to do and being dissatisfied by the 'uneven' standard of teaching in a day centre. A future orientation was also implicit in activities participants hoped would maintain or improve functioning. Even mundane tasks, like sorting medicines, could be understood as efforts to maintain functioning and efficacy.

Where participants found activities they valued that linked them with others, this was often helped by public or community action through centres and clubs. This highlights the importance of policies that facilitate engagement for older disabled people (Carpentier et al, 2010). Boredom and confinement at home were often a motivation for joining a centre but low expectations of a club, day centre or disability centre could be confounded. The findings suggest positive aspects of later life with disability (for participants from the DwithA as well as the AwithD group), which are not much explored in scholarship. This points to the need to explore the individual and societal factors that make this possible for some people and not others.

Challenges to living a meaningful life occurred in areas of connections and participation – areas already identified as challenges to meaning for the 'third age' (Weiss and Bass, 2002). However, challenges are *greater* for older disabled people. This is due to limitations of impairment and being faced with disablist, contextual barriers to participation, simultaneously, in many cases, with loss of intimates. Furthermore, the need for meaningful orientations may go unrecognised, in part, due to links made in dominant discourses between absence of impairment and health, and able-bodiedness, personal growth and engagement (Lloyd, 2015; Gibbons, 2016). Older people who do not fit models like 'positive ageing' or the 'third age' are left outside these frames, though not in their own interpretations. Thus, boundaries in public policies and in sociocultural discourse between the 'third' and 'fourth' ages were not well marked in the interpretations of participants. Instead, they continued to identify with goals of self-development, remaining active and staying socially connected, which are essentially processes that help sustain a sense of meaning in life.

Findings discussed here also illuminate debates about the 'fourth age', such as its characterisation as an 'event horizon', 'terminal destination' or 'black hole' (Gilleard and Higgs, 2010a: 122–3). As discussed in Chapter 5, several participants found it difficult to address the possibility of a future when they could not care for themselves. Arguably, these approaches were attempts, as Lloyd et al (2014: 17) say, to keep 'from being sucked into the black hole'. However, the accounts of several participants who might already be considered to be in the 'fourth age' suggest an imaginative engagement in such a future – preparing for a time of becoming totally blind or of a move to a care setting. There was a sense of this as ultimately outside one's control but there was also a clear-sighted engagement, involving sadness and vulnerability, as well as agency, imagination and effort.

Participants were creatively engaging with such a future, seeking to exert whatever control they could and trying to make their lives comprehensible. This suggests that there may be many event horizons and that there can be efforts to imaginatively know and cope with each. As Lloyd (2015) reflects on debates about the 'fourth age', what matters most is to better understand people's experience. Even among the oldest participants, the experience was about wanting a life that made sense and was more dynamic and agentic than conventional depictions of the last stage of life as a residual 'fourth age'.

The chapter developed a counter-narrative of ageing and the lifecourse that seeks to integrate disablement processes as a 'normal' part of life. It is necessary to recognise both the challenges of disablement processes in older age and the ongoing efforts to perceive value and meaning in life. The findings discussed support calls to develop alternative cultural narratives of ageing that integrate the challenges that disablement processes represent and the efforts made in response, and for resistance to framings of disability as wholly negative (see Cruikshank, 2003: 23; Baars, 2010; Laceulle and Baars, 2014). For example, Laceulle and Baars (2014: 40) suggest the need for a moral discourse on self-realisation, recognising the 'intrinsic connection between self-realisation and a search for meaning'. These authors clarify that they are not discussing 'self-realisation' as it has come to be associated with the 'third age' and with a consumer and leisure lifestyle that can be exclusionary (Laceulle and Baars, 2014: 40–1). Public policies bifurcated in terms of 'healthy' or 'active' ageing, on the one hand, and care and dependency, on the other, fail to recognise that common needs for continuing to live meaningful lives subsist among all older people. As well as socialising, opportunities for purposeful activity, self-development and contribution are all needed.

Although the present study did not evaluate centres attended by participants, its findings suggest that, for the most part, they offered valued social contact and opportunities, in several cases, for purposeful activity that helped people to compensate for other losses and exclusions. Participants were clear-sighted about the value of centres and often about their shortcomings also. Overall, these findings are consistent with the suggestion that older people's day centres have positive effects on quality of life (Orellana et al, 2020). Negative experiences associated with disability care settings mean that 'much received wisdom' in relation to disability is that centres are a poor substitute for mainstream activities (Barnes, 2011: 164). However, this study supports the need for social care to encompass shared public spaces and collective aspects of care (Needham, 2014: 105). It also suggests that societies need to facilitate and support older disabled people to stay involved in all aspects of community life in ways they find meaningful.

In this and the previous two chapters, the arguments made include people ageing with disability and people experiencing disability with ageing, though sometimes signalling that there are differences or different emphases between the two groups. In Chapter 8, I address the last of the study's research questions by drawing out those differences.

8

Comparison: disability with ageing and ageing with disability

Introduction

In this chapter, I draw on the findings of the empirical study to compare the experiences of the two groups of study participants: the AwithD group and the DwithA group. In previous chapters, arguments made included both groups, sometimes signalling that there were variations in experiences or different emphases in the case of the AwithD group of participants – and it is on those differences that this chapter focuses. This chapter addresses the third research question of the present study: 'In what ways do the social processes (as opposed to the medical processes) of first experiencing disability with ageing differ from those of ageing with disability?' I start by briefly considering heterogeneity in the AwithD group and then introduce approaches to comparison between these two experiences. The main part of this chapter uses as subheadings the subjects of each of the three previous chapters – disabling bodies, disabling or enabling contexts, and responding to challenges – and, of necessity, repeats some of the discussion of those chapters.

Both groups could perceive themselves as disabled by their bodies and their contexts. This included loss of intimates, lack of material resources or supportive public services, and inaccessible physical environments. Both groups could be disabled by discrediting attitudes of other people and by overarching framings of disability as a diminished state of being (Campbell, 2001). However, many of those factors had detrimentally shaped life for longer for participants from the AwithD group. The discussion suggests that while differences have often been stressed in scholarship, there are also commonalities between the two experiences.

Both groups wanted similar outcomes for their lives, including connection with other people, meaningful activity and inclusion in what is considered the mainstream of life. While pointing to similarities, I do not lose sight of the cumulative disadvantage experienced by people living with disability over the long term (AwithD group), which can make later life extremely challenging. It should also be remembered that some participants in this study whom I categorised as experiencing disability with ageing (DwithA group) had experienced disability for a relatively long time too given that some had experienced disability onset in their late 40s or 50s. (The recruitment criteria are discussed again in more detail in the 'Methodological annexe'.)

Heterogeneity in ageing with disability

At the outset, I acknowledge again that the two participant categorisations employed throughout this book are somewhat arbitrary given that age and disability are phenomena that occur throughout the lifespan and overlap. Instead of categorising participants into just two categories (AwithD and DwithA), further categories could have been identified based on different timings of disability onset (see Putnam, 2017). All of this contributes to the challenges of trying to balance what is similar and what is different across the two participant groups.

The vast majority of study participants were white Irish and none identified as lesbian, gay, bisexual, transgender or queer (LGBTQ). In that respect, the study participants were quite homogeneous. However, in terms of gender, geographical location and socio-economic class, they varied (see 'Methodological annexe'). The AwithD group of participants, especially, was also heterogeneous in a range of other ways. This is unsurprising given that this is true of disabled people generally. Generalisations about people from the AwithD group are therefore difficult (Sheets, 2005). All AwithD participants had experienced physical and/or sensory impairment from birth, childhood or adulthood, though before midlife (age 45). All were living in Ireland in the community, not in residential settings. However, their lifecourse trajectories were diverse.

Participants from the AwithD group included people experiencing a range of conditions and impairments, with different timings of disability onset, people never employed and people who worked until the age at which they became eligible for a pension. Some participants had been sent away to schools/care homes/hospitals as babies or children. They often experienced these as difficult times in which education, health or well-being were neglected. For some, these experiences had been traumatic. Some participants never participated in formal education, or education stopped upon a childhood diagnosis, and they did not go on to work outside the home. These early experiences radically affected the lifecourse of some participants. Others had lived lifecourse trajectories that might be perceived as more standardised, with transitions that involved education, work and retirement. Participants from this group also varied in their levels of engagement with disability services and activism. All of this makes generalisation and comparison complex, and suggests that there is much scope for further research with this group and with intersectional aspects of these experiences across the lifespan.

Background: comparing ageing with disability and disability with ageing

Part of the rationale for the study informing this book was that it is unclear if the social processes of ageing are different for people ageing with long-standing disability (AwithD) and people first experiencing disability with ageing (DwithA) (Putnam, 2002; Freedman, 2014). Such engagement as there is on this issue often comes from a health or rehabilitation perspective. At a population level, little is known about people from the AwithD group, and research engaging with their subjective experiences is quite limited (Jeppsson Grassman et al, 2012; Clarke and Latham, 2014; Putnam et al, 2016).

Two contrasting hypotheses about the experience of ageing with disability are posited in some literatures. The first is the idea of 'double difference' (Jeppsson Grassman, 2013: 30) or 'double jeopardy', arising from the overlay of ageing processes on disability. The second is the concept of age as 'leveller', suggesting that there are advantages from applying strategies acquired from living with disability to processes of ageing (Reyes, 2009; Bishop and Hobson, 2015). From medical sociology, there is also the assumption of Williams (2000: 50) that ageing with disability might be an experience of continuity, *not* disruption (as discussed in Chapter 5).

Researchers in gerontology and rehabilitation counselling suggest that experiences of people from the DwithA and AwithD groups are different (Garabagiu, 2009; Grist, 2010; Westwood and Carey, 2019). Different aetiologies tend to be highlighted, along with different social and material conditions. As discussed already, in medical terms, disability in older age is linked to chronic illness, whereas disability at younger ages is more associated with congenital or developmental conditions or injury. People from the AwithD group can also experience further or secondary health conditions, and some people experience early onset of age-related conditions (Sheets, 2010; Iezzoni, 2014). There is little exploration of the social consequences of experiencing secondary conditions with ageing (see Newbronner and Atkin, 2018).

There are also social and material differences between the two groups. The DwithA group is assumed to age after a life of social inclusion, through employment and/or marriage, and may have accumulated social and financial resources (National Council on Ageing and Older People and National Disability Authority, 2006). For people from the AwithD group, worsening health and impairment often occur against a backdrop of generally poorer health and social disadvantage (Iezzoni, 2014). Thus, the AwithD group is often disadvantaged through lack of material resources, including housing, pensions and savings, and social resources, including engagement, care or support (Westwood and Carey, 2019). Few empirical studies compare experiences of people from the two groups. Among the exceptions are Grist's (2010) psychological study of adaptation to physical disability, and Bülow and Svensson's (2013) study focusing on experiences of mental health conditions.

Some scholarship now also posits that there may be experiences in common between the two groups (Bickenbach et al, 2012: 1; Molton and Ordway, 2019). Examining 'persistent disability over a long time period', Verbrugge et al (2017) outline prevalence and correlates, and also suggest that when disability is experienced for a long time, social and emotional consequences might be similar for all age groups. They conclude that some goals and issues will vary by age 'but overarching life issues are the same', and that experiences of disability could have significant social and health disadvantages if experienced for a long time irrespective of when onset occurred (Verbrugge et al, 2017: 767).

Disabling bodies: comparing the two groups

In Chapter 5, I discussed how participants from both groups (DwithA and AwithD) experienced bodily changes with ageing that could fundamentally affect their lives, challenge their sense of self and lead to an increasing sense of uncertainty about daily life, functioning and the future. The experience, I argued, amounted to a sense of biographical disruption (Bury, 1982, 1997), particularly as the concept has been expanded to mean not necessarily a single or unexpected event (Larsson and Jeppsson Grassman, 2012). Chapter 5 also signalled that people from the AwithD group had heterogeneous experiences of bodies.

For some participants in the AwithD group, worsening or additional impairment represented a kind of double jeopardy. This is because worsening of conditions, or onset of additional impairments, compounded challenges of existing conditions, sometimes magnifying a sense of isolation and making activities and participation more difficult. An example discussed was the case of Hazel (aged 80, AwithD), visually impaired from her 30s, who now found life very isolating due to onset of hearing impairment. Another example came from Helen (aged

68, AwithD), for whom anticipated worsening in health was "a big concern", associated with fears of being unable to care for herself at all or being confined to bed. For these participants, even though they had coped with many challenges, life lived with impairment did not seem to make it easier to face further impairment or ill health. This is similar to Simcock's (2017) conclusions in respect of older people who were deaf-blind.

Some participants among the AwithD group had experienced the kinds of challenges described earlier at various points in the lifespan. Several did not know whether recent bodily symptoms were attributable to existing conditions or due to ageing. Participants talked about experiencing pain, fatigue or balance issues, and had often lived with a sense of uncertainty for a long time. For example, Blanaid (aged 60, AwithD), who had fallen many times, said she had always lived with the risk of falling. Thus, what Grenier (2012: 177) refers to as a 'permanent state of uncertainty' associated with being older and impaired could be the experience at younger ages for some disabled people (see Mattlin, 2016).

Bülow and Svensson (2013) described these processes as the 'fourth age' coming earlier to people with long-standing disability. Like participants in other empirical studies (Bode et al, 2012; Jeppsson Grassman, 2013), some members of the AwithD group were not very old, chronologically, but felt that their functioning resembled much older people. For example, the youngest participant in the study, Liz (age 55, AwithD), described the stroke she had at age 42 as "an old person's stroke" because it was severe, and likened her functioning to that of her mother, who was in her 80s. For these younger participants, bodily changes were sometimes linked to ageing, or to time advancing, but also to the progression or worsening of conditions. Thus, they could describe an experience of 'decline' or 'deterioration' but not always use 'age' as a discursive resource. This meant that for this group, 'age' was not always available to 'buffer' the concept of self (Kelley-Moore, 2010: 105).

Some participants among the AwithD group did not experience standard later-life transitions like retirement (or they had occurred at a much earlier time) and they could appear to age outside typical generational categories (Priestley, 2006). Participants who had experienced adult-onset disability often perceived it as a significant turning point where the chronological trajectory anticipated for their lives was disrupted – as biographical disruption in a classical sense (Bury, 1982, 1997). As argued in Chapter 5, participants from the DwithA group could have similar perceptions of sudden onset of disability even if it happened in late older age. However, for participants experiencing onset earlier, many areas of life could have been affected, such as early careers or parenting of children. Thus, the consequences were likely to have been broader for people experiencing disability earlier in life. For example, Blanaid (aged 61, AwithD) experienced onset of a progressive condition at age 30 and started her narrative of her life with that experience:

> 'Well, I'll start when my life changed, and that was at the age of 30. I had ... children, and I was a ... teacher [talks about the effects of symptoms, and medication over several years]. ... So, I had to come out of teaching, and that was devastating to me. So, that was kind of the real changing point in my life and changed my whole perspective and my whole relationship with people in life because I became a dependent person in certain situations. And my husband then became kind of the mother at home.'

For Blanaid, giving up work was the real "changing point", when relationships and her "perspective" changed and she became a "dependent person". She had to rely on her husband and others for help with her children. Blanaid also felt that relationships with key intimates had deteriorated over time, as she has been unable to participate alongside them in activities.

However, similar points of crisis and change could punctuate the adult experience of people with lifelong disability. For example, April (aged 65, AwithD) described a period in her early 40s when experiences of pain and fatigue associated with post-polio syndrome were confusing and difficult, involving challenges in looking after herself and her children. She discussed the change to using a wheelchair: "The first year I hated it [wheelchair]. I used to sit in the corner, reversed into the corner in the sitting room. I'd be staying like this watching the television but I wasn't watching the television. I was miles away but I was staring at the screen." April perceived this as an affront to her sense of self as someone who was independent and cared for others. This was so even though it came in a lifecourse highly affected by reactions to her having experienced polio as a toddler, as she had spent childhood mostly in hospital and her family had sent her to an orphanage at age 12.

The degree of change in older age was perceived relative to the individual life. People who had lived lives of great confinement or exclusion, or lives with multiple health or impairment challenges, could perceive less change or loss. For a small number, like Babs (aged 67,

AwithD) (whose case was discussed in Chapter 6 and in later sections of this chapter), there was little sense of biographical disruption occasioned by worsening impairment or health issues with ageing. Even though Babs experienced ongoing health issues, such challenges were part of an embodied sense of self over a long period (see also Lloyd et al, 2020). Unlike most experiences within the AwithD group of participants, the accounts of that small number support the position suggested by Williams (2000: 49–50) that ageing experiences of people with lifelong disability might be one of continuity, *not* disruption, or that adversity could mediate perceptions of the impact of impairment or chronic illness in later life.

However, even participants whose lives had been experienced as very confined could still have valued activities and 'competencies' to lose. They could still fear losing independence and they could still try to maintain a sense of continuity with former routines. For example, Teresa (aged 87, AwithD), who was born with physical impairment, lived all her adult life in her family home. She was proud of having learned to read, a key outlet for her, though she never attended school. However, since gradually experiencing visual impairment, reading was no longer possible. In recent years, Teresa also experienced her mobility as more impaired and had started using a wheelchair. She was facing the prospect of greater dependence ("The idea of going into an old people's home, that is what was getting me down") and, as she perceived it, negative impacts of worsening impairment on relationships. However, Teresa retained a sense of continuity by listening to audiobooks obtained from the library. She also simultaneously enjoyed greater community involvement through having joined an older people's group in her 50s. Teresa experienced both disruption and greater inclusion.

All participants (DwithA and AwithD) emphasised activities and outlets that were still available, and even if they had a sense of themselves as changed in some respects, they still tended to have a continuous sense of self. None wanted to be defined by their bodies and all participants made efforts to engage in activities and to participate with others where they could.

Impaired bodies that did not 'disable'

A small number of AwithD participants experienced bodies as not (or minimally) disabling – impaired, yes, but not disabling. In this respect, they were different from other participants in the present study. For example, Len (aged 69, AwithD), a wheelchair user following an accident in his teens, felt that impairment caused him no difficulty, pointing to how he drove an adapted car and lived in an accessible house. Len perceived minimal changes in his body with ageing. Visually impaired from birth, Desmond (aged 72, AwithD) suggested that as long as he uses his new hearing aids, his body caused him "zero problem".

This group tended to think of retirement as the most significant transition of recent years. They focused on leisure or volunteering opportunities (sometimes through disability organisations), and identified with peers who might be considered in the 'third age' (see Weiss, 1997). The perceptions of these participants resembled those from a study with lifelong disabled people who were living 'rather active "third-age lives"' and were like 'any retired person' (Jeppsson Grassman, 2013: 30). In the present study, the lives of the participants concerned were organised over decades such that they experienced disability minimally on a day-to-day basis. These participants, all male, also tended to have worked until standard retirement ages. They may have had the financial resources to have organised their immediate surroundings to minimise disabling aspects. However, these participants still experienced various environmental or relational barriers to participation. For example, Len referred to occasional difficulties accessing parking or buildings. These participants had learned to live with these issues but still considered them unjust.

These accounts might tend to confirm the thesis that lifelong disability builds coping skills and resilience that help people to cope with older age (Reyes, 2009; Iwakuma, 2001), or to support the proposition of Williams (2000: 50) that the AwithD experience might be one of continuity, *not* disruption. However, while this subgroup of participants was clearly resilient and used to dealing with challenges (as were many other AwithD participants), they also did not appear to be experiencing health or significant additional impairment challenges *at this stage in their ageing process*. The stability of their conditions and minimal changes with the passage of time set their bodily experiences apart from others. There had been no biographical disruption and their accounts echo a social model approach in which 'disability' is created by external barriers. However, it is clear that ageing with disability is a heterogeneous experience at the bodily level. There is much scope for revealing a range of experiences among people ageing with disability – and, indeed, for their perspectives to inform societies as populations age and the experience of disability increases.

Disabling or enabling contexts: comparing the two groups

In Chapter 6, I discussed how participants could be disabled or enabled by the contexts in which their lives were lived, using four interlinked headings: social/familial factors; support and care; physical environments; and sociocultural meanings in everyday interactions. Both participant groups (DwithA and AwithD) could be disabled by factors that disable people of all ages, such as inaccessible homes and public transport, and through being discredited by others in daily interactions.

Social/familial factors

In terms of social and familial factors, there were many similarities between participants from the AwithD and DwithA groups. Both understood how they functioned as part of a relational or social unit, particularly with a spouse if they had one. However, the AwithD participants were less likely to be married, or to have been married, than the DwithA participants were. Loss of intimates is a particular characteristic of disability experienced in older age. This also points to challenges for people from the AwithD group, who are less likely to have married and more likely to experience deaths among their informal care networks (Loprest and Maag, 2007; Westwood and Carey, 2019). However, for some participants, changes in the health of family members had led to a kind of inversion over time in caring relationships as they had come to be carers for parents. For example, Teresa (aged 87, AwithD) said of her mother: "I became more independent and it was I that was kind of looking after her instead of the other way around." Furthermore, some participants from the AwithD group, and some among the DwithA group, suggested that relationships had disimproved over time due to disability or worsening impairment. This again signals how public policies need to engage with the AwithD experience and, indeed, to include a focus on anyone experiencing disability over the long term.

Support and care

Having access to financial resources or, alternatively, supportive public provision facilitated functioning and participation, and reduced perceptions of disability. Against the backdrop of anomalies in separate public policies on ageing and on disability in Ireland (see Leahy, 2018; see also Chapter 4), the experiences of public services of the AwithD group were varied. To experience disability in older age is expensive (Cullinan et al, 2013; Morciano et al, 2014). This means that anyone ageing with a legacy of financial disadvantage may live in very difficult circumstances, with lives curtailed by the lack of even the smallest resources. The account of Liz (aged 55, AwithD) from Chapter 6 showed this. She was living in a partially accessible house and was largely unable to get out, even to avail of physiotherapy, for want of money to install a ramp or to pay for taxis.

There were also positive experiences of public support and care, including warm long-term relations with people providing home care, and public services played a crucial role in the lives of many participants (from the AwithD and DwithA groups). The positive role that public services could play was very evident among a very small number of participants in the AwithD group who had remained in disability services after age 65. They could have been made 'older' as young adults but have gone on to benefit from a 'lowering of generational significance' as an older disabled person (Priestley, 2003a: 146).

These inversions were, for example, obvious in the case of Babs (aged 67, AwithD), whose case was discussed in Chapter 6. Following a childhood spent in hospitals and residential settings, she attended a day centre for older people for over two decades starting in her 20s, and then moved to a care home at age 50 and to a supported-living apartment at age 60, benefitting at that stage from a change in disability policy towards decongregation of institutional settings. In relation to her move out of the care home, Babs quoted a social worker who had said: "You do things backwards." By this, he meant leaving a nursing home at a stage when others might be going in. Babs was highly amused by this. With the support of carers and a personal assistant, Babs lived independently. The best thing about life nowadays was being her own "person" and "the boss", describing gaining more "confidence" by learning to do things for herself (like preparing vegetables and taking the bus) as points when she really felt "great".

Thus, public policy models could now help translate aspirations for a 'third age' type of lifestyle into a reality for some participants. While not typical (in terms of levels of formal support), Babs's case indicates how people experiencing disability at the level of the body maximally could also have the most positive perceptions of life nowadays – provided they had appropriate supports. This is consistent with Larsson's (2013: 66) findings that with the right environmental, financial and other supportive conditions, older people with significant impairment can take an active part in social life.

However, within the AwithD group generally, as with the DwithA group of participants, supports did not typically include personal assistance and could be perceived as inflexible. For example, Tony (aged 83, AwithD) described how his allotted home-help hours (two hours per week) clashed with his allotted time in the communal laundry of his housing complex, both on the same day he had a valued outlet at a day centre. He described a life in which opportunities for socialising had diminished and inflexible service provision risked diminishing participation further. Again, the legacy of disadvantage typically experienced by people living with disability over the long term means that there must be particular attention placed within public policies on this group.

Physical environments

Both AwithD and DwithA participants took accessible homes and environments for granted if they had them, perceiving themselves as less disabled as a result. However, environments that involved barriers for disabled people generally (like unlowered footpaths, inaccessible transport or cultural spaces that lacked hearing technology) were disabling of participants (AwithD and DwithA groups). The accounts of participants from both groups suggested experiences of disability in a classical social model sense of oppression (see UPIAS and The Disability Alliance, 1976; Brisenden, 1998 [1986]). One difference – and a paradoxical one given how they are not generally considered 'disabled' – was that participants from the DwithA group tended to stress difficulties encountered in physical environments.

Of course, that is not to say that participants from the AwithD group did not experience disablist exclusion due to environmental factors. In fact, where a new impairment was experienced on top of an existing one, there could be a whole new set of barriers to negotiate. People among the AwithD group who depended on public services and lacked resources (say, for taxis or for home adaptations or private provision of care) could continue to be very negatively affected by environmental barriers. For example, Tony (aged 83, AwithD) escaped 'disability' categorisation in some respects in early life through experiencing impairment largely in appearance rather than functioning, to use the distinction made by Davis (1995). He lived in a local authority bedsit for 'seniors', which was not fully accessible for a rollator or wheelchair, and was thus not capable of supporting change over time – the exact opposite of what people's needs are as they age (for both DwithA and AwithD groups). Tony described challenges and precariousness involved in preparing breakfast in a kitchen too narrow to accommodate his rollator. He used one hand to hold himself upright by grasping the worktop while working with his free hand. Knowing that his bedsit could not accommodate a wheelchair, Tony anticipated a move to a nursing home due to progressive worsening of his mobility.

The approach to senior housing that Tony experiences reflects a bureaucratic approach in which the status of disability is 'frozen' (Rickli, 2016: 126–7) and in which older disabled people are categorised as 'elderly', not 'disabled' (Jönson and Larsson, 2009). This does not meet the needs of either group. Neither do various environmental barriers – partially accessible public transport, for example – which both groups contended with.

Sociocultural meanings in everyday interactions

The two groups experienced some differences due to sociocultural meanings made of impairment, ageing and the lifecourse, experiences that occur, as already argued, as part of larger societal and cultural processes in which constructions of ageing and of disability are intertwined, as is their social devaluation. Contrasts between the experiences of the two groups were notable in this area, as already discussed in Chapter 6. Coinciding with disability onset, participants from the DwithA group could experience exclusion (from physical environments) and they could be othered even within families and community groups, experiencing psycho-emotional disablism (Thomas, 2007, 2015; Reeve, 2012). These participants could perceive themselves as crossing a boundary into a discredited social category, as ableism constructs disability as a diminished state (Campbell, 2001). Thus, the social construction of disability could construct ageing and the lifecourse.

However, invalidating and discrediting processes were part of the AwithD experience in the long term. For example, Janice (aged 66, AwithD), who lived with multiple sclerosis, described decades of explaining and educating others. She still felt that people talked over her and that they could still be "afraid" around her, and she has to reassure them that they will not "catch anything". This can be the experience of disabled people generally (Reeve, 2012: 81). For Simon (aged 66, AwithD), other people's perceptions of him as a visually impaired person had always made him feel "vulnerable", and he thought that was how others still saw him. Lives could have been influenced by societal framings of disability over decades, as disablism and internalised prejudice, or negative stereotypes of what it means to have an impairment, could have resulted in self-imposed restrictions (Reeve, 2012). For example, Tony (aged 83, AwithD) talked about never having had a relationship with a "lassie", which he attributed to sensitivity about his appearance when younger: "I used to be very sensitive about growing up and I'd be saying, 'Who would be bothered with a happy fellow like me?' This would run in my head." Tony also knew that attitudes to disability had changed over time, and he reflected that disabled people do marry nowadays. However, Tony lived alone and experienced an increasingly narrow social network in recent years, for example, describing buying cakes in case of callers but having to throw them out as people seldom called.

Some participants among the AwithD group experienced positive changes with ageing in aspects of life. This arose in the context of social constructions of age and the lifecourse affecting meanings made of disability (Kelley-Moore, 2010). It could involve perceptions of re-entering the standardised lifecourse, as the physical appearance or lives of AwithD participants came to resemble those of their age peers more. I used the case of Helen (aged 68, AwithD) to illustrate this experience (see Chapter 6). Helen described how life was more difficult in recent years (due to worsening impairment and pain) but also better in some ways because being older made her appearance less notable and helped her to resist others' judgements.

Positive experiences could also be associated with finding new ways to participate in communities, sometimes with groups of older people and often due to public or community actions. Among both DwithA and AwithD groups, some participants had positive perceptions of joining centres or clubs due especially to connecting with others and accessing opportunities for purposeful activity (see Chapter 7). However, for participants among the AwithD group who had lived lives that had been very confined or isolated, it could be their first time (or their first time in decades) engaging in communal activities with their age peers. The degree of both 'disruption' and (what might be called) 'normalisation' that participants experienced was perceived relative to the degree of exclusion experienced at earlier life stages. As argued in Chapter 6, this therefore says as much about the degree to which social norms isolate and exclude disabled people as it does about perceptions of greater belonging or 'normalisation' on the part of the individuals concerned.

Blanaid (aged 61, AwithD), among the youngest study participants, joined the local older people's centre and said, "I love being part of the older generation." She positioned herself within a chronological categorisation as "older" despite narratives of decline. This is in contrast to Carmel (aged 69, DwithA), whose experience was discussed in Chapter 6, who can be said to have opted for a 'disability' identity over an 'ageing' one. However, Blanaid's perspective was different, as it was influenced by years of relative isolation and by her perception that for decades she had had no identity other than "just a person with [name of condition]". She explained that joining an older person's centre entailed the possibility for a new identification as part of a community that accepts her and a new sense of purpose: "It's such a good focus for people and you've somewhere to go and you belong. And when you walk in the door, you're just accepted as you are and you're a different person from the person sitting at home in the kitchen. ... So, you've a function and a focus."

Something similar might be said of Teresa (aged 87, AwithD), who joined her local older people's centre in her 50s. She said: "It really opened a new life for me and I went on holidays with them and everything. ... Well I was going out and I was meeting people and I was getting to sing songs and I went on holidays then." This was a new outlet for Teresa, who perceived that her adulthood had been very confined ("I might only get out once a year"). Living on her own for the first time since her late 70s, Teresa also conveyed a sense of pride in being independent: "I am on my own. And I am independent." Like Babs, her characterisation of herself now suggests identification with valorised notions of independence, and her emphasis on the social and leisure aspects of life evokes descriptions of the 'third age' or 'positive' ageing.

These processes of becoming increasingly similar to one's age peers for the AwithD group are consistent with experiences reported in other studies (Jeppsson Grassman, 2013: 31; Pollington cited in Simcock, 2017). One way to engage with these experiences is found in the notion that disabled people operate on 'crip time', which can involve not only a slower pace of movement, but also encounters with barriers over which one has no control (Kafer, 2013: 26). Thus, participants could also be said to experience their lifecourse in crip time, as disability disrupts normative understandings of time and the lifecourse (see Ljuslinder et al, 2020).

It is also worth stressing that these positive changes were experienced by participants for whom bodies might make life more precarious and difficult, and who continued to have to negotiate barriers to participation. There could be both a 'double jeopardy' *and* (what might be called) 'normalisation'. There could be a sense of biographical disruption, especially associated with the prospect of increasing dependence, and a sense of re-entering the standardised lifecourse at the same time.

The issue of a **disability identity** was also relevant to the meanings made by participants of their experiences, and has again already been discussed in Chapter 6. The picture that emerged was complex but there were more similarities than is generally appreciated between the two groups. For their part, the DwithA group of participants could resist prejudice or disablism (without framing it in those terms), and for some, a disability consciousness could be said to be evolving in response to exclusion, as well as through involvement with mainstream disability organisations in some cases (see Chapter 6).

Empirical studies with people ageing with disability (AwithD group) suggest that maintaining a strong sense of a 'disability' identity distinguishes the experience (Jeppsson Grassman et al, 2012; Cooper and Bigby, 2014). While the AwithD group of participants in the present study were likely to use terms like 'disabled' of themselves and to value contact with other disabled people or activism, they did not tend to stress their 'disability' identities. These participants stressed their experiences as part of the mainstream. For example, Eileen (aged 66, AwithD) said the thing she most wanted was to be treated as "normal". However, 'disability' could mean contact with supportive others and could still be a useful concept – providing analytical or political approaches informed by disability activism, say, understanding 'disability' as encompassing social/environmental barriers. As April (aged 65, AwithD) said, "It is society that disables you." Not all AwithD participants had had much involvement with disability organisations earlier in life. However, for others, organising and activities (like sports) associated with disability were how they had met their spouses, or had led to lifelong friendships and activities. For several, long-term involvement in groups advocating for disabled people, or providing support to them, continued to be a valued outlet for connection and contribution.

All participants wanted to be seen as 'full human beings' (Morris, 2001: 10). Implicit in this is a rejection of the idea of an exclusive 'normalcy' (see Davis, 2013b; Shakespeare, 2014a: 99). Instead, participants communicated a sense that there is more to them than any label, as well as a desire to live lives they perceived as mainstream, as connected to others and as meaningful. That being said, the category 'disability' was useful and provided empowering, analytical approaches informed by disability activism for many people within the AwithD group (and for some within the DwithA group), who also valued collective experiences with other disabled people, involving shared experiences and knowledge. Again, both groups could experience shared social experiences that could be both positive and negative, which is what contributes to the formation of a disability identity, as articulated by Siebers (2017 [2013]) (discussed in Chapter 6).

Responding to challenges: comparing the two groups

In response to the twin challenges of disablement (onset or worsening) and reduced social networks, Chapter 7 showed that participants often sought to remake their lives to perceive them as meaningful. Under this heading, there were more similarities than differences between the two participant groups (AwithD and DwithA). A cycle of losses could reduce a sense of life as meaningful. Participants' responses evidence how they sought to function in ways that enabled them to perceive their lives as meaningful. This was discussed (in Chapter 7) by reference, especially, to the needs for meaning articulated by Baumeister (1991) and Derkx (2013, 2016; Derkx et al, 2020). These were the need for purpose, moral worth, self-worth, efficacy, connectedness, comprehensibility (or coherence) and excitement. Thus, both groups expressed the need for a meaningful life through efforts to minimise the effects on identity of disablement processes (or worsening impairment), to resist othering or exclusion, and to maintain a sense of continuity. They made efforts to continue everyday activities (which they could invest with new meaning), to maintain activities and to participate in new ones, to make their own decisions, to connect with others, and to contribute to families and communities where they could. For some participants from the AwithD group, continuing involvement with a disability organisation was a meaningful expression of the need for purpose, connection, self-worth and moral worth. For example, Babs (aged 67, AwithD) enjoyed volunteering with a disability organisation to give talks to social care students about her experiences as a disabled person, "because if we don't get up and talk, no one will know, you know".

The DwithA group could experience a threat to a sense of coherence and meaning in life, associated with a sense of having been consigned to a discredited social category. What was different for some participants from the AwithD group was that perceptions of re-entering the standardised lifecourse (against a backdrop of exclusion) could help with a sense that life now made more sense or had value. For these participants from the AwithD group, physical segregation from family and work, reinforcing perceptions of cultural difference, had characterised their whole lives (Finkelstein, 1991). Some participants had gained a sense of validation or self-worth, and moral worth or efficacy, from finding that they could now identify with social and leisure activities associated with a 'third age' lifestyle, or with values of autonomy and independence. Sometimes, joining groups of older people brought a new sense of connection and belonging. Participants sometimes perceived that needing support was now the norm not only for them, but also for their chronological peers. Thus, participants could distance themselves from 'discourses of dependency and otherness' (Priestley, 2006) and sometimes identify with 'positive', 'active' framings of later life. These processes helped, I suggest, with perceptions that life made sense or was meaningful.

Thus, both groups (DwithA and AwithD) identified with qualities associated with the 'third age' (or similar discourses of 'positive' ageing), especially with goals of self-development, activity and social connectedness. Their identities were not just based on bodies or impairments. Binary notions of 'third' and 'fourth' ages are further problematised by the fact that some AwithD participants had perceived precariousness and 'decline' (usually associated with the 'fourth age') for decades.

Where participants from the AwithD group found activities they valued that linked them with others, this tended to be facilitated either by public services that included supports such as personal assistance, which was unusual, or, more typically, through centres/clubs for older people or disabled people, or through advocacy organisations of disabled people. This highlights the need for communal action to support older disabled people from both groups, and (as Chapter 7 argued) for shared public spaces, collective aspects of support and care, and recognition that older disabled people continue to seek meaningful (not tokenistic) activities and outlets for contribution.

Discussion and conclusions

This chapter illustrated that while participants ageing with disability (AwithD group), especially, had heterogeneous experiences, there were similarities and differences between the two groups (DwithA and AwithD). Both experienced contextual barriers to participation, including losses of intimates, inaccessible physical environments and lack of material resources or supportive public services. Both could experience disablism due to discrediting attitudes of others. External barriers were sometimes stressed by people from the DwithA group but had detrimentally shaped lives of the AwithD participants for longer, for whom experiences of impairment, disablism and social exclusion across the lifespan could have significant negative consequences in older age. Both groups also engaged in processes of reinterpretation within their contexts and sought to experience their lives as meaningful.

The discussion showed some of the inversions, or disruptions to the normative lifecourse, that could be part of the experience of the

AwithD group of participants. This could involve a kind of bodily ageing (or 'fourth age') 'before time', or being 'aged' by sociocultural meanings or public policy responses early in life. Public policy approaches informed by service norms within disability services had even reversed those 'ageing' processes later in life for a small group of participants – as they moved out of residential care at a stage when the response to other older people might be that they should move in. Ageing with disability could also involve experiencing transitions in older age as re-entering the standardised lifecourse following a lifetime of exclusion from standard institutions and rites of passage, or of being out of synch with them. This was often achieved through joining older people's centres or clubs, where public services or community organising facilitated this. As Chapter 6 suggested, the discussion here is meant not to signal acceptance of interpretations of the normative lifecourse based on an able-bodied ideal, but instead to reflect participants' perceptions of these changes within their contexts. It also highlights the exclusions of disabled people that are taken for granted in normalising (or non-disabled) society. In addition, it points to the possibility of reinterpretation and reconstruction of the normative lifecourse from the perspective of ageing with disability.

Responding to the research question as to how the social processes of the two groups compare, while there are differences, the *outcomes* both want for their lives are similar, as are many of the difficulties and barriers faced. At a most fundamental level, both groups share similar aspirations for their lives – for connection with others, for inclusion in the mainstream of life and for having lives they value or perceive as meaningful. Many of the differences between the two groups arise from sociocultural meanings made of impairment at different points of the lifespan. As already argued, these arise as part of an ableist societal tendency to valorise independent adulthood and to devalue other social categories (Priestley, 2002, 2003a, 2006). Both groups could engage in dynamic processes of trying to recreate meaningful structures for their lives in response to loss and change. For some AwithD participants, engaging with activism or volunteering with a disability organisation was a long-standing commitment that helped with perceptions of purpose and connection to others.

While it is not true to suggest that the two experiences are the same, it may be true that biomedical determinations of different aetiologies, between early and late onset of disability, have led to assumptions of more difference in social experiences of the two groups than is the case. Unquestioned ideas that disabled people are very different from other people may also play a role in influencing some of this thinking.

Similarities are especially evident when the focus is on what people want from their lives. This is consistent with Townsend's (1981a: 93, emphasis in original) argument for emphasising not biology, but the *outcome*, of disability in older age. Even if scholarship and public policies tend to approach people from the DwithA and AwithD groups as if they are very different, the emphasis on activity, self-development and connection with others enshrined in 'positive' ageing models resonated with participants from both groups (see also Chapter 5). Both engaged in constant processes of social identity formation in interaction with broader societal discourses and ideologies. Both can have a complex relationship to the idea of a 'disability' identity; both can also experience disablist exclusion. Not meeting standard 'successful' ageing criteria does not preclude either group from identifying with them – or, indeed, from being othered by them. Accounts of both groups challenge the 'third age'–'fourth age' binary. They also challenge siloed approaches to scholarship and policy.

Suggesting that the two experiences share some things in common is compatible with what I already argued in respect of community and public policy approaches to people from the AwithD group: there must be a particular focus on them or on anyone experiencing disability over the long term. We need to become more aware of how experiences of disability earlier in life have wide-ranging consequences for later life, and we need to know more about the subjective experiences involved. Many questions about ageing with disability, including intersectional issues, remain relatively unexplored (Lamb, 2015). There is no doubt that assumptions about disability generally lead to resource inequalities and social discrimination (Kafer, 2013: 14). The accounts of some participants ageing with disability illustrate how lack of material and social resources could make later life very difficult. It must also be acknowledged that participants categorised as belonging to the AwithD group were not the only ones to experience cumulative disadvantage. Some participants within the DwithA group, whose experiences were discussed in earlier chapters, also had very limited resources (social and financial) in older age that resulted in many difficulties and limitations (see also Scharf, 2009).

There is scope for people ageing with disability to inform societies more broadly as populations age and the experience of disability increases. As Westwood and Carey (2019) argue, the expertise from experience of people ageing with long-standing disability is an asset that could inform people experiencing disability for the first time in older age. However, getting there would require confronting the denial that deprives society of knowledge and resources that would help many people to live well with disability in older age.

9

Conclusion

Introduction

This book, framed within a critical gerontological perspective, has aimed to contribute to elucidating experiences of disability in older age, drawing on an inductive empirical study. This chapter summarises key issues and empirical findings, and suggests some future directions for scholarship and public policies. At the outset, the book outlined a series of paradoxes inherent in the attempt to engage with the issue of disability and ageing, and, indeed, paradox and inversion were themes that the book engaged with at many points.

Chief among these is the fact that social science approaches to ageing are dominated by issues to do with older age lived without impairment. Despite how anticipated economic costs of health and social care dominate responses to population ageing, relatively little is known about subjective experiences of the people most concerned – older people experiencing disability or chronic illness (or people who might be considered to be in the so-called 'fourth age'). While there are many studies on impairment in later life, they are often limited to medical or functionalist perspectives. Paradox is also inherent in the fact that older people experiencing impairment are rarely considered 'disabled', as well as in siloed approaches to ageing and disability in theorising, activism and policymaking.

Part I contextualised the book and the empirical findings that inform it. Chapter 2 showed that fundamentally different ideas about what disability is inform different fields. This represents a barrier to more conversations that cross existing boundaries in scholarship and in other areas. The chapter suggested that if understood more widely as an explanatory framework for disability in older age, interactional or biopsychosocial approaches to definition could facilitate an understanding of disability as more than a personal problem (discussed again later).

The review of the academic literature from different fields (see Chapter 3) confirmed the point made in the book's introduction that there is little theorising that addresses ageing and disability together. Critical approaches in both fields use similar approaches but intersect only to a limited degree. It also confirmed the need for more empirical engagement with subjective experiences of disability in older age.

The policy review in Chapter 4 discussed the separation of policy frameworks on disability and ageing, which means that societies differ in how they respond to 'disability' experienced at different points of the lifespan. Increasing numbers of people ageing with disability create a growing challenge to the two policy frameworks to intersect and to learn from each other. The chapter argues for developing greater understanding of similarities as well as differences across different service-user groups, and for more collective responses. I consider public policies again later in this chapter.

Part II presented evidence from an empirical study with participants rarely considered together in research – people ageing with disability (AwithD) and people first experiencing disability with ageing (DwithA). The study's participants were all experiencing physical or sensory disability. Its key finding can be summed up briefly as follows: with ageing, people experience disability (or greater disablement) in their bodies and in their contexts, which can challenge their sense of meaning in life, often in combination with losses of intimates. They respond by engaging in challenging and dynamic processes of trying to remake lives they perceive as meaningful.

The study evidenced that the perception of bodies that now 'limited' participants (or limited them more than previously) was a central part of the experience for most participants, and could be associated with a sense of finitude and lack of control, and of fears of greater dependency (see Chapter 5). However, participants did not want to be defined by their bodies, and they often emphasised what they could still do. Divisions between the so-called 'third' and 'fourth' ages were not well marked in their perceptions. In a seeming contradiction, participants could identify both with 'decline' and with 'positive' ageing discourses. The chapter suggests that the extent to which dominant discourses of ageing are ableist, and consequently discrediting of older disabled people, is under-recognised.

Although disability in older age tends to be largely subject to medical analysis and individual framing, Chapter 6 evidenced how a range of contextual factors actively disabled and limited participants' potential, as they do of all disabled people. These included disablist social relations, inaccessible environments and lack of material resources. People who lacked social and financial resources could experience disability maximally. In that chapter, I also considered the issue of a 'disability' identity in older age, suggesting that the experience is more nuanced and fluid than has been assumed to date.

Chapter 7 showed how participants responded to the twin challenges of disablement (or worsening disability) and loss of intimates and social networks. Both could reduce perceptions of life as meaningful and, in combination, were particularly challenging, forcing change in how participants perceived meaning in their lives. Using an approach to 'meaning in life' with its basis in humanism (Derkx, 2013; Derkx et al, 2020), the study highlights agentic responses, involving ongoing processes of interpretation and reinterpretation. This can involve finding positive aspects of later life lived with disability, especially through connecting with others and finding purposeful activity. That participants engage in such processes problematises 'positive' or active ageing discourse – typically associated with absence of impairment – and policies on ageing organised around an axis of able-bodiedness. The chapter amounts to evidence for a counter-narrative of ageing and the lifecourse that recognises both the challenges of disablement processes in older age and ongoing efforts to perceive value and meaning in life.

While it is always difficult to balance similarities and differences, in Chapter 8, I compared the experience of the two groups of participants (DwithA and AwithD). I suggested that while people in the AwithD group especially had heterogeneous experiences, similarities could also be seen when the focus was on what outcomes participants wanted for their lives. Both groups faced many similar difficulties and barriers. At a most fundamental level, both shared aspirations that include connection with others, inclusion in what was perceived as the mainstream and having lives they valued or perceived as meaningful. Key differences arise from sociocultural meanings made of impairment at different stages of the lifespan. People experiencing disability first with ageing (DwithA group) started to experience disablism and exclusion with impairment onset but those processes had shaped the AwithD experience for longer.

Towards critical responses

By focusing on how older disabled people interpreted change and reacted to it, the findings discussed throughout this book challenge some of the assumptions or informing paradigms of separate academic fields. These include overwhelmingly biological explanations of impairment in older age that dominate gerontology, and normative notions of the nature of the lifecourse, especially about the residual nature of the so-called 'fourth age'. It also shows how the ageing with disability experience can challenge ideas of the normative lifecourse. The book shows how transitions experienced in older age are more complex and varied than those that have received most attention in lifecourse scholarship to date. It also points to the need for more exploration of subjective experiences of later life lived with disability and for those experiences to influence policies. It highlights the need for more theoretical engagement within different fields with disablement processes in later life and the cultural meanings made of them, and for more exploration of how older disabled people can continue to live lives of value and meaning.

There is a particular need for research on experiences of people ageing with long-standing disability (AwithD group) in order to engage with their (diverse) experiences of ageing and of public policies at the intersection of separate frameworks on disability and on ageing. Heterogeneity among this group signals scope for revealing a wide spectrum of experience. Their experiences could inform both scholarship and societies more broadly.

I argue throughout the book for a realistic engagement with the nature of humanity, including its limitations, but not *only* its limitations. The book's arguments point to the need for greater recognition in scholarship of the challenges of disablement processes in older age *and* the ongoing efforts of older disabled people to perceive value and meaning in their lives, as well as the range of barriers that actively limit them in doing so. As suggested in Chapter 1, this may require critical challenges to orthodoxies in both disability studies and social gerontology. The fields of ageing and disability are distinct and each has strengths. However, neither has yet engaged comprehensively with subjective experiences of older people experiencing physical and sensory disability in ways that reveal the range of factors that constitute disability, on the one hand, or of what it means to live a life of value and meaning despite challenges, which can be personal and societal, on the other.

Scholars within disability studies who resist the notion that most people will experience 'disability' with age, or universalising ideas of impairment, tend to see this as risking obscuring hierarchies and oppressive structural factors. It is important that scholarship should not elide difference or lead to trivialising the experience of any disabled people. However, the intent of this book has not been to argue that everyone is impaired to some degree, which overlooks patterns of discrimination and exclusion. It does not seek to universalise disability in that way. Rather, it is informed by the fact that the likelihood of disability increases with age and it seeks to focus attention on the causes, consequences and understandings of disability in older age (among both DwithA and AwithD groups). After all, older disabled people, including people living with severe levels of impairment, constitute an enormous group and make up a large proportion of disabled people, one that is under-acknowledged but that will grow with population ageing (see Chapter 4).

The extent to which constructions of ageing and of disability, and the social devaluation of each, are intertwined and linked to fears of human vulnerability means that these issues would benefit from approaches that address them across the lifespan for both disabled people generally and for older disabled people (AwithD and DwithA groups). Ideally, more conversations between disparate areas of scholarship would result in engagement with disability in older age as a personal, embodied, social, cultural, political and socio-economic phenomenon.

Yoshizaki-Gibbons (2019) has called for more engagement with ageing within critical disability studies, and Siebers (2008: 81) has argued that the primary objective for disability studies should be to awaken more political consciousness to the concept of ableism, which, he suggested, has yet to be accepted into general usage. If Siebers is correct, it would seem appropriate to explore whether political ideas of who is encompassed within the category 'disabled' can be expanded to include people who first experience it in older age (as well as, of course, people ageing with disability). This could help address the issue highlighted decades ago by Abberley (1987: 15) that levels of disability are minimised by overlooking disability associated with ageing (see also Townsend, 1981a).

For this author, the aim would be to marshal more interest in and more support for the issues affecting all disabled people in order to foster both the inclusive responses to disability that are long overdue and approaches to ageing that are both inclusive and realistic in not being organised around an axis of able-bodiedness. For this to happen, scholarship is needed that makes links between the fields of ageing and disability, or that at least engages in conversations across boundaries, even if those conversations can be fraught, as Lamb (2015) suggests. I next consider some areas that offer this potential for critical scholarship.

Some starting points

In general terms, applying a critical or cultural disability lens contributes a valuable analysis of how society *actively* disables and limits the potential of disabled people, and about what disability reveals about culture. There is potential for much more analysis of the role that ableist ideologies and disablism play in processes of disablement in older age, in denial of human rights and in the very creation of the so-called 'fourth age' as a time of withdrawal from society. Another insight from critical disability studies that could usefully inform critical gerontology is how disability is not necessarily all negative – that different ways of being in the world can be sources of satisfaction, creativity and meaning.

Critical gerontology (like critical disability studies) focuses on interpretation. It also focuses on materiality. This perspective is associated with attempts to transcend individual, medicalised framings of impairment in older age and to direct attention to social, political, economic and cultural factors. More of this engagement is needed both at a macro level (see, for example, Kelley-Moore, 2010) and at the level of subjective interpretations (see Chapter 6). However, ageing forces engagement with physiology, 'not least because of the ultimate undeniability of death' (Twigg, 2004: 63). For this author, it is a strength of critical gerontology that it can engage not only with discourse, but also with material issues of the body and with existential questions. Engagement with aspects of the experience perceived as negative as well as positive is important for a realistic engagement with all aspects of later life. Indeed, it is possible, as West and Glynos (2016) argue, that including issues of death and dying could change our outlook on ageing and on life in general.

More engagement at the intersections of ageing and disability should lead to a broadening out of enquiry rather than a narrowing to existing areas of commonality. At the risk of appearing to narrow the focus, I refer next to several strands within scholarship that offer potential. This discussion, of necessity, involves concision and a certain amount of generalisation of complex issues and distinctions.

Scholarship that applies concepts that have been developed within disability studies to ageing, or that brings a cultural disability lens to constructions of disability in older age, is an obvious avenue to be further explored. This would include ideas of normalcy, disablism or ableism being applied to discourses of ageing (and their manifestations in public policies) and to constructions of disability in older age. Explorations of intersections of ageism and disablism are also needed, as is engagement with bodies that are both older and disabled. There are examples from different perspectives already seeking to open conversations in these areas (Chivers, 2011; Gibbons, 2016; McGrath et al, 2017; Yoshizaki-Gibbons, 2019). The development by Gibbons of the concept of 'compulsory youthfulness' (drawing on the work of McRuer) is an example of scholarship linking ageism and ableism.

Engagement within disability scholarship with dementia can be seen as an area where common ground is already being sought, and this could also be applied to other forms of impairment experienced in older age. Thomas and Milligan (2018) suggest that scholarship should explore how a dementia diagnosis brings the phenomena of ageism and disablism together. Consideration has also been given as to what conceptual understanding of disability would best inform moving to considerations of dementia as disability (Shakespeare et al, 2019).

From a lifecourse perspective, Priestley (2003a) pioneered exploration of ageing and disability. Contributing to a dialogue across the fields of ageing and disability, Kahana and Kahana (2017: 78) suggest that approaches to the lifecourse are needed that validate people living with illness and disability across the lifespan. Grenier et al (2016) challenge age-based understandings of the lifecourse and the construction of disabled people and older people within it, as well as interpretations of disability as inherently negative. However, there is much more scope for challenges to the construction of the normative lifecourse from a disability (or crip) perspective (see Ljuslinder et al, 2020). Intersectional lifecourse perspectives could be important in this endeavour. These are starting points from which to develop more engagement that challenges interpretations of lifecourse transitions and patterns that are based on an able-bodied ideal, something that needs to be shaped, I would suggest, by diverse experiences of disability in older age.

Feminist perspectives and intersectional approaches represent obvious avenues for bridging boundaries between traditionally separate fields, opening more potential to perceive disability in older age as a political category, not an individual pathology or tragedy, as well as explicating how multiple dimensions of inequality (such as gender, class, ethnicity and sexuality) intersect with age. Berghs et al (2019: 1037–8) argue that 'the time has come to think of what unifies' in discussing reductions in the rights and entitlements of disabled people, and suggest that it may be time to welcome 'greater diversity and intersectionality of identities across the life-course'.

While the disciplines of feminist disability studies and feminist gerontology have largely remained disparate fields, there is scholarship pointing to the possibility of more links between the two. These include Morell's (2003) application to older age of arguments from Wendell's (1996) theorising of the rejected body. Other examples (from within disability studies) of starting points may be identified in the scholarship of Garland-Thomson and Kafer. For example, Kafer (2013: 8) argues that anxiety about ageing can be seen as a symptom of compulsory able-bodiedness/able-mindedness and she tries to make space for both the bodily and the contextual. Kafer (2013) engages with feminism, crip and queer studies to argue that the value of a future that includes disability goes unrecognised. Her arguments are among those that influence Sandberg and Marshall's (2017) critique of 'successful' ageing. Kafer's (2013: 3, 27) proposition that disability futures go unrecognised, encapsulated in her phrase that 'disability too often serves as the agreed-upon limit of our projected futures', seems particularly relevant to disability experiences of later life and to how we engage with (and fail to engage with) experiences of the so-called 'fourth age'.

It is difficult to envisage a way forward without empirical research with older disabled people. As Yoshizaki-Gibbons (2019) argues, older disabled people should be centred in emancipatory research and praxis. Addressing injustice requires identifying and understanding the experience of social groups that have been disadvantaged by social arrangements (Vehmas and Watson, 2014: 647). Greater understanding is also needed if people of all ages are going to come to accept the aspects of ageing that are disabling and to resist disability as wholly negative (Morell, 2003: 80). The articulation of individual experience can lead to the growth of communities of common interest. It would be interesting to see separate fields engaging in empirical research that explores experiences that might traditionally be considered to fit more readily within the other field. That is to say, gerontology might engage more with experiences of ageing with disability (something that has already started) and disability studies with experiences of disability with ageing. Both, of course, could also explore experiences across both categories.

As mentioned already, critical gerontology includes a focus not just on discourse, but also on materiality and physiology. Those characterised as realists (or critical realists) within critical disability studies also acknowledge the material aspects of the experience of disability. They also tend to approach 'disability' as something that can be experienced in older age. For example, Shakespeare (2006: 64) considers that 'across the life span, everyone experiences impairment and limitation', adding that disabilities differ in their impact and that it is important to respect real differences, particularly the extent to which people are affected by suffering and restriction. For Shakespeare (2014a), the social and the biological are always intertwined, and he calls for more empirical research on how disabled people experience embodiment. He highlights the need for responses informed by lived experience that account for a human nature that has limitations and vulnerabilities, and is ultimately mortal, while also acknowledging that life with disability can involve possibilities for adaptation and flourishing (Shakespeare, 2014a). Similarly, for Siebers (2008: 5, 71), able-bodiedness is a 'temporary identity' and he suggests that disability studies must account for both the negative and positive valences of disability, and focus on speaking 'about, for, and with disabled people'.

Scholarship within critical gerontology mirrors calls in disability studies (primarily among those considered realists) for more empirical research with how disabled people experience embodiment. Although they may use different terminology, this can be seen among scholars who challenge the lack of engagement with 'real bodies' of older people, allowing the unproblematised support of positive cultural images that fail to validate people who do not meet those standards (Holstein and Minkler, 2007: 16). Another example is evident in calls for more engagement with how people negotiate the 'fourth age' and for their experiences to influence public policies (Lloyd, 2012, 2015; Lloyd et al, 2014).

An issue that underlies all the discussion in this book concerns conceptual models of disability (discussed in Chapter 2). This is a significant issue because the fields of disability and of ageing tend to operate from radically different ideas about what disability is, constituting different starting points in the framing of scholarship, research and, indeed, policy and activism. At one end of the spectrum, much recent scholarship in disability studies apprehends disability as entirely culturally and discursively created, while, at the other, gerontology is in many ways still all about the material body, with biomedical definitions dominant. Clearly, the engagement with discursive constructions of disability within critical disability studies has something of a counterpart within approaches to the body in older age in critical gerontology (see Twigg, 2004; Pickard, 2014). However, scholarship on ageing that includes material issues of mind and body represents a significant challenge for conversations across the two fields.

As argued already, basing gerontological research exclusively on medicalised diagnostic categories also misses opportunities to identify issues common across a range of categories, and it risks overlooking the role of broader cultural, socio-economic and political factors in the causation of disability. Gerontologists should, I suggest, be explicit about what model of disability informs their engagement with impairment. Categories based on the medical model and used even in social gerontology (such as the 'fourth age' or 'frailty') are inimical to approaches within disability studies, are not ones that anyone is likely to want to identify with and therefore provide no interpretive resources for self or collective identity.

On the basis that it would represent a step forward for approaches to ageing, in Chapter 2, I suggested that interactional or biopsychosocial understandings of what disability is in older age would allow for recognition of issues other than the biological and might lay the groundwork for a more unified agenda on disability between different fields. This would also be consistent with international human rights approaches to disability, such as the definition used in the UN Convention of the Rights of Persons with Disabilities. This could help to build wider support for universally accessible built environments and laws designed to offer equal protection to all people. Other conceptual models offering potential for a more unified approach, such as that found in the field of environmental gerontology, were also discussed in Chapter 2.

Adopting shared conceptual models of disability might also help move towards development of more realistic and inclusive approaches to ageing. As argued throughout this book, binary understandings of what it is to age, characterising good health and absence of impairment as 'success' and the sine qua non of a good life, occur within prevailing concepts of autonomy and independence, fears of human vulnerability, and ableism. From within critical gerontology, Grenier et al (2017) argue instead for approaches that develop from acknowledgement of fragility and limitations. Others emphasise subjective perceptions of meaning and value at all stages of older age over conventional paradigms. For example, Baars (2017) suggests that there is a deficit in approaching ageing due to the lack of recognition of vulnerabilities and limitations, on the one hand, and of potential for creativity and fulfilment, on the other. For him, ageing is drained of its 'meanings' when life is characterised as residual beyond hectic adulthood. This scholarship is consistent with key findings of the study that informs this book (see Chapter 7). Part of the broader picture is that cultural framings of all disabled people fail to present them as ordinary people trying to carve out meaningful lives like everybody else (Riddell and Watson, 2003: 3).

Overall, the argument for trying to open up conversations across traditional boundaries in scholarship is: to move towards a more realistic engagement with what it is to age and to live a life of meaning at all of life's stages; to present a more complete picture of the diverse experiences that are involved in disability and ageing; and to contribute to a more realistic societal engagement with disability as an issue relevant to all human beings. Reactions to negative constructions of both ageing and disability have led to emphasising the potential for independence and autonomy, to distancing between the fields of disability and ageing, and to distancing most of all from 'deep' older age, or from ageing lived with chronic illness or disability. However, ageing is a multifaceted phenomenon that benefits from being approached from multiple perspectives. This requires that we rethink antitheses – disabled person–older person, 'third age'–'fourth age', growth–decline, independence–dependence and vulnerability–strength – as well as antithetical stances within and between areas of scholarship.

Critical gerontologists are already challenging medicalised understandings of older age that inform unquestioned assumptions that everything that is valuable in life requires absence of ill health or impairment, and highlighting the role of socio-economic and cultural factors in the construction of disability in older age. However, critical scholarship sometimes avoids engagement with moral or existential issues, and a paucity of approaches to ageing emphasising value and meaning in life's last stages continues to be a significant societal deficit. Engaging in theorising of personal meaning in life from a humanistic perspective offers potential to better communicate understandings of how a sense of a meaningful life is achieved at any stage of life, including in its last stage, and of how it can also be threatened. As this perspective is relevant to disabled and non-disabled people as well as to people of all ages, it has potential for bridging different fields and for developing shared understandings of what is important to people at all of life's stages. It could also help to highlight how processes of social identity formation and reinterpretation are always ongoing, processes that require the exercise of creativity and agency, and, because of this, it could be employed to challenge 'decline' narratives of ageing.

However, in the absence of acknowledgement that fragility, vulnerability and, yes, death are inherent in the human condition, we are unlikely to achieve much other than to push more difficult issues (and the people perceived to embody them) further to the margins. These issues can be difficult and challenging for individuals (and, indeed, for researchers); however, they are not synonymous with weakness, tragedy, absence of agency or lack of a sense of meaning in life, and our collective responses to them are strongly influenced by broader sociocultural contexts. Thus, instead, they reveal how we understand and structure care, social relations, lifecourse transitions and cultural narratives of both disability and ageing. They should, I suggest, also help us to re-imagine human potential across the lifespan.

The COVID-19 pandemic has highlighted that existing models of ageing and approaches to theorising ageing are limited and are easily turned upside-down in policies and public conversations at times of crisis. It showed that despite decades of focus on positive ageing (in its various forms) within theorising, public policies and societal discourse, older people could suddenly be consigned to a single group – all termed 'the elderly' and 'vulnerable'. It has shown how easily certain lives – people who are older and people with underlying conditions – can become linked in public discourse, and, unfortunately, how both groups can be easily discounted or devalued at times. The pandemic has also highlighted the need for collective responses within and across countries. Instead of valorising self-sufficiency above all else, connectedness, collective approaches and belonging are the most authentic ways to address the fragility that inheres in all our lives. All of this should bring home the need for developing discourses of disability and ageing that model how life (lived with adequate support) can continue to be experienced as meaningful and rewarding, and that also facilitate integration of more difficult aspects of the experiences concerned.

Implications for public policy

This final section draws together key points on public policies referred to in previous chapters. The review of international policies in Chapter 4 suggests that problems arise in policies both because of artificial bureaucratic distinctions based on chronological age, *and* from applying approaches associated with disability activism to the social care of older people without sufficient scrutiny of all the issues involved. Many countries have moved to individualised or personalised approaches to social care, associated with disability activism but also implemented as a means to reduce costs in anticipation of demographic ageing. Often undertaken concurrently with funding reductions, this has had consequences, including, in several cases, institutionalising ageism (with age ceilings applied in access to some services and supports). While the personalisation of care results in more choice and flexibility for some disabled people, as Kelly (2010) argues, the needs of others are unaccounted for within the type of political demands that have dominated disability activism. These include demands for direct payments, which implicitly position rational, independent decision-making as the ultimate 'ability'.

There are examples of bridging initiatives between the separate policy frameworks of disability and ageing which signal that there may be gains in bringing the two policy worlds closer together, or at least in having more interchange and learning between them. To do this would involve interrogation of their respective definitions, informing philosophies and concepts, and resulting standards and practices, including their use of technology. These exchanges could benefit all older disabled people, and they are vital for people ageing with disability (AwithD group), who require an active interchange between the two sectors. This highlights the need for more research linked to policymaking that bridges the fields of disability and ageing. As Putnam (2014) suggests, building capacity to conduct bridging research should be a high priority for practitioners, policymakers and scholars working on ageing and disability.

Several of the study's findings challenge societies to respond to ageing with a more communal approach that emphasises the social, not the biological. These include the fact that older disabled people experienced exclusion due to inaccessible physical environments and due to disablist social relations in families and in communities. Death among intimates and reducing social networks could also result in experiencing more disablement, which, the book argues, is a systemic issue in older age that requires collective responses. Experience of suffering and disruption that the study evidences, and the fact that participants engaged in dynamic processes in response, represents a challenge for governments and communities to support all older people to meet the need for lives of value and meaning.

Public services played a major role in the lives of many participants, and some service models and community organising could help translate aspirations for a meaningful life into more of a reality. These included approaches that were supportive and facilitative of choice making and control, and of participation and connection with others. Not least, this means that public policies must aim to ensure that all the participation opportunities that communities offer are inclusive of all older disabled people. They also need to educate more about how ableism as well as unacknowledged disablism and ageism operate as barriers to greater participation.

Community centres (for older people and disabled people) were also important in the lives of many participants, and the nature of those services and the quality of activities they offered had a big impact, as did the relationships they involved. They could also play a role in forming the collective identification of participants, and contact with other disabled people or disability activism could be empowering (even for people first experiencing disability later in life). Participants valued provision of accessible transport, kindness and competence of staff, activities involving challenge and learning, and social opportunities that connected them to others and enabled them to contribute. Thus, the findings highlight the importance of social and collective aspects of support and care, and suggest that services should also aim to provide opportunities for self-development and contribution. Public approaches to ageing therefore need to have a broad approach, encompassing community, environmental, housing, cultural and other aspects.

Policies for ageing populations need a specific engagement with experiences of people ageing with disability (AwithD), or with people experiencing disability over the long term, because of the cumulative disadvantage involved. Otherwise, their position from age 65 on may be worked out in ways that are not transparent or consistent. There also needs to be a particular focus on anyone ageing without social and financial resources. Finally, people ageing with disability (and, indeed, other older disabled people) may be able to contribute a more holistic appreciation of what it means to live a fulfilling life with disability in older age, something absent in dominant 'positive' or 'active ageing' discourse and policies. We need to articulate what these concepts mean for older disabled people. This is an issue for those promoting international policy approaches, as well as for national governments.

Concluding remarks

The key finding of the present study that older disabled people are engaged in processes of seeking to have lives they perceive as meaningful represents a challenge for governments and societies. Another challenge is represented by the fact that the emphasis on the social that informs theorising, models and policy frameworks on disability is at least as valuable for older disabled people as it is for disabled people generally. Finally, that similar barriers exclude disabled people of all ages, and that the social devaluation of ageing and disability are intertwined, points to the need for more unified approaches to disability. Instead, lives would be better if societies were more accepting of disability as a normal part of life at some stage, not some kind of individual failure, and if all older people were recognised as still involved in both challenge and growth. This requires a reorientation in general thinking about ageing and disability, and recognition of how disability is an issue for all ages.

Methodological annexe

Here I outline the methodology and key methods used in the empirical study that informs the book, introduced already in Chapter 5. I set out the inclusion and exclusion criteria for participation, and summarise key participant demographic details. Finally, I briefly outline the processes of analysis and refer to ethical issues and limitations.

Methodology

One strength of qualitative research is its ability to explicate the meaning of something from the viewpoint of the people involved. As an objective of this study was to explore experiences and meanings made of disablement processes, a biographical narrative method and an inductive constructivist grounded theory method were appropriate. Narrative research conveys tacit assumptions and norms of individuals and cultural groups (Wengraf, 2001). Biographical narrative was therefore a method that could, among other things, focus on how participants made sense of events and actions in their lives, empower them to co-determine important issues, and illuminate the impact of social structures on them (Elliott, 2005).

Grounded theory serves as a way to learn about the worlds we study and a method for developing theories to understand them (Charmaz, 2014: 17). A grounded theory method fitted with the research questions because it is suited to attempts to understand the process by which actors construct meaning out of intersubjective experience (Suddaby, 2006: 634). Charmaz developed what she terms a constructivist approach to grounded theory (Charmaz, 2000, 2014; see also Silverman, 2010). For Charmaz (2014: 154, 277), a constructivist approach assumes that researchers engage in an interpretive portrayal of the studied world, that is, neither the data nor theories are *discovered*; rather, we construct grounded theories through past and present involvements and interactions with people, perspectives and research practices. Thus, for Charmaz (2014: 14), 'subjectivity is inseparable from social existence', and she explains that her constructivist approach aligns with the form that social constructionism takes today, also distinguishing her position from those who take a radical subjectivist stance. The emphasis that Charmaz places on subjectivity of the researcher fits well with a critical gerontological approach, in which researchers reflect on their own roles in the production of knowledge (Holstein and Minkler, 2007; Ziegler and Scharf, 2014: 158).

Charmaz (2014: 15) envisages a flexible approach to address different research questions, and outlines the following steps pursued by grounded theorists:

1. conduct data collection and analysis simultaneously in an iterative process;
2. analyse actions and processes rather than themes and structure;
3. use comparative methods;
4. draw on data to develop new conceptual categories;
5. develop inductive abstract analytic categories through systematic data analysis;
6. emphasise theory construction rather than description or application of current theories;
7. engage in theoretical sampling;
8. search for variation in the studied categories or process; and
9. pursue developing a category rather than covering a specific empirical topic.

I progressed through all the aforementioned steps except for item 7 (theoretical sampling), which was very limited in this study. Charmaz (2014: 5) views actions 1 to 5 as 'evidence of a grounded theory study' rather than evidence of grounded theory. I characterise my approach as a grounded theory study. The categories set up at the outset of this study (DwithA and AwithD) were intended to enable comparison between groups whose experiences are generally thought to be different. However, while I did pursue my 'analytic direction' (Charmaz, 2014: 99) in later interviews, emphasising these categories meant a sampling process that was more purposive than theoretical.

Intensive interviewing is the most typical approach to interviews used by grounded theorists (Charmaz, 2014: 85). Following pilot interviews, I used an open-ended or narrative interview, also called 'unstructured interactive interviews' (Corbin and Morse, 2003). I used an open-ended question at the outset to help build rapport and to enable participants to set the agenda. The initial opening question was an invitation to tell one's life story. This approach helped to open up enquiry and was helpful in conducting a genuinely grounded enquiry (Timonen et al, 2018). I afterwards asked questions and sought clarifications based on the stories told. I ended interviews with disability questions from the Irish Census (discussed later). Interviews were audio-recorded and transcribed verbatim.

Recruitment and inclusion criteria

I sought to get away from medical-model framings based on diagnostic categories and, other than seeking participants experiencing physical or sensory disability, I did not consider the cause of impairment important. The focus on experiences of physical and sensory disability was for conceptual and practical reasons. For example, rates of physical disability and sensory disability are among those that increase most with age (Central Statistics Office, 2017; see also Table E9006, Central Statistics Office, 2020). Also, experiences of physical disability are particularly neglected in research into ageing with disability (Bishop and Hobson, 2015), and the area of sensory disability is most neglected of all (Simcock, 2017).

When it came to defining what is 'older', there were options. A threshold of age 65+ was most obvious for both groups. For the AwithD group, however, a lower age threshold might have been appropriate because of possible secondary conditions with ageing and more rapid ageing. Age thresholds used in empirical studies with this group differ. For example, Cooper and Bigby (2014: 422) took age 50+ as older, Bishop and Hobson (2015) used age 65+, and Zarb and Oliver (1993) relied on self-identification as 'older'. I chose an age threshold for both groups of 65+, which does not imply acceptance of the administratively defined notion of age 65 as the entry point to older age. It was more difficult to access participants in the AwithD group. Thus, three people ageing with disability who were not aged 65 were included (aged, respectively, 55, 60 and 61) on pragmatic grounds.

Another question was how long someone had to have experienced disability to be said to be in the AwithD group, and, correspondingly, how early or late one might have experienced disability to be considered in the DwithA group. Literature suggests that people experiencing disability from birth or in early to midlife are considered to age with disability (AwithD) (Verbrugge and Yang, 2002; Naidoo et al, 2012). Correspondingly, people experiencing disability in mid- or late life are considered to experience disability with ageing (DwithA), with midlife characterised as ages 45 to 64 (Verbrugge and Yang, 2002). I also considered the age thresholds used in a range of empirical studies with people from the AwithD group, which varied considerably (Zarb and Oliver, 1993; Jeppsson Grassman et al, 2012; Holme, 2013; Cooper and Bigby, 2014; Bishop and Hobson, 2015). They included having experienced disability for at least three years before age 65 (Bishop and Hobson, 2015, in a study with people with adult-onset disability) to having lived with impairment for at least 40 years (Cooper and Bigby, 2014), and having considered oneself disabled for at least 20 years (Zarb and Oliver, 1993). I opted for the following categorisations:

1. **Group 1 (AwithD)**: people ageing with disability, meaning they first experienced disability between birth and age 45 ($n = 18$); and
2. **Group 2 (DwithA)**: people who began to experience disability with ageing (from age 45) ($n = 24$).

All but one participant from Group 1 (AwithD) had lived with disability for at least 20 years, and most participants in Group 2 (DwithA) had experienced disability onset after age 60.

I recruited the majority of participants through disability and age-sector organisations. I worked with staff or volunteers, who were asked to invite people to participate who met the following criteria for the DwithA group:

1. men or women aged 65 years or over;
2. having long-standing disability experienced with ageing (that is, since aged 45);
3. the principal disability experienced to be of mobility or dexterity, sight, or hearing (that is, one or more);
4. living at home (alone or with family or others);
5. cognitively and physically able to participate;
6. able to give informed consent; and
7. willing to participate in the study.

By 'long-standing' was meant having lasted for six months or more, or tending to reoccur regularly, in line with the 2011 Irish Census questionnaire (Central Statistics Office, 2012a). In practice, participants' experiences of disability tended to be much longer than this.

For the AwithD group, I used the same criteria as already listed, save for item 2, which in this case was:

2. experiencing long-standing disability, the onset of which occurred before age 45.

One of the disability centres, unusually in an Irish context, included clients experiencing disability onset after age 65. Another mainly worked with lifelong Deaf people but also ran self-support groups for people experiencing hearing impairment after age 65. I used personal contacts to reach a small number of other participants, principally to include people not involved in disability/older people's centres. I conducted pilot interviews with three people from this group and also took advice from them on the study design and communications.

There were several considerations in relation to how the study would determine if participants were 'disabled'. It could be hypothesised that AwithD participants might self-identify as 'disabled', though that could not be taken for granted. However, the DwithA group would be unlikely to do so. I took two approaches:

- accessing most participants through gatekeepers, who identified potential participants as disabled; and
- including specific questions at the interview stage that would seek self-reported information.

Disability surveys typically do not rely on disability self-identification and instead seek self-reporting on conditions and functional difficulties (United Nations Department of Economic and Social Affairs, 2008; Priestley et al, 2016: 3). I decided to use disability questions (questions 16 and 17) from the 2011 Irish national Census (Central Statistics Office, 2012a) for categorisation purposes. Question 16 enquires about the nature of 'long-lasting conditions or difficulties' and specifies seven possible disability types that are phrased in general terms, not diagnostic categories.[1] Question 17 enquires about four types of limitations to functioning.[2] If people answered 'yes' to any of the categories in either question, they would be categorised as disabled according to the Census.

Thus, disability categorisation questions were added to a largely unstructured narrative interview format, intended to conform to how disability rates are calculated at a national (and supranational) level. The questions were straightforward and relatively brief. Testing and consulting on them during pilot interviews suggested that they could be incorporated at the end of an otherwise largely unstructured interview without difficulty. I added a question about self-reported level of difficulty (from a five-point scale of 'no difficulty' to 'a lot of difficulty' and 'cannot do at all') alongside Census questions 16 and 17. This was because disability severity is linked to significantly less social participation (Gannon et al, 2005). This scale had been used in the Irish National Disability Survey and is similar to that recommended in international approaches to measurement of disability prevalence (see United Nations Washington Group on Disability Statistics, 2008).

As acknowledged in Chapter 5, these categorisation measures are somewhat crude. To cultural or critical disability scholars, they may represent attempts to solidify firm definitions based on bodily issues, where disability is a malleable category constructed through discourse. However, not to attempt categorisation would have been to leave open the question as to whether study participants, particularly people first experiencing disability with ageing, could be considered within the category 'disabled' at all, even in medical or functional terms.

There were other aspects to the study, including interviews with a small group of older people not experiencing disability, as well as with policymakers and service providers. I refer throughout the book to some findings from the policy aspect of the study (see Leahy, 2018).

Participant profile

All participants were living in their homes in the community; several lived in housing complexes for seniors or for disabled people. They were interviewed between 2015 and 2017. Table 1 sets out key participant characteristics.

Ages and gender

There were 42 participants, with an age range of 55–90 years. The mean age was 74.1 and the median was 72.5. There were 18 among the AwithD group whose ages ranged from 55 to 90, including three aged under 65. There were 24 participants among the DwithA group, whose ages ranged from 65 to 88. There were more women than men (F = 25; M = 17). This was justifiable as, according to the 2011 Census, of the 204,069 people aged 65+ who were disabled in Ireland, almost 60 per cent were women, while men represented just over 40 per cent (Central Statistics Office (2012d), calculated from CSO online database CD801). These are almost identical to the sample proportions.

Impairment types and severity

Participants were experiencing a range of impairment types, including mobility issues and hearing and vision impairment. Participants' narratives referred to a range of diagnoses. For example, mobility issues could relate to conditions that included cerebral palsy, amputation (due to accident or an underlying condition), stroke or arthritis, or

Table 1: Participant characteristics

	Disability with ageing (DwithA): onset after age 45 ($N = 24$)	Ageing with disability (AwithD): onset before age 45 ($N = 18$)	All participants ($N = 42$)
Sex			
Male	12	5	17
Female	12	13	25
Total	**24**	**18**	**42**
Age			
50s	0	1	1
60s	7	9	16
70s	8	3	11
80s	9	4	13
90s	0	1	1
Age range	65–88	55–90	55–90
Family status			
Single	4	7	11
Married	11	3	14
Widowed	6	5	11
Separated/ divorced	3	3	6
Geographical locations			
City	14	11	25
Town	2	2	4
Village	4	2	6
Rural	4	3	7
Socio-economic status			
Low	7	8	15
Medium	10	7	17
High	7	3	10
Disability type (primary)			
Mobility	19	14	33
Vision	2	4	6
Hearing	1	0	1
Other	2	0	2

(continued)

Table 1: Participant characteristics (continued)

	Disability with ageing (DwithA): onset after age 45 (N = 24)	Ageing with disability (AwithD): onset before age 45 (N = 18)	All participants (N = 42)
Decade of disability onset			
Birth	–	6	6
0–9	–	2	2
10–19	–	3	3
20–29	–	1	1
30–39	–	3	3
40–44	–	3	3
45–49	2	–	2
50–59	8	–	8
60–69	4	–	4
70–79	6	–	6
80–89	4	–	4
Highest level of disability severity (self-reported level of difficulty)[a]			
No difficulty	1	3	4
Just a little	4	1	5
Moderate level	7	3	10
A lot of difficulty	5	3	8
Cannot do at all	6	8	14

Note: [a] One participant did not complete the Census questionnaire because she had to cut the interview short and, unfortunately, died before a second interview was arranged.

to progressive conditions like multiple sclerosis. Visual impairment could also have a range of causes; it could be congenital or arise from an accident or a condition like macular degeneration. Alternatively, participants could be vague about the exact cause of a mobility or sensory issue (especially if experienced gradually with ageing). Some were very clear when onset had occurred; others described gradual onset and could not say exactly when conditions started. Many participants were experiencing more than one impairment, and, if so, I asked which caused most difficulty.

A difficulty with mobility was the commonest primary type of disability identified, and a difficulty with vision was the second commonest (33 and 6 participants, respectively). A total of 32 participants (around three quarters) identified more than one disability type. Their narratives often involved interconnecting experiences of, say, mobility difficulties and pain or hearing/sight impairment, to which the list of 'primary' disability types listed in Table 1 does not altogether do justice.

A total of 22 participants (just over half) could be categorised as experiencing disability at the most severe level on the basis that in at least one domain, they experienced 'a lot of difficulty' or 'cannot do at all'. There were 11 people in this category in both DwithA and AwithD groups. In assessing severity of impairment, I did not include responses to one part of question 17 of the Census – about working or attending school or college – as most participants did not consider this relevant to them.

Other demographic information

Participants lived in a range of locations (cities, towns, villages and rural areas) and they were mixed in terms of family status – in being single, married, widowed or separated/divorced. None identified as LGBTQ. All but one was white Irish. In this respect, they were quite homogeneous and reflect a particular demographic in Ireland at present.

I took a pragmatic approach to categorisation for socio-economic status (SES) based on participants' life narratives, using the occupational status categorisation from the Irish Central Statistics Office (2012b, 2012c). I grouped participants into three categories of high, middle and low SES based on their last occupation (adopting the approach of Timonen et al (2013)). Thus, 15 (36 per cent) were categorised as having low SES, 17 (40 per cent) as having middle SES, and ten (24 per cent) as having high SES. Following Census guidelines, participants who had never worked were categorised into an SES category based on either their partner's SES or that of their family of origin.

Data analysis and development of categories

I listened back to recordings, read and reread transcripts, and made memos during all stages of the analysis, including immediately after each interview and immediately after coding each new transcript. I also considered similarities and differences in each case. Charmaz (2014: 140) advises keeping 'your involvement in mind as you proceed' and these reflections contributed to the development of categories or to a slightly higher level of abstraction.

I started coding and comparison almost as soon as interviews started, and I continued as I interviewed. Initial coding resulted in hundreds of different sub-codes and over 5,200 coded segments. I engaged in constant comparison to find similarities and differences (Charmaz, 2014: 132). The analysis process is not a linear one. However, stated in linear terms, another stage in a constructivist analysis is focused coding, requiring 'decisions about which initial codes make most analytic sense', and thinking about the ones that may be promising 'tentative categories' (Charmaz, 2014: 138, 140).

The open codes could be encompassed by three main categories:

1. **Category 1:** disabling bodies
2. **Category 2:** disabling/enabling contexts
3. **Category 3:** responding to challenges

The overarching concept that encompasses the three is '**seeking to remake lives that make sense**', which 'renders the data most effectively' (Charmaz, 2014: 247). Thus, the story of the data I identified was that processes of disablement and (often) the simultaneous loss of intimates and shrinking social circles could create a sense that life was less meaningful, and participants were engaged in a process of responding by seeking to remake lives that make sense.

Ethical issues

As some participants could be characterised as vulnerable, the ethical approval process was rigorous. The relevant Maynooth University Ethics Committee approved the study, as did the ethics committee of one disability organisation which helped with recruitment.

Information about the study was made available in accessible formats and, in all cases, I checked that participants had read the information before interview (or were otherwise familiar with the contents) and whether they had any questions. I checked that they were comfortable with being audio-recorded. Interviewees signed consent forms except in the case of visually impaired participants, where I recorded the consent process, something anticipated in the ethical approvals.

Limitations

The different categories set up at the outset were perhaps both a strength and a limitation: inevitably, there are smaller numbers of representative interviewees in each category than there might otherwise have been. The limitations of this are particularly obvious for one category (AwithD) given that participants were so diverse. On the other hand, the categories enabled exploration of different lifecourse experiences of disability and of similarities and differences between the groups. Another issue is that only people who had the ability to verbally communicate participated and so the sample is biased towards people able-bodied enough to share their stories.

An obvious limitation is the relative homogeneity of the sample in terms of race/ethnic origin and sexual orientation. Another possible limitation is that I recruited more women in one category – AwithD – than men (F = 13; M = 5). While the greater number of women in the study is justifiable overall, as it reflects the wider demographic context (discussed already), it would have been preferable to have had a better balance between men and women in the AwithD sample. However, this would have required a much longer fieldwork timetable.

Notes

[1] Question 16 of the 2011 Irish national Census regarding 'long-lasting conditions or difficulties' includes the following categories: (1) blindness or a serious vision impairment; (2) deafness or a severe hearing impairment; (3) a difficulty with basic physical activities such as walking, climbing stairs, reaching, lifting or carrying; (4) an intellectual disability; (5) difficulty with learning, remembering or concentrating; (6) psychological or emotional condition; (7) a difficulty with pain, breathing or any other chronic illness or condition (see Central Statistics Office, 2012a).

[2] Question 17 of the 2011 Irish national Census regarding 'difficulty in doing' includes the following limitations: (1) dressing, bathing or getting around inside the home; (2) going outside the home alone to shop or visit a doctor's surgery; (3) working at a job or business or attending school or college; (4) participating in other activities, for example, leisure or using transport (see Central Statistics Office, 2012a).

References

Abberley, P. (1987) 'The concept of oppression and the development of a social theory of disability', *Disability, Handicap & Society*, 2(1): 5–19.

AGE Platform Europe (2017) *Feedback on Draft of General Comment on Article 5 Equality & Non-discrimination Submission by AGE Platform Europe*, Brussels: AGE Platform Europe.

AGE Platform Europe (2019) *Questionnaire on the Rights of Older People with Disabilities: Contribution AGE Platform Europe*, Brussels: Age Platform Europe. Available at: www.age-platform.eu/sites/default/files/AGE_contribution_on_rights_of_older_persons_with_disabilities-April2019.pdf

Amundson, R. (1992) 'Disability, handicap, and the environment', *Journal of Social Philosophy*, 23(1): 105–19.

Applebaum, R. and Mahoney, K. (2016) 'Expanding self direction and its impact on quality', *Public Policy & Aging Report*, 26(4): 138–42. Available at: http://dx.doi.org/10.1093/ppar/prw022

Arber, S. and Ginn, J. (1995) 'Gender differences in informal caring', *Health & Social Care in the Community*, 3(1): 19–31.

Arvig, T. (2006) 'Meaning in life for individuals with physical disabilities', *Psychological Reports*, 98 (3): 683–8.

Aubrecht, K. and Keefe, J. (2016) 'The becoming subject of dementia', *Review of Disability Studies: An International Journal*, 12(2/3): 137–54.

Aubrecht, K., Kelly, C. and Rice, C. (2020) 'Introduction', in Aubrecht, K., Kelly, C. and Rice, C. (eds) *The Aging–Disability Nexus*, Toronto: UBC Press.

Australian Institute of Health and Welfare (2006) *National Evaluation of the Aged Care Innovative Pool Disability Aged Care Interface Pilot: Final Report. Aged Care Series No. 12, Cat. No. AGE 50*, Canberra: Australian Institute of Health and Welfare.

Ayalon, L. and Tesch-Römer, C. (2018) 'Introduction to the section: ageism – concept and origins', in Ayalon, L. and Tesch-Römer, C. (eds) *Contemporary Perspectives on Ageism*, Cham, Switzerland: Springer Open, pp 1–10.

Baars, J. (2010) 'Philosophy of aging, time, and finitude', in Cole, T., Ray, R. and Kastenbaum, R. (eds) *A Guide to Humanistic Studies in Aging: What Does It Mean to Grow Old*, Baltimore, MD: Johns Hopkins University Press, pp 105–20.

Baars, J. (2017) 'Aging: learning to live a finite life', *The Gerontologist*, 57(5): 969–76.

Baars, J. and Phillipson, C. (2014) 'Connecting meaning with social structure: theoretical foundations', in Baars, J., Dohmen, J., Grenier, A. and Phillipson, C. (eds) *Ageing, Meaning and Social Structure: Connecting Critical and Humanistic Gerontology*, Bristol: Policy Press, pp 11–30.

Baars, J., Dannefer, D., Phillipson, C. and Walker, A. (2006) *Aging, Globalization, and Inequality: The New Critical Gerontology*, Amityville, NY: Baywood.

Baltes, P.B. and Baltes, M.M. (1990a) *Successful Aging: Perspectives from the Behavioural Sciences*, Cambridge: Cambridge University Press.

Baltes, P.B. and Baltes, M.M. (1990b) 'Psychological perspectives on successful aging: the model of selective optimization with compensation', in Baltes, P.B. and Baltes, M.M. (eds) *Successful Aging: Perspectives from the Behavioural Sciences*, Cambridge: Press Syndicate of University of Cambridge, pp 1–34.

Barnes, C. (1997) 'A legacy of oppression: a history of disability in Western culture', in Barton, L. and Oliver, M. (eds) *Disability Studies: Past, Present and Future*, Leeds: The Disability Press, pp 3–24.

Barnes, C. (1998) 'The social model of disability: a sociological phenomenon ignored by sociologists', in Shakespeare, T. (ed) *The Disability Reader: Social Science Perspectives*, London: Cassell, pp 65–78.

Barnes, C. and Mercer, G. (1996) 'Introduction: exploring the divide', in Barnes, C. and Mercer, G. (eds) *Exploring the Divide: Illness and Disability*, Leeds: The Disability Press, pp 11–16.

Barnes, C. and Mercer, G. (2006) *Independent Futures. Creating User-Led Disability Services in a Disabling Society*, Bristol: Policy Press.

Barnes, C. and Mercer, G. (2010) *Exploring Disability*, 2nd edn, Cambridge: Polity Press.

Barnes, M. (2011) 'Abandoning care? A critical perspective on personalisation from an ethic of care', *Ethics and Social Welfare*, 5(2): 153–67.

Baumeister, R.F. (1991) *Meanings of Life*, New York: Guilford Press.

Baumeister, R.F. (2005) *The Cultural Animal: Human Nature, Meaning, and Social Life*, Oxford: Oxford University Press.

Baumeister, R.F., Maranges, H.M. and Vohs, K.D. (2017) 'Human self as information agent: functioning in a social environment based on shared meanings', *Review of General Psychology*, 22(1): 36–47.

Bê, A. (2012) 'Feminism and disability: a cartography of multiplicity', in Watson, N., Roulstone, A. and Thomas, C. (eds) *Routledge Handbook of Disability Studies*, London: Routledge, pp 363–75.

Bê, A. (2016) 'Disablism in the lives of people living with a chronic illness in England and Portugal', *Disability & Society*, 31(4): 465–80.

Bê, A. (2019) 'Disabled people and subjugated knowledges: new understandings and strategies developed by people living with chronic conditions', *Disability & Society*, 34(9–19): 1334–52.

Becker, G. (1997) *Disrupted Lives. How People Create Meaning in a Chaotic World*, Los Angeles, CA: University of California Press.

Becker, G. and Kaufman, S.R. (1995) 'Managing an uncertain illness trajectory in old age: patients' and physicians' views', *Medical Anthropology Quarterly*, 9(2): 165–87.

Bengtson, V.L., Putney, N.M. and Johnson, M.L. (2005) 'The problem of theory in gerontology today', in Johnson, M.L. (ed) *The Cambridge Handbook of Age and Ageing*, Cambridge: Cambridge University Press, pp 3–20.

Beresford, P. (2008) *What Future for Care?*, York: Joseph Rowntree Foundation.

Berghs, M., Atkin, K.M., Graham, H.M., Hatton, C. and Thomas, C. (2016) 'Implications for public health research of models and theories of disability: a scoping study and evidence synthesis', *Public Health Research*, 4(8).

Berghs, M., Atkin, K., Hatton, C. and Thomas, C. (2019) 'Do disabled people need a stronger social model: a social model of human rights?', *Disability & Society*, 34(7/8): 1034–9.

Bernard, M. and Scharf, T. (2007) 'Critical perspectives on ageing societies', in Bernard, M. and Scharf, T. (eds) *Critical Perspectives on Ageing Societies*, Bristol: Policy Press, pp 3–12.

Bickenbach, J. (2011) 'The world report on disability', *Disability & Society*, 26(5): 655–8.

Bickenbach, J., Chatterji, S., Badley, E.M. and Ustun, T.B. (1999) 'Models of disablement, universalism and the international classification of impairments', *Social Science & Medicine*, 48(9): 1173–87.

Bickenbach, J., Bigby, C., Salvador-Carulla, L., Heller, T., Leonardi, M., LeRoy, B., Mendez, J., Putnam, M. and Spindel, A. (2012) 'The Toronto declaration on bridging knowledge, policy and practice in aging and disability: Toronto, Canada, March 30, 2012', *International Journal of Integrated Care*, 12 (8).

Bigby, C. (2002) 'Ageing people with a lifelong disability: challenges for the aged care and disability sectors', *Journal of Intellectual and Developmental Disability*, 27(4): 231–41.

Bigby, C. (2008) 'Beset by obstacles: a review of Australian policy development to support ageing in place for people with intellectual disability', *Journal of Intellectual and Developmental Disability*, 33(1): 76–86.

Bishop, K. and Hobson, S.J.G. (2015) 'Perceptions of aging for persons with adult-onset disability', *Journal of Canadian Gerontological Nursing Association*, 37(4): 6–19.

Bode, C., Taal, E., Westerhof, G.J., van Gessel, L. and van de Laar, M.V. (2012) 'Experience of aging in patients with rheumatic disease: a comparison with the general population', *Aging & Mental Health*, 16(5): 666–72.

Boudiny, K. (2013) '"Active ageing": from empty rhetoric to effective policy tool', *Ageing and Society*, 33(6): 1077–98.

Bowling, A. and Dieppe, P. (2005) 'What is successful ageing and who should define it?', *British Medical Journal*, 331(7531): 1548–51.

Bowling, A., Farquhar, M. and Grundy, E. (2008) 'Associations with changes in level of functional ability. Results from a follow-up survey at two and a half years of people aged 85 years and over at baseline interview', *Ageing and Society*, 14(1): 53–73.

Brennan, C., Traustadóttir, R., Anderberg, P. and Rice, J. (2016) 'Are cutbacks to personal assistance violating Sweden's obligations under the UN Convention on the Rights of Persons with Disabilities?', *Laws*, 5(2).

Brisenden, S. (1998 [1986]) 'Independent living and the medical model of disability', in Shakespeare, T. (ed) *The Disability Reader: Social Science Perspectives*, London: Cassell, pp 20–7.

Bülow, P. and Svensson, T. (2013) 'Being one's illness: on mental disability and ageing', in Jeppsson Grassman, E. and Whitaker, A. (eds) *Ageing with Disability: A Lifecourse Perspective*, Bristol: Policy Press, pp 73–90.

Burchardt, T. (2000) *The Dynamics of Being Disabled. CASEpaper 36*, London: Centre for Analysis of Social Exclusion, London School of Economics.

BURDIS (Burden of Disease Network Project) (2004) *Disability in Old Age: Final Report, Conclusions and Recommendations*, Jyvaskyla: Jyvaskyla University Press.

Bury, M. (1982) 'Chronic illness as biographical disruption', *Sociology of Health and Illness*, 4(2): 167–82.

Bury, M. (1988) 'Meanings at risk: the experience of arthritis', in Anderson, R. and Bury, M. (eds) *Living with Chronic Illness: The Experience of Patients and Their Families*, London: Unwin Hyman, pp 89–116.

Bury, M. (1991) 'The sociology of chronic illness: a review of research and prospects', *Sociology of Health and Illness*, 13(4): 451–68.

Bury, M. (1997) *Health and Illness in a Changing Society*, London: Routledge.

Bury, M. (2000) 'Health, ageing and the lifecourse', in Williams, S.J., Gabe, J. and Calnan, M. (eds) *Health, Medicine and Society: Key Theories, Future Agendas*, London: Routledge, pp 87–100.

Butler, R.N. (1969) 'Age-ism: another form of bigotry', *Gerontologist*, 9(4.1): 243–6.

Calasanti, T.M. (2019) 'On the intersections of age, gender and sexualities in research on ageing', in King, A., Almack, K. and Jones, R.L. (eds) *Intersections of Ageing, Gender and Sexualities: Multidisciplinary International Perspectives*, Bristol: Policy Press, pp 13–30.

Calasanti, T.M. and Slevin, K.F. (2006) 'Introduction: age matters', in Calasanti, T., Slevin, M. and Kathleen, F. (ed) *Age Matters: Realigning Feminist Thinking*, New York: Taylor and Francis, pp 1–18.

Caldwell, J.T., Lee, H. and Cagney, K.A. (2019) 'Disablement in context: neighborhood characteristics and their association with frailty onset among older adults', *The Journals of Gerontology: Series B*, 74(7): e40–9.

Campbell, F.K. (2001) 'Inciting legal fictions: "disability's" date with ontology and the ableist body of the law', *Griffith Law Review*, 10(1): 42–62.

Campbell, F.K. (2008) 'Exploring internalized ableism using critical race theory', *Disability & Society*, 23(2): 151–62.

Campbell, F.K. (2009) *Contours of Ableism: The Production of Disability and Abledness*, Basingstoke: Palgrave Macmillan.

Campbell, F.K. (2017) 'Queer anti-sociality and disability unbecoming: an ableist relations project?', in Sircar, O. and Jain, D. (eds) *New Intimacies, Old Desires: Law, Culture and Queer Politics in Neoliberal Times*, New Delhi: Zubaan, pp 280–316.

Cancian, F.M. and Oliker, S.J. (2000) *Caring and Gender*, Walnut Creek, CA: Rowman & Littlefield.

Carey, G., Malbon, E., Olney, S. and Reeders, D. (2018) 'The personalisation agenda: the case of the Australian National Disability Insurance Scheme', *International Review of Sociology*, 28(1): 20–34.

Carpentier, N., Bernard, P., Grenier, A. and Guberman, N. (2010) 'Using the life course perspective to study the entry into the illness trajectory: the perspective of caregivers of people with Alzheimer's disease', *Social Science & Medicine*, 70(10): 1501–8.

Carter Anand, J., Davidson, G., Macdonald, G., Kelly, B., Clift-Matthews, V., Martin, A. and Rizzo, M. (2012) *The Transition to Personal Budgets for People with Disabilities: A Review of Practice in Specified Jurisdictions*, Dublin: National Disability Authority.

Central Statistics Office (2012a) *Profile 8: Our Bill of Health – Health, Disability and Carers in Ireland*, Dublin: Stationery Office.

Central Statistics Office (2012b) *This is Ireland: Highlights from Census 2011, Part 2 Appendix 4*, Dublin: Stationery Office.

Central Statistics Office (2012c) *Census 2011 Profile 3: At Work. Statistical Tables and Appendices Pages 74/75*, Dublin: Stationery Office.

Central Statistics Office (2012d) Online database interactive tables: CD801: Persons with a disability as a percentage of all population by age group, sex, census year and statistic. Available at: www.cso.ie/en/census/census2011reports/census2011profile8ourbillofhealth-healthdisabilityandcarersinireland/

Central Statistics Office (2017) 'Census of population 2016 – profile 9 health, disability and carers'. Available at: www.cso.ie/en/releasesandpublications/ep/p-cp9hdc/p8hdc/

Central Statistics Office (2020) Online database interactive tables: E9006, population 2011 to 2016. Available at: https://data.cso.ie/

Chamberlayne, P., Bornat, J. and Wengraf, T. (2000) 'Introduction: the biographical turn', in Chamberlayne, P., Bornat, J. and Wengraf, T. (eds) *The Turn to Biographical Methods in Social Science. Comparative Issues and Examples*, London: Routledge, pp 1–30.

Chambers, P. (2000) 'Widowhood in later life', in Bernard, M., Philips, J., Machin, L. and Harding Davies, V. (eds) *Women Ageing: Changing Identities, Challenging Myths*, London: Routledge, pp 127–48.

Charmaz, K. (1983) 'Loss of self: a fundamental form of suffering in the chronically ill', *Sociology of Health & Illness*, 5(2): 168–95.

Charmaz, K. (1995) 'The body, identity, and self: adapting to impairment', *The Sociological Quarterly*, 36(4): 657–80.

Charmaz, K. (2000) 'Grounded theory: objectivist and constructivist methods', in Denzin, N.K. and Lincoln, Y.S. (eds) *Handbook of Qualitative Research*, 2nd edn, Thousand Oaks, CA: Sage, pp 509–36.

Charmaz, K. (2005) 'Grounded theory in the 21st century: applications for advancing social justice', in Denzin, N.K. and Lincoln, Y.S. (eds) *The Sage Handbook of Qualitative Research*, 3rd edn, Thousand Oaks, CA: Sage, pp 507–36.

Charmaz, K. (2014) *Constructing Grounded Theory*, 2nd edn, London: Sage.

Chicoine, B., McGuire, D. and Rublin, S.S. (1999) 'Specialty clinic perspectives', in Janicki, M.P. and Dalton, A.J. (eds) *Dementia, Aging and Intellectual Disabilities*, Philadelphia, PA: Brunner/Mazel, pp 278–93.

Chivers, S. (2011) *The Silvering Screen: Old Age and Disability in Cinema*, Toronto: Toronto University Press.

Chivers, S. (2020) 'Cripping care advice: Austerity, advice literature and the troubled link between disability and old age', in Aubrecht, K., Kelly, C. and Rice, C. (eds) *The Aging–Disability Nexus*, Toronto: UBC Press, pp 51–64.

Clarke, P. and Latham, K. (2014) 'Life course health and socioeconomic profiles of Americans aging with disability', *Disability and Health Journal*, 7(1 – Supplement): S15–23.

Clegg, A., Young, J., Iliffe, S., Rikkert, M.O. and Rockwood, K. (2013) 'Frailty in elderly people', *The Lancet*, 381(9868): 752–62.

Cohen, E.S. (1988) 'The elderly mystique: constraints on the autonomy of the elderly with disabilities', *The Gerontologist*, 28(Supplement): 24–31.

Cooper, M. and Bigby, C. (2014) 'Cycles of adaptive strategies over the life course', *Journal of Gerontological Social Work*, 57(5): 421–37.

Corbin, J. and Morse, J.M. (2003) 'The unstructured interactive interview: issues of reciprocity and risks when dealing with sensitive topics', *Qualitative Inquiry*, 9(3): 335–54.

Corker, M. (1999) 'Differences, conflations and foundations: the limits to "accurate" theoretical representation of disabled people's experience?', *Disability & Society*, 14(5): 627–42.

Corker, M. and French, S. (1999) 'Reclaiming discourse in disability studies', in Corker, M. and French, S. (eds) *Disability Discourse*, Buckingham: Open University Press, pp 1–11.

Couture, M., Carbonneau, H. and Raymond, É. (2020) 'Perceived benefits of social participation among older adults living with congenital disabilities or disabilities acquired prior to adulthood', *Loisir et Société*, 43(1): 5–15.

Coyle, C.E. and Mutchler, J.E. (2017) 'Aging with disability: advancement of a cross-disciplinary research network', *Research on Aging*, 39(6): 683–92.

Crimmins, E.M. and Beltrán-Sánchez, H. (2010) 'Mortality and morbidity trends: is there compression of morbidity?', *Journal of Gerontology: Social Sciences*, 66B(1): 75–86.

Cross, M. (2013) 'Demonised, impoverished and now forced into isolation: the fate of disabled people under austerity', *Disability and Society*, 28(5): 719–23.

Crow, L. (1996) 'Including all of our lives: renewing the social model of disability', in Barnes, C. and Mercer, G. (eds) *Exploring the Divide*, Leeds: The Disability Press, pp 55–72.

Cruikshank, M. (2003) *Learning to Be Old: Gender, Culture, and Aging*, Lanham, MD: Rowman & Littlefield.

Cruikshank, M. (2008) 'Aging and identity politics', *Journal of Aging Studies*, 22(2): 147–51.

Cullinan, J., Gannon, B. and O'Shea, E. (2013) 'The welfare implications of disability for older people in Ireland', *The European Journal of Health Economics*, 14(2): 171–83.

Cumming, E. and Henry, W. (1961) *Growing Old: The Process of Disengagement*, New York: Basic Books.

Da Roit, B. and Le Bihan, B. (2010) 'Similar and yet so different: cash-for-care in six European countries' long-term care policies', *Milbank Quarterly*, 88(3): 286–309.

Daniels, R., van Rossum, E., de Witte, L. and van den Heuvel, W. (2008) 'Frailty in older age: concepts and relevance for occupational and physical therapy', *Physical & Occupational Therapy in Geriatrics*, 27(2): 81–95.

Dannefer, D. and Lin, J. (2014) 'Commentary: contingent ageing, naturalisation and some rays of intellectual hope', in Baars, J., Dohmen, J., Grenier, A. and Phillipson, C. (eds) *Ageing, Meaning and Social Structure: Connecting Critical and Humanistic Gerontology*, Bristol: Policy Press, pp 181–95.

Dannefer, D. and Settersten, R.A. (2010) 'The study of the life course: implications for social gerontology', in Dannefer, D. and Phillipson, C. (eds) *The Sage Handbook of Social Gerontology*, London: Sage, pp 3–19.

Darling, R.B. and Heckert, D.A. (2010) 'Orientations toward disability: differences over the lifecourse', *International Journal of Disability, Development and Education*, 57(2): 131–43.

Davis, L.J. (1995) *Enforcing Normalcy: Disability, Deafness, and the Body*, London: Verso.

Davis, L.J. (2013a) 'The end of identity politics: on disability as an unstable category', in Davis, L.J. (ed) *The Disability Studies Reader*, New York: Routledge.

Davis, L.J. (2013b) 'Introduction: normality, power and culture', in Davis, L.J. (ed) *The Disability Studies Reader*, New York: Routledge.

Department of Health and Children (2008) *Tackling Chronic Disease – A Policy Framework for the Management of Chronic Disease*, Dublin: Department of Health.

Derkx, P. (2013) 'Humanism as a meaning frame', in Pinn, A.B. (ed) *What Is Humanism and Why Does It Matter*, Durham: Acumen, pp 42–57.

Derkx, P. (2016) 'Humanism and meaning in life', paper presented at the 'Communities in Later Life: Engaging with Diversity. 45th Annual BSG Conference', Stirling, Scotland.

Derkx, P., Bos, P., Laceulle, H. and Machielse, A. (2020) 'Meaning in life and the experience of older people', *International Journal of Ageing and Later Life*, 14(1): 37–66.

Dittman-Kohli, F. (1990) 'The construction of meaning in old age. Possibilities and constraints', *Ageing and Society*, 10: 279–94.

Duppen, D., Machielse, A., Verté, D., Dury, S., De Donder, L. and D-Scope Consortium (2019) 'Meaning in life for socially frail older adults', *Journal of Community Health Nursing*, 36(2): 65–77.

Edmondson, R. (2015) *Ageing, Insight and Wisdom: Meaning and Practice across the Lifecourse*, Bristol: Policy Press.

Elder, G.H., Jr. (1975) 'Age differentiation and the life course', *Annual Review of Sociology*, 1: 165–90.

Elder, G.H., Jr., Kirkpatrick Johnson, M. and Crosnoe, R. (2003) 'The emergence and development of life course theory', in Mortimer, J. and Shanahan, M. (eds) *Handbook of the Life course*, New York: Springer, pp 3–19.

Elliott, J. (2005) *Using Narrative in Social Research: Qualitative and Quantitative Approaches*, London: Sage.

Erevelles, N. and Minear, A. (2010) 'Unspeakable offenses: untangling race and disability in discourses of intersectionality', *Journal of Literary & Cultural Disability Studies*, 4(2): 127–45.

Esping-Andersen, G. (1990) *The Three Worlds of Welfare Capitalism*, Cambridge: Polity Press.

Estes, C.L. (1979) *The Aging Enterprise*, San Francisco, CA: Jossey Bass.

Estes, C.L., Biggs, S. and Phillipson, C. (2003) *Social Theory, Social Policy and Ageing: A Critical Introduction*, Buckingham: Open University Press.

European Network of National Human Rights Institutions (2016) *The CRPD and Older Persons with Disabilities: The Transition to Community-Based Long-Term Care Services*, Brussels: ENNHRI.

European Network on Independent Living (2015) *Personal Assistance Services Across Europe*, Brussels: European Network on Independent Living.

European Network on Independent Living (2018) 'Submission by the European Network on Independent Living to the 9th session of the Open-ended Working Group on Aging. Topic: autonomy and independence'. Available at: https://enil.eu/news/enil-submission-on-older-people-and-independent-living/

Faircloth, C.A. (2003) 'Introduction: different bodies and the paradox of aging: locating aging bodies in images and everyday experience', in Faircloth, C.A. (ed) *Aging Bodies: Images and Everyday Experience*, Walnut Creek, CA: Altamira, pp 1–26.

Featherstone, M. (1991) 'The body in consumer culture', in Featherstone, M., Hepworth, M. and Turner, B.S. (eds) *The Body, Social Process and Cultural Theory*, London: Sage, pp 170–96.

Featherstone, M. and Hepworth, M. (1991) 'The mask of ageing and the postmodern life course', in Featherstone, M., Hepworth, M. and Turner, B.S. (eds) *The Body: Social Process and Cultural Theory*, London: Sage, pp 371–89.

Featherstone, M. and Hepworth, M. (1995) 'Images of positive ageing', in Featherstone, M. and Wernick, M. (eds) *Images of Ageing*, London: Routledge, pp 29–47.

Feely, M. (2016) 'Disability studies after the ontological turn: a return to the material world and material bodies without a return to essentialism', *Disability & Society*, 31(7): 863–83.

Ferraro, K.F. (2001) 'Aging and role transitions', in Binstock, R.H. and George, L.K. (eds) *Handbook of Aging and the Social Sciences*, 5th edn, New York: Academic Press, pp 313–30.

Fillit, H. and Butler, R.N. (2009) 'The frailty identity crisis', *Journal of the American Geriatrics Society*, 57(2): 348–52.

Fine, M. and Glendinning, C. (2005) 'Dependence, independence or inter-dependence? Revisiting the concepts of "care" and "dependency"', *Ageing and Society*, 25(4): 601–21.

Finkelstein, A., Tenenbaum, A. and Bachner, Y.G. (2020) ' "I will never be old": adults with Down syndrome and their parents talk about ageing-related challenges', *Ageing & Society*, 40(8): 1788–807.

Finkelstein, V. (1981) 'Disability and the helper/helped relationship: an historical view', in Brechin, A., Liddiard, P. and Swain, J. (eds) *Handicap in a Social World*, London: Hodder & Stoughton, pp 12–22.

Finkelstein, V. (1991) 'Disability: an administrative challenge? (The health and welfare heritage)', in Oliver, M. (ed) *Social Work: Disabled People and Disabling Environments*, London: Jessica Kingsley, pp 19–39.

Finkelstein, V. (1998) 'Emancipating disability studies', in Shakespeare, T. (ed) *The Disability Reader: Social Science Perspectives*, London: Cassell, pp 28–49.

Freedman, V.A. (2014) 'Research gaps in the demography of aging with disability', *Disability and Health Journal*, 7(1): S60–3.

Freedman, V.A., Martin, L.G. and Schoeni, R.F. (2002) 'Recent trends in disability and functioning among older adults in the United States: a systematic review', *Jama*, 288(24): 3137–46.

Fried, L.P. and Guralnik, J.M. (1997) 'Disability in older adults: evidence regarding significance, etiology, and risk', *Journal of the American Geriatrics Society*, 45: 92–100.

Fried, L.P., Tangen, C.M., Walston, J., Newman, A.B., Hirsch, C., Gottdiener, J., Seeman, T., Tracy, R., Kop, W.J. and Burke, G. (2001) 'Frailty in older adults: evidence for a phenotype', *The Journals of Gerontology Series A: Biological Sciences and Medical Sciences*, 56(3): M146–57.

Gadsby, E.W., Segar, J., Allen, P., Checkland, K., Coleman, A., McDermott, I. and Peckham, S. (2013) 'Personal budgets, choice and health – a review of international evidence from 11 OECD countries', *International Journal of Public and Private Health Care Management*, 3(3): 15–28.

Gannon, B., Nolan, B. and Economic and Social Research Institute (2005) *Disability and Social Inclusion in Ireland*, Dublin: National Disability Authority and the Equality Authority.

Garabagiu, A. (2009) 'Bridging knowledge in long term care 2009: Council of Europe actions to promote the rights and full inclusion of ageing people with disabilities', *International Journal of Integrated Care*, 9(Supplement)(e24): 1–7.

Garland-Thomson, R. (2002) 'Integrating disability, transforming feminist theory', *NWSA Journal*, 14(3): 1–32.

Garland-Thomson, R. (2016) 'Becoming disabled: roughly one in five Americans lives with a disability. So where is our pride movement?', *New York Times*. Available at: www.nytimes.com/2016/08/21/opinion/sunday/becoming-disabled.html

Garland-Thomson, R. (2019) 'Critical disability studies: a knowledge manifesto', in Ellis, K., Garland-Thomson, R., Kent, M. and Robertson, R. (eds) *Manifestos for the Future of Critical Disability Studies*, London: Routledge.

Gibbons, H.M. (2016) 'Compulsory youthfulness: intersections of ableism and ageism in "successful aging" discourses', *Review of Disability Studies: An International Journal*, 12(2/3): 70–88.

Gilleard, C. (2018) 'Suffering: the darker side of aging', *Journal of Aging Studies*, 44: 28–33.

Gilleard, C. and Higgs, P. (2000) *Cultures of Ageing: Self, Citizen, and the Body*, Harlow: Prentice Hall.

Gilleard, C. and Higgs, P. (2010a) 'Aging without agency: theorizing the fourth age', *Aging & Mental Health*, 14(2): 121–8.

Gilleard, C. and Higgs, P. (2010b) 'Frailty, disability and old age: a re-appraisal', *Health*, 15(5): 475–90.

Gilleard, C. and Higgs, P. (2013) 'The fourth age and the concept of a "social imaginary": a theoretical excursus', *Journal of Aging Studies*, 27(4): 368–76.

Glasby, J. (2011) *Whose Risk Is It Anyway? Risk and Regulation in an Era of Personalisation*, York: Joseph Rowntree Foundation.

Glasby, J. and Littlechild, R. (2016) *Direct Payments and Personal Budgets: Putting Personalisation into Practice*, 3rd edn, Bristol: Policy Press.

Glendinning, C. (2010) 'Continuous and long-term care: European perspectives', in Dannefer, D. and Phillipson, C. (eds) *The Sage Handbook of Social Gerontology*, London: Sage, pp 551–72.

Glendinning, C., Challis, D., Fernández, J.-L., Jacobs, S., Jones, K., Knapp, M., Manthorpe, J., Moran, N., Netten, A., Stevens, M. and Wilberforce, M. (2008) *Evaluation of the Individual Budgets Pilot Programme: Summary Report*, York: Social Policy Research Unit, University of York.

Gobbens, R.J., Luijkx, K.G., Wijnen-Sponselee, M.T. and Schols, J.M. (2010) 'In search of an integral conceptual definition of frailty: opinions of experts', *Journal of the American Medical Directors Association*, 11(5): 338–43.

Goodley, D. (2011) *Disability Studies: An Interdisciplinary Introduction*, London: Sage.

Goodley, D. (2013) 'Dis/entangling critical disability studies', *Disability & Society*, 28(5): 631–44.

Goodley, D. (2014) *Dis/Ability Studies: Theorising Disablism and Ableism*, Abingdon: Routledge.

Goodley, D., Lawthom, R., Liddiard, K. and Runswick-Cole, K. (2019) 'Provocations for critical disability studies', *Disability & Society*, 34(6): 972–97.

Graham, K. (2015) 'Cash payments in context: (self-)regulation in the new social relations of assistance', *Disability & Society*, 30(4): 597–613.

Grammenos, S. (2018) *European Comparative Data on Europe 2020 & People with Disabilities. Final Report on Behalf of the European Network of Academic Experts in the Field of Disability (ANED)*, Brussels: ANED (European Commission). Available at: www.disabilityeurope.net/theme/statistical-indicators

Grenier, A. (2006) 'The distinction between being and feeling frail: exploring emotional experiences in health and social care', *Journal of Social Work Practice*, 20(3): 299–313.

Grenier, A. (2007) 'Constructions of frailty in the English language, care practice and the lived experience', *Ageing and Society*, 27(3): 425–45.

Grenier, A. (2012) *Transitions and the Lifecourse: Challenging the Constructions of 'Growing Old'*, Bristol: Policy Press.

Grenier, A. (2020) 'The conspicuous absence of the social, emotional and political aspects of frailty: the example of *The White Book on Frailty*', *Ageing & Society*, 40(11): 2338–54.

Grenier, A. and Phillipson, C. (2014) 'Rethinking agency in late life: structural and interpretive approaches', in Baars, J., Dohmen, J., Grenier, A. and Phillipson, C. (eds) *Ageing, Meaning and Social Structure*, Bristol: Policy Press, pp 55–79.

Grenier, A., Griffin, M. and McGrath, C. (2016) 'Aging and disability: the paradoxical positions of the chronological life course', *Review of Disability Studies: An International Journal*, 12 (2/3): 11–27.

Grenier, A., Lloyd, L. and Phillipson, C. (2017) 'Precarity in late life: rethinking dementia as a "frailed" old age', *Sociology of Health & Illness*, 39(2): 318–30.

Grist, V.L. (2010) 'The relationships between age of disability onset, adaptation to disability, and quality of life among older adults with physical disabilities', unpublished thesis, Florida State University. Available at: http://diginole.lib.fsu.edu/etd/3953

Grue, J. (2017) 'Now you see it, now you don't: a discourse view of disability and multidisciplinarity', *ALTER – European Journal of Disability Research*, 11(3): 168–78.

Gullette, M.M. (2004) *Aged by Culture*, Chicago, IL: University of Chicago Press.

Gullette, M.M. (2010) 'Ageism and social change: the new regime of decline', in Cole, T.R., Ray, R. and Kastenbaum, R. (eds) *A Guide to Humanistic Studies in Ageing: What Does It Mean to Grow Old?*, Baltimore, MD: Johns Hopkins University Press, pp 319–40.

Hagestad, G.O. and Settersten, R.A. (2017) 'Aging: it's interpersonal! Reflections from two life course migrants', *Gerontologist*, 57(1): 136–44.

Hahn, H. (1986) 'Public support for rehabilitation programs: the analysis of US disability policy', *Disability, Handicap and Society*, 1(2): 121–37.

Hahn, H. (1993) 'The political implications of disability definitions and data', *Journal of Disability Policy Studies*, 4(2): 41–52.

Hallgrimsdottir, B. and Ståhl, A. (2016) 'The impact of measures taken in the outdoor environment on an ageing population: a panel study over a ten-year period', *Ageing & Society*, 38(2): 217–39.

Hareven, T.K. (1978) *Transitions: The Family and the Life Course in Historical Perspective*, New York: Academic Press.

Havighurst, R.J. and Albrecht, R. (1953) *Older People*, London: Longman.

Health Service Executive Working Group on Congregated Settings (2011) *Time to Move on from Congregated Settings: A Strategy for Community Inclusion*, Dublin: Health Service Executive.

Heath, N.A. (2018) 'Extending the concept of successful ageing to persons ageing with disabilities', unpublished PhD thesis, University of Melbourne, Australia.

Heikkinen, R.-L. (2000) 'Ageing in an autobiographical context', *Ageing and Society*, 20(4): 467–83.

Heinz, W.R. (2004) 'From work trajectories to negotiated careers: the contingent work life course', in Mortimer, J.T. and Shanahan, M.J. (eds) *Handbook of the Life Course*, Boston, MA: Springer Science and Business, pp 185–204.

Hendricks, J. (2010) 'Age, self, and identity in the global century', in Dannefer, D. and Phillipson, C. (eds) *The Sage Handbook of Social Gerontology*, London: Sage, pp 251–64.

Henning-Smith, C. (2016) 'Where do community-dwelling older adults with disabilities live? Distribution of disability in the United States of America by household composition and housing type', *Ageing and Society*, 37(6): 1227–48.

Hiam, L., Dorling, D., Harrison, D. and McKee, M. (2017) 'Why has mortality in England and Wales been increasing? An iterative demographic analysis', *Journal of the Royal Society of Medicine*, 110: 153–62.

Higgs, P. and Gilleard, C. (2015) *Rethinking Old Age: Theorising the Fourth Age*, London: Palgrave Macmillan.

Higgs, P. and Rees-Jones, I. (2009) *Medical Sociology and Old Age: Towards a Sociology of Health in Later Life*, London: Routledge.

Hill, M. (2006) *Social Policy in the Modern World: A Comparative Text*, Malden, MA, and Oxford: Blackwell.

Hinojosa, R., Boylstein, C., Rittman, M., Sberna, Hinojosa, M. and Faircloth, C.A. (2008) 'Constructions of continuity after stroke', *Symbolic Interaction*, 31(2): 205–24.

Hockey, J.L. and James, A. (1993) *Growing Up and Growing Old: Ageing and Dependency in the Life Course*, London: Sage.

Hockey, J.L. and James, A. (2003) *Social Identities across the Lifecourse*, Basingstoke: Palgrave Macmillan.

Hoeyberghs, L.J., Schols, J.M.G.A., Verté, D. and De Witte, N. (2020) 'Psychological frailty and quality of life of community dwelling older people: a qualitative study', *Applied Research in Quality of Life*, 15: 1395–1412.

Holme, L. (2013) 'Disability, identity and ageing', in Jeppsson Grassman, E. and Whitaker, A. (eds) *Ageing with Disability: A Lifecourse Perspective*, Bristol: Policy Press, pp 35–53.

Holstein, J.A. and Gubrium, J.F. (2000) *Constructing the Life Course*, 2nd edn, Plymouth: General Hall.

Holstein, M.B. (2015) *Women in Late Life: Critical Perspectives on Gender and Age*, Lanham, MD: Rowman and Littlefield.

Holstein, M.B. and Cole, T.R. (1996) 'Reflections on age, meaning and chronic illness', *Journal of Aging and Identity*, 1: 7–22.

Holstein, M.B. and Minkler, M. (2003) 'Self, society, and the "new gerontology"', *The Gerontologist*, 43(6): 787–96.

Holstein, M.B. and Minkler, M. (2007) 'Critical gerontology: reflections for the 21st century', in Bernard, M. and Scharf, T. (eds) *Critical Perspectives on Ageing Societies*, Bristol: Policy Press, pp 13–26.

Hosking, D.L. (2008) 'Critical disability theory', paper presented at the '4th Biennial Disability Studies Conference', Lancaster University.

Hubbard, G., Kidd, L. and Kearney, N. (2010) 'Disrupted lives and threats to identity: the experiences of people with colorectal cancer within the first year following diagnosis', *Health*, 14(2): 131–46.

Hughes, B. (2009) 'Wounded/monstrous/abject: a critique of the disabled body in the sociological imaginary', *Disability & Society*, 24(4): 399–410.

Hughes, B. and Paterson, K. (1997) 'The social model of disability and the disappearing body: towards a sociology of impairment', *Disability & Society*, 12(3): 325–40.

Hung, L.W., Kempen, G.I.J.M. and De Vries, N.K. (2010) 'Cross-cultural comparison between academic and lay views of healthy ageing: a literature review', *Ageing & Society*, 30(8): 1373–91.

Hunt, P. (1998 [1966]) 'A critical condition', in Shakespeare, T. (ed) *The Disability Reader: Social Science Perspectives*, London: Cassell, pp 7–19.

Hupkens, S., Machielse, A., Goumans, M. and Derkx, P. (2018) 'Meaning in life of older persons: an integrative literature review', *Nursing Ethics*, 25(8): 973–91.

Hutchinson, K., Roberts, C. and Daly, M. (2018) 'Identity, impairment and disablement: exploring the social processes impacting identity change in adults living with acquired neurological impairments', *Disability & Society*, 33(2): 175–96.

Iezzoni, L.I. (2014) 'Policy concerns raised by the growing US population aging with disability', *Disability and Health Journal*, 7(1): S64–8.

Irwin, S. (1999) 'Later life, inequality and sociological theory', *Ageing and Society*, 19(6): 691–715.

Irwin, S. (2001) 'Repositioning disability and the life course: a social claiming perspective', in Priestley, M. (ed) *Disability and the Life Course: Global Perspectives*, Cambridge: Cambridge University Press, pp 15–25.

Isherwood, L.M., King, D.S. and Luszcz, M.A. (2017) 'Widowhood in the fourth age: support exchange, relationships and social participation', *Ageing and Society*, 37(1): 188–212.

Iwakuma, M. (2001) 'Ageing with disability in Japan', in Priestley, M. (ed) *Disability and the Life Course: Global Perspectives*, Cambridge: Cambridge University Press, pp 219–30.

Iwarsson, S., Wahl, H.-W., Nygren, C., Oswald, F., Sixsmith, A., Sixsmith, J., Zsuzsa, S. and Tomsone, S. (2007) 'Importance of the home environment for healthy aging: conceptual and methodological background of the European ENABLE–AGE project', *The Gerontologist*, 27(1): 78–84.

Jasper, R., Hughes, J., Roberts, A., Chester, H., Davies, S. and Challis, D. (2019) 'Commissioning home care for older people: scoping the evidence', *Journal of Long-Term Care*: 176–93.

Jenkins, R. (2008) *Social Identity*, 3rd edn, Abingdon: Routledge.

Jensen, M.P., Devlin, H.C., Vowles, K.E. and Molton, I.R. (2019) 'Assessing perceived success in valued living in individuals with long-term physical health conditions', *Journal of Aging and Health*, 31(10): 195S–213S.

Jeppsson Grassman, E. (2013) 'Time, age and the failing body: a long life with disability', in Jeppsson Grassman, E. and Whitaker, A. (eds) *Ageing with Disability: A Lifecourse Perspective*, Bristol: Policy Press, pp 17–34.

Jeppsson Grassman, E. and Whitaker, A. (eds) (2013) *Ageing with Disability: A Lifecourse Perspective*, Bristol: Policy Press.

Jeppsson Grassman, E., Holme, L., Larsson, T.A. and Whitaker, A. (2012) 'A long life with a particular signature: life course and aging for people with disabilities', *Journal of Gerontological Social Work*, 55(2): 95–111.

Johnson, E.K., Cameron, A., Lloyd, L., Evans, S., Darton, R., Smith, R., Atkinson, T. and Porteus, J. (2020) 'Ageing in extra-care housing: preparation, persistence and self-management at the boundary between the third and fourth age', *Ageing and Society*, 40(12): 2711–31.

Jönson, H. and Larsson, A.T. (2009) 'The exclusion of older people in disability activism and policies – a case of inadvertent ageism?', *Journal of Aging Studies*, 23(1): 69–77.

Kafer, A. (2003) 'Compulsory bodies: reflections on heterosexuality and able-bodiedness', *Journal of Women's History*, 15(3): 77–89.

Kafer, A. (2013) *Feminist, Queer, Crip*, Bloomington, IN: Indiana University Press.

Kahana, J.S. and Kahana, E. (2017) *Disability and Aging: Learning from Both to Empower the Lives of Older Adults*, Boulder, CO: Lynne Reinner.

Kane, R. and Kane, R. (2005) 'Ageism in healthcare and long-term care', *Generations*, 29(3): 49–54.

Katz, S. (2005) *Cultural Aging: Life Course, Lifestyle, and Senior Worlds*, Toronto: Broadview Press.

Katz, S. (2020) 'Precarious life, human development and the life course: critical intersections', in Grenier, A., Phillipson, P. and Settersten, R.A. (eds) *Precarity and Ageing: Understanding Insecurity and Risk in Later Life*, Bristol: Policy Press, pp 41–65.

Katz, S. and Calasanti, T. (2015) 'Critical perspectives on successful aging: does it "appeal more than it illuminates"?', *The Gerontologist*, 55(1): 26–33.

Keefe, B. (2018) 'Can a unified service delivery philosophy be identified in aging and disability organizations? Exploring competing service delivery models through the voices of the workforce in these organizations', *Journal of Aging & Social Policy*, 30(1): 48–71.

Kelley-Moore, J.A. (2010) 'Disability and ageing: the social construction of causality', in Dannefer, D. and Phillipson, C. (eds) *The Sage Handbook of Social Gerontology*, London: Sage, pp 96–110.

Kelley-Moore, J.A., Schumacher, J.G., Kahana, E. and Kahana, B. (2006) 'When do older adults become "disabled"? Social and health antecedents of perceived disability in a panel study of the oldest old', *Journal of Health and Social Behavior*, 47(2): 126–41.

Kelly, C. (2010) 'Wrestling with group identity: disability activism and direct funding', *Disability Studies Quarterly*, 30(3/4).

Kelly, C. (2016) *Disability Politics and Care: The Challenge of Direct Funding*, Vancouver: UBC Press.

Kelly, M.P. and Field, D. (1996) 'Medical sociology, chronic illness and the body', *Sociology of Health & Illness*, 18(2): 241–57.

Kennedy, J. (2000) 'Responding to the disparities between disability research and aging research', *Journal of Disability Policy Studies*, 11(2): 120–3.

Kennedy, J. and Minkler, M. (1998) 'Disability theory and public policy: implications for critical gerontology', *International Journal of Health Services*, 28(4): 757–76.

Kennedy, J. and Minkler, M. (1999) 'Disability theory and public policy: implications for critical gerontology', in Minkler, M. and Estes, C.L. (eds) *Critical Gerontology: Perspectives from Political and Moral Economy*, New York: Baywood.

Kohli, M. (1986) 'The world we forgot: a historical review of the life course', in Marshall, V.W. (ed) *Later Life: The Social Psychology of Ageing*, Beverly Hills, CA: Sage, pp 271–301.

Kohli, M. (2007) 'The institutionalization of the life course: looking back to look ahead', *Research in Human Development*, 4(3/4): 253–71.

Krause, N. (2004) 'Stressors arising in highly valued roles, meaning in life, and the physical health status of older adults', *The Journals of Gerontology Series B: Psychological Sciences and Social Sciences*, 59(5): S287–97.

Krause, N. (2009) 'Meaning in life and mortality', *The Journals of Gerontology Series B: Psychological Sciences and Social Sciences*, 64(4): 517–27.

Krause, N. (2012) 'Meaning in life and healthy aging', in Wong, P.T.P. (ed) *The Human Quest for Meaning: Theories, Research and Application*, 2nd edn, New York: Routledge, pp 409–32.

Kuh, D. (2007) 'A life course approach to healthy aging, frailty, and capability', *The Journals of Gerontology Series A: Biological Sciences and Medical Sciences*, 62(7): 717–21.

La Plante, M.P. (2014) 'Key goals and indicators for successful aging of adults with early-onset disability', *Disability and Health Journal*, 7(1): S44–50.

Laceulle, H. (2014) 'Self-realisation and ageing: a spiritual perspective', in Baars, J., Dohmen, J., Grenier, A. and Phillipson, C. (eds) *Ageing, Meaning and Social Structure: Connecting Critical and Humanistic Gerontology*, Bristol: Policy Press, pp 97–118.

Laceulle, H. (2016) 'Becoming who you are. Aging, self-realization and cultural narratives about later life', dissertation, University of Humanistic Studies, The Netherlands.

Laceulle, H. and Baars, J. (2014) 'Self-realization and cultural narratives about later life', *Journal of Aging Studies*, 31: 34–44.

Lakhani, A., McDonald, D. and Zeeman, H. (2018) 'Perspectives of self-direction: a systematic review of key areas contributing to service users' engagement and choice-making in self-directed disability services and supports', *Health and Social Care in the Community*, 26: 295–313.

Lamb, E.G. (2015) 'Age and/as disability: a call for conversation', *Age, Culture, Humanities*, 2: 313–22.

Lamb, S. (2014) 'Permanent personhood or meaningful decline? Toward a critical anthropology of successful aging', *Journal of Aging Studies*, 29: 41–52.

Larsson, A.T. (2013) 'Is it possible to "age successfully" with extensive physical impairments?', in Jeppsson Grassman, E. and Whitaker, A. (eds) *Ageing with Disability: A Lifecourse Perspective*, Bristol: Policy Press.

Larsson, A.T. and Jeppsson Grassman, E. (2012) 'Bodily changes among people living with physical impairments and chronic illnesses: biographical disruption or normal illness?', *Sociology of Health & Illness*, 34(8): 1156–69.

Larsson, A.T. and Jönson, H. (2018) 'Ageism and the rights of older people', in Ayalon, L. and Tesch-Römer, C. (eds) *Contemporary Perspectives on Ageism*, Cham: Springer, pp 369–82.

Laslett, P. (1996 [1989]) *A Fresh Map of Life: The Emergence of the Third Age*, 2nd edn, Basingstoke: Palgrave Macmillan.

Lawson, A. and Beckett, A.E. (2021) 'The social and human rights models of disability: towards a complementarity thesis', *The International Journal of Human Rights*, 25(2): 348–79.

Lawton, M.P. and Nahemow, L. (1973) 'Ecology and the aging process', in Eisdorfer, C. and Lawton, M.P. (eds) *The Psychology of Adult Development and Aging*, Washington, DC: American Psychological Association, pp 619–74.

Le Bihan, B. (2016) 'France anticipates ageing society through new piece of legislation', ESPN Flash Report 2016/18.

Leahy, A. (2018) 'Too many "false dichotomies"? Investigating the division between ageing and disability in social care services in Ireland: a study with statutory and non-statutory organisations', *Journal of Aging Studies*, 44: 34–44.

Leahy, A. (2020) 'Time to confront the portrait in the attic? Reflections on theories and discourses of ageing sparked by the COVID-19 crisis', *Ageing Issues*, 9 April. Available at: https://ageingissues.wordpress.com/2020/04/09/time-to-confront-the-portrait-in-the-attic-reflections-on-theories-and-discourses-of-ageing-sparked-by-covid-19/

Litwin, H. and Levinson, M. (2018) 'The association of mobility limitation and social networks in relation to late-life activity', *Ageing and Society*, 38(9): 1771–90.

Ljuslinder, K., Ellis, K. and Vikström, L. (2020) 'Cripping time: understanding the life course through the lens of ableism', *Scandinavian Journal of Disability Research*, 22(1): 35–8.

Lloyd, A., Haraldsdottir, E., Kendall, M., Murray, S.A. and McCormack, B. (2020) 'Stories from people living with frailty', *Ageing & Society*, 40(12): 2732–53.

Lloyd, L. (2004) 'Mortality and morality: ageing and the ethics of care', *Ageing and Society*, 24(2): 235–56.

Lloyd, L. (2010) 'The individual in social care: the ethics of care and the "personalisation agenda" in services for older people in England', *Ethics and Social Welfare*, 4(2): 188–200.

Lloyd, L. (2012) *Health and Care in Ageing Societies: A New International Approach*, Bristol: Policy Press.

Lloyd, L. (2015) 'The fourth age', in Twigg, J. and Martin, W. (eds) *Routledge Handbook of Cultural Gerontology*, 1st edn, London: Routledge, 261–8.

Lloyd, L., Calnan, M., Cameron, A., Seymour, J. and Smith, R. (2014) 'Identity in the fourth age: perseverance, adaptation and maintaining dignity', *Ageing and Society*, 34(1): 1–19.

Loja, E., Costa, M.E., Hughes, B. and Menezes, I. (2013) 'Disability, embodiment and ableism: stories of resistance', *Disability & Society*, 28(2): 190–203.

Loprest, P. and Maag, E. (2007) 'The relationship between early disability onset and education and employment', *Journal of Vocational Rehabilitation*, 26: 49–62.

Luborsky, M.R. (1994) 'The cultural adversity of physical disability: erosion of full adult personhood', *Journal of Aging Studies*, 8(3): 239–53.

MacDonald, S.J., Deacon, L., Nixon, J., Akintola, A., Gillingham, A., Kent, J., Ellis, G., Mathews, D., Ismail, A., Sullivan, S., Dore, S. and Highmore, L. (2018) '"The invisible enemy": disability, loneliness and isolation', *Disability & Society*, 33(7): 1138–59.

Manthorpe, J. and Iliffe, S. (2015) 'Frailty – from bedside to buzzword?', *Journal of Integrated Care*, 23(3): 120–8.

Marshall, V.W. and Mueller, M.M. (2002) *Rethinking Social Policy for an Aging Workforce and Society: Insights from the Life Course Perspective*, CPRN Discussion Paper No. W/18, Ottawa: Canadian Policy Research Networks.

Mattlin, B. (2016) 'A disabled life is a life worth living', *New York Times*, 5 October. Available at: www.nytimes.com/2016/10/05/opinion/a-disabled-life-is-a-life-worth-living.html

Mayer, K.U. (1986) 'Structural constraints on the life course', *Human Development*, 29(3): 163–70.

McCallion, P. and McCarron, M. (2015) 'People with disabilities entering the third age', in Iriarte, E.G., McConkey, R. and Gilligan, R. (eds) *Disability and Human Rights: Global Perspectives*, London: Macmillan International.

McGrath, C., Laliberte Rudman, D., Polgar, J., Spafford, M.M. and Trentham, B. (2016) 'Negotiating "positive" aging in the presence of age-related vision loss (ARVL): the shaping and perpetuation of disability', *Journal of Aging Studies*, 39: 1–10.

McGrath, C., Laliberte Rudman, D., Trentham, B., Polgar, J. and Spafford, M.M. (2017) 'Reshaping understandings of disability associated with age-related vision loss (ARVL): incorporating critical disability perspectives into research and practice', *Disability and Rehabilitation*, 39(19): 1990–8.

McRuer, R. (2006) *Crip Theory: Cultural Signs of Queerness and Disability*, New York: New York University Press.

Meekosha, H. and Shuttleworth, R. (2009) 'What's so "critical" about critical disability studies?', *Australian Journal of Human Rights*, 15(1): 47–75.

Meekosha, H., Shuttleworth, R. and Soldatic, K. (2013) 'Disability and critical sociology: expanding the boundaries of critical social inquiry', *Critical Sociology*, 39(3): 319–23.

Meijering, L., Lettinga, A.T., Nanninga, C.S. and Milligan, C. (2017) 'Interpreting therapeutic landscape experiences through rural stroke survivors' biographies of disruption and flow', *Journal of Rural Studies*, 51: 275–83.

Miller, P., Parker, S. and Gillinson, S. (2004) *Disablism: How to Tackle the Last Prejudice*, London: Demos.

Minkler, M. and Estes, C.L. (1999) 'Introduction', in Minkler, M. and Estes, C.L. (eds) *Critical Gerontology: Perspectives from Political and Moral Economy*, Amityville, NY: Baywood, pp 1–13.

Minkler, M. and Fadem, P. (2002) '"Successful aging": a disability perspective', *Journal of Disability Policy Studies*, 12(4): 229–35.

Mitchell, D.T. and Snyder, S.L. (1997) 'Introduction: disability studies and the double bind of representation', in Mitchell, D.T. and Snyder, S.L. (eds) *The Body and Physical Difference: Discourses of Disability*, Ann Arbor, MI: University of Michigan Press, pp 1–31.

Mitra, S. and Shakespeare, T. (2019) 'Remodeling the ICF', *Disability and Health Journal*, 12(3): 337–9.

Molton, I.R. and Ordway, A. (2019) 'Aging with disability: populations, programs, and the new paradigm: an introduction to the special issue', *Journal of Aging and Health*, 31(IOS): 3S–20S.

Molton, I.R. and Yorkston, K.M. (2017) 'Growing older with a physical disability: a special application of the successful aging paradigm', *The Journals of Gerontology: Series B*, 72(2): 290–9.

Monahan, D. and Wolf, D. (2014) 'The continuum of disability over the lifespan: the convergence of aging with disability and aging into disability', *Disability and Health Journal*, 7(1 – Supplement): S1–3.

Moody, H.R. (1993) 'Overview: what is critical gerontology and why is it important', in Cole, H. (ed) *Voices and Visions of Aging: Toward a Critical Gerontology*, New York: Springer.

Moody, H.R. and Sasser, J. (2012) *Aging: Concepts and Controversies*, Thousand Oaks, CA: Sage.

Morciano, M., Hancock, R. and Pudney, S. (2014) 'Disability costs and equivalence scales in the older population in Great Britain', *Review of Income and Wealth*, 61(3): 494–514.

Morell, C.M. (2003) 'Empowerment and long-living women: return to the rejected body', *Journal of Aging Studies*, 17(1): 69–85.

Morris, J. (1991) *Pride against Prejudice: Transforming Attitudes to Disability: A Personal Politics of Disability*, London: The Women's Press.

Morris, J. (1993) *Independent Lives? Community Care and Disabled People*, London: Macmillan.

Morris, J. (2001) 'Impairment and disability: constructing an ethics of care that promotes human rights', *Hypatia*, 16(4): 1–16.

Morris, J. (2006) 'Independent living: the role of the disability movement in the development of government policy', in Glendinning, C. and Kemp, P.A. (eds) *Cash and Care: Policy Challenges in the Welfare State*, Bristol: Policy Press, pp 235–48.

Moulaert, T. and Biggs, S. (2012) 'International and European policy on work and retirement: reinventing critical perspectives on active ageing and mature subjectivity', *Human Relations*, 66(1): 23–43.

Murphy, K., O'Shea, E., Cooney, A. and Casey, D. (2007) *The Quality of Life of Older People with a Disability in Ireland*, Report No. 99, Dublin: National Council on Ageing and Older People.

Murphy, R. (1987) *The Body Silent*, New York: Henry Holt and Company.

Nagi, S.Z. (1976) 'An epidemiology of disability among adults in the United States', *The Milbank Memorial Fund Quarterly Health and Society*, 54(4): 439–67.

Naidoo, V., Putnam, M. and Spindel, A. (2012) 'Key focal areas for bridging the fields of aging and disability: findings from the Growing Older with a Disability Conference', *International Journal of Integrated Care*, 12(8).

National Audit Office (2016) *Personalised Commissioning in Social Care. Report by the Comptroller and Auditor General*, London: HMSO.

National Council on Ageing and Older People and National Disability Authority (2006) *Proceedings of the Seminar: The Interface between Ageing and Disability*, Dublin: National Council on Ageing and Older People & National Disability Authority.

Naue, U. and Kroll, T. (2010) 'Bridging policies and practice: challenges and opportunities for the governance of disability and ageing', *International Journal of Integrated Care*, 10(2).

Needham, C. (2014) 'Personalization: from day centres to community hubs?', *Critical Social Policy*, 34(1): 98–108.

Newbronner, E. and Atkin, K. (2018) 'The changing health of thalidomide survivors as they age: a scoping review', *Disability and Health Journal*, 11(2): 184–91.

Nicholson, C. (2009) 'Holding it together: a psycho-social exploration of living with frailty in old age', unpublished thesis, City University of London.

Nicholson, C., Meyer, J., Flatley, M., Holman, C. and Lowton, K. (2012) 'Living on the margin: understanding the experience of living and dying with frailty in old age', *Social Science & Medicine*, 75(8): 1426–32.

Nicholson, C., Meyer, J., Flatley, M. and Holman, C. (2013) 'The experience of living at home with frailty in old age: a psychosocial qualitative study', *International Journal of Nursing Studies*, 50(9): 1172–9.

Oldman, C. (2002) 'Later life and the social model of disability: a comfortable partnership?', *Ageing and Society*, 22(6): 791–806.

Oliver, M. (1990) *The Politics of Disablement*, Basingstoke: Macmillan.

Oliver, M. (1996) *Understanding Disability: From Theory to Practice*, Basingstoke: Macmillan Press.

Oliver, M. and Barnes, C. (2012) *The New Politics of Disablement*, Basingstoke: Palgrave Macmillan.

Orellana, K., Manthorpe, J. and Tinker, A. (2020) 'Day centres for older people: a systematically conducted scoping review of literature about their benefits, purposes and how they are perceived', *Ageing & Society*, 40(1): 73–104.

Pack, R., Hand, C., Laliberte Rudman, D. and Huot, S. (2019) 'Governing the ageing body: explicating the negotiation of "positive" ageing in daily life', *Ageing & Society*, 39: 2086–108.

Phillipson, C. (1982) *Capitalism and the Construction of Old Age*, London: Macmillan.

Phillipson, C. (2002) *Transitions from Work to Retirement: Developing a New Social Contract*, Bristol: Policy Press.

Phillipson, C. (2013) *Ageing*, Cambridge: Polity Press.

Phillipson, C. (2015) 'The political economy of longevity: developing new forms of solidarity for later life', *The Sociological Quarterly*, 56(1): 80–100.

Phillipson, C. (2020) 'Austerity and precarity: individual and collective agency in later life', in Grenier, A., Phillipson, C. and Settersten, R.A. (eds) *Precarity and Ageing: Understanding Insecurity and Risk in Later Life*, Bristol: Policy Press, pp 215–46.

Phillipson, C. and Baars, J. (2007) 'Social theory and social ageing', in Bond, J., Peace, S., Dittmann-Kohli, F. and Westerhof, G.J. (eds) *Ageing in Society*, 3rd edn, London: Sage, pp 68–84.

Phillipson, C. and Walker, A. (1987) 'The case for a critical gerontology', in DeGregorio, S. (ed) *Social Gerontology, New Directions*, London: Croom Helm.

Pickard, S. (2014) 'Biology as destiny? Rethinking embodiment in "deep" old age', *Ageing and Society*, 34(8): 1279–91.

Pike, B., O'Nolan, G. and Farragher, L. (2016) *Individualised Budgeting for Social Care Services for People with a Disability: International Approaches and Evidence on Financial Sustainability*, Dublin: Health Research Board.

Pirhonen, J., Ojala, H., Lumme-Sandt, K. and Pietilä, I. (2016) ' "Old but not that old": Finnish community-dwelling people aged 90+ negotiating their autonomy', *Ageing and Society*, 36(8): 1625–44.

Pound, P., Gompertz, P. and Ebrahim, S. (1998) 'Illness in the context of older age: the case of stroke', *Sociology of Health & Illness*, 20(4): 489–506.

Prideaux, S., Roulstone, A., Harris, J. and Barnes, C. (2009) 'Disabled people and self-directed support schemes: reconceptualising work and welfare in the 21st century', *Disability & Society*, 24(5): 557–69.

Priestley, M. (2000) 'Adults only: disability, social policy and the life course', *Journal of Social Policy*, 29(3): 421–39.

Priestley, M. (2001) 'Epilogue', in Priestley, M. (ed) *Disability and the Life Course: Global Perspectives*, Cambridge: Cambridge University Press, pp 240–8.

Priestley, M. (2002) 'Whose voices? Representing the claims of older disabled people under New Labour', *Policy & Politics*, 30(3): 361–72.

Priestley, M. (2003a) *Disability: A Life Course Approach*, Cambridge: Polity.

Priestley, M. (2003b) ' "It's like your hair going grey", or is it? Impairment, disability and the habitus of old age', in Ridddell, S. and Watson, N. (eds) *Disability, Culture and Identity*, Harlow: Pearson, pp 53–66.

Priestley, M. (2006) 'Disability and old age: or why it isn't all in the mind', in Goodley, D. and Lawthom, R. (eds) *Disability and Psychology: Critical Introductions and Reflections*, Basingstoke: Palgrave Macmillan, pp 84–93.

Priestley, M. and Rabiee, P. (2001) *Building Bridges: Disability and Old Age. End of Award Report: ESRC Small Grant Number: R000223581*, Leeds: University of Leeds. Available at: https://disability-studies. leeds.ac.uk/wp-content/uploads/sites/40/2011/10/bridgesreport.pdf

Priestley, M., Corker, M. and Watson, N. (1999) 'Unfinished business: disabled children and disability identity', *Disability Studies Quarterly*, 19(2): 87–98.

Priestley, M., Stickings, M., Loja, E., Grammenos, S., Lawson, A., Waddington, L. and Fridriksdottir, B. (2016) 'The political participation of disabled people in Europe: rights, accessibility and activism', *Electoral Studies*, 42: 1–9.

Psarra, E. and Kleftaras, G. (2013) 'Adaptation to physical disabilities: the role of meaning in life and depression', *The European Journal of Counselling Psychology*, 2(1): 77–99.

Putnam, M. (2002) 'Linking aging theory and disability models: increasing the potential to explore aging with physical impairment', *The Gerontologist*, 42(6): 799–806.

Putnam, M. (2007) 'Moving from separate to crossing aging and disability service networks', in Putnam, M. (ed) *Aging and Disability: Crossing Network Lines*, New York: Springer, pp 5–17.

Putnam, M. (2011) 'Perceptions of difference between aging and disability service systems consumers: implications for policy initiatives to rebalance long-term care', *Journal of Gerontological Social Work*, 54(3): 325–42.

Putnam, M. (2014) 'Bridging network divides: building capacity to support aging with disability populations through research', *Disability and Health Journal*, 7(1): S51–9.

Putnam, M. (2017) 'Extending the promise of the Older Americans Act to persons aging with long-term disability', *Research on Aging*, 39(6): 799–820.

Putnam, M. and Stoever, A. (2007) 'Facilitators and barriers to crossing network lines: a Missouri case study', in Putnam, M. (ed) *Aging and Disability: Crossing Network Lines*, New York: Springer Publishing, pp 19–54.

Putnam, M., Molton, I.R., Truitt, A.R., Smith, A.E. and Jensen, M.P. (2016) 'Measures of aging with disability in US secondary data sets: results of a scoping review', *Disability and Health Journal*, 9(1): 5–10.

Puts, M.T.E., Lips, P. and Deeg, D.J.H. (2005) 'Sex differences in the risk of frailty for mortality independent of disability and chronic diseases', *Journal of the American Geriatrics Society*, 53(1): 40–7.

Puts, M.T.E., Shekary, N., Widdershoven, G., Heldens, J. and Deeg, D.J.H. (2009) 'The meaning of frailty according to Dutch older frail and non-frail persons', *Journal of Aging Studies*, 23(4): 258–66.

Rabiee, P. (2013) 'Exploring the relationships between choice and independence: experiences of disabled and older people', *British Journal of Social Work*, 43(5): 872–88.

Rabiee, P. and Glendinning, C. (2014) 'Choice and control for older people using home care services: how far have council-managed personal budgets helped?', *Quality in Ageing and Older Adults*, 15(4): 210–19.

Rabiee, P., Baxter, K. and Glendinning, C. (2016) 'Supporting choice: support planning, older people and managed personal budgets', *Journal of Social Work*, 16(4): 453–69.

Raymond, É. and Grenier, A. (2013) 'Participation in policy discourse: new form of exclusion for seniors with disabilities?', *Canadian Journal on Aging*, 32(2): 117–29.

Raymond, É., Grenier, A. and Hanley, J. (2014) 'Community participation of older adults with disabilities', *Journal of Community & Applied Social Psychology*, 24(1): 50–62.

Reed, K., Hocking, C. and Smythe, L. (2010) 'The interconnected meanings of occupation: the call, being-with, possibilities', *Journal of Occupational Science*, 17(3): 140–9.

Reeve, D. (2012) 'Psycho-emotional disablism: the missing link?', in Watson, N., Roulstone, A. and Thomas, C. (eds) *Routledge Handbook of Disability Studies*, 1st edn, Abingdon: Routledge, pp 78–92.

Reker, G.T. and Wong, P.T.P. (2012) 'Personal meaning in life and psychosocial adaptation in the later years', in Wong, P.T.P. (ed) *The Human Quest for Meaning: Theories, Research, and Applications*, 2nd edn, New York: Routledge, pp 433–56.

Rembis, M. (2015) 'Disability studies', *The Year's Work in Critical and Cultural Theory*, 23(1): 162–89. Available at: https://doi.org/10.1093/ywcct/mbv007

Rembis, M. (2019) *Disability: A Reference Handbook*, Santa Barbara, CA: ABC-CLIO.

Reyes, R. (2009) 'Aging with a spinal cord injury', Spinal Cord Injury Forum, Northwest Regional Spinal Cord Injury System, University of Washington.

Rickli, F. (2016) ' "No longer disabled" – reflections on a transitional process between disability and aging in Switzerland', *Review of Disability Studies: An International Journal*, 12(2/3): 122–36.

Riddell, S. and Watson, N. (2003) 'Disability, culture and identity: introduction', in Riddell, S. and Watson, N. (eds) *Disability, Culture and Identity*, Harlow: Pearson Education, pp 1–18.

Riddell, S., Priestley, M., Pearson, C., Mercer, G., Barnes, C., Jolly, D. and Williams, V. (2006) *Disabled People and Direct Payments: A UK Comparative Study*. Available at: www.docs.hss.ed.ac.uk/education/creid/Projects/10i_Directpyts_FinalRpt_I.pdf

Ridolfo, H. (2010) Constructing a disabled identity: the influence of impairment, social factors and reflected appraisals, unpublished thesis, University of Maryland.

Romo, R.D., Wallhagen, M.I., Yourman, L., Yeung, C.C., Eng, C., Micco, G., Pérez-Stable, E.J. and Smith, A.K. (2013) 'Perceptions of successful aging among diverse elders with late-life disability', *The Gerontologist*, 53(6): 939–49.

Roulstone, A. (2015) 'Personal independence payments, welfare reform and the shrinking disability category', *Disability and Society*, 30(5): 673–88.

Rowe, J.W. and Kahn, R.L. (1987) 'Human aging: usual and successful', *Science*, 237(4811): 143–9.

Rowe, J.W. and Kahn, R.L. (1997) 'Successful aging', *The Gerontologist*, 37(4): 433–40.

Ryff, C.D. and Singer, B. (1998) 'The contours of positive human health', *Psychological Inquiry*, 9(1): 1–28.

Salvador-Carulla, L., Putnam, M., Bigby, C. and Heller, T. (2012) 'Advancing a research agenda for bridging ageing and disability', *International Journal of Integrated Care (IJIC)*, 12(Oct–Dec): 1.

Sandberg, L.J. (2013) 'Affirmative old age: the ageing body and feminist theories on difference', *International Journal of Ageing and Later Life*, 8(1): 11–40.

Sandberg, L.J. and Marshall, B.L. (2017) 'Queering aging futures', *Societies*, 7(3): 21.

Sanders, C., Donovan, J. and Dieppe, P. (2002) 'The significance and consequences of having painful and disabled joints in older age: co-existing accounts of normal and disrupted biographies', *Sociology of Health & Illness*, 24(2): 227–53.

Santiago, L.M., Gobbens, R.J., Mattos, I.E. and Bittencourt Ferreira, D. (2019) 'A comparison between physical and biopsychosocial measures of frailty: prevalence and associated factors in Brazilian older adults', *Archives of Gerontology and Geriatrics*, 81: 111–18.

Scharf, T. (2001) 'Social gerontology in Germany: historical trends and recent developments', *Ageing & Society*, 21(4): 489–505.

Scharf, T. (2009) 'Too tight to mention: unequal income in older age', in Cann, P. and Dean, M. (eds) *Unequal Ageing: The Untold Story of Exclusion in Old Age*, Bristol: Policy Press, pp 25–52.

Scharf, T., Phillipson, C., Smith, A.E. and Kingston, P. (2002) *Growing Older in Socially Deprived Areas: Social Exclusion in Later Life*, London: Help the Aged.

Sellon, A.M. (2018) 'Volunteerism among older adults with mobility-limiting disabilities: an exploratory study', unpublished thesis, University of Kansas.

Settersten, R.A. (2002) 'Social sources of meaning in later life', in Weiss, R. and Bass, S. (eds) *Challenges of the Third Age: Meaning and Purpose in Later Life*, New York: Oxford University Press, pp 55–79.

Settersten, R.A. (2005) 'Linking the two ends of life: what gerontology can learn from childhood studies', *Journal of Gerontology, Series B*, 60(4): S173–80.

Settersten, R.A. (2006) 'Aging and the life course', in Binstock, R.H. and George, L.K. (eds) *Handbook of Aging and the Social Sciences*, Boston, MA: Boston Academic Press.

Settersten, R.A. and Trauten, M. (2009) 'The new terrain of old age: hallmarks, freedoms and risks', in Bengtson, V., Gans, D., Putney, N. and Silverstein, M. (eds) *Handbook of Theories of Aging*, 2nd edn, New York: Springer, pp 455–70.

Shakespeare, T. (1994) 'Cultural representation of disabled people: dustbin for disavowal?', in Barton, L. and Oliver, M. (eds) *Disability Studies: Past, Present and Future*, Leeds: The Disability Press, pp 217–33.

Shakespeare, T. (2000a) *Help*, Birmingham: Venture Press.

Shakespeare, T. (2000b) 'The social relations of care', in Lewis, G., Gerwitz, S. and Clarke, J. (eds) *Rethinking Social Policy*, London: Sage, pp 52–65.

Shakespeare, T. (2006) *Disability Rights and Wrongs*, London: Routledge.

Shakespeare, T. (2013) 'The social model of disability', in Davis, L.J. (ed) *The Disability Studies Reader*, 4th edn, New York: Routledge.

Shakespeare, T. (2014a) *Disability Rights and Wrongs Revisited*, 2nd edn, Abingdon: Routledge.

Shakespeare, T. (2014b) 'Nasty, brutish and short? On the predicament of disability and embodiment', in Bickenbach, J.E., Franzisca, F. and Schmitz, B. (eds) *Disability and the Good Human Life*, New York: Cambridge University Press.

Shakespeare, T. and Watson, N. (2002) 'The social model of disability: an outdated ideology?', *Research in Social Science and Disability*, 2: 9–28.

Shakespeare, T. and Watson, N. (2010) 'Beyond models: understanding the complexity of disabled people's lives', in Scambler, G. and Scambler, S. (eds) *New Directions in the Sociology of Chronic and Disabling Conditions*, London: Palgrave Macmillan, pp 57–78.

Shakespeare, T., Watson, N. and Alghaib, O.A. (2017) 'Blaming the victim, all over again: Waddell and Aylward's biopsychosocial (BPS) model of disability', *Critical Social Policy*, 37(1): 22–4.

Shakespeare, T., Zeilig, H. and Mittler, P. (2019) 'Rights in mind: thinking differently about dementia and disability', *Dementia*, 18(3): 1075–88.

Shao, J., Zhang, Q., Lin, T., Shen, J. and Li, D. (2014) 'Well-being of elderly stroke survivors in Chinese communities: mediating effects of meaning in life', *Aging and Mental Health*, 18(4): 435–43.

Shaw, L.R., Chan, F. and McMahon, B.T. (2012) 'Intersectionality and disability harassment: the interactive effects of disability, race, age, and gender', *Rehabilitation Counselling Bulletin*, 55(2): 82–91.

Sheets, D. (2005) 'Aging with disabilities: ageism and more', *Generations*, 29(3): 37–41.

Sheets, D. (2010) 'Aging with physical disability', *International Encyclopedia of Rehabilitation*. Available at: https://citeseerx.ist.psu.edu/viewdoc/download?doi=10.1.1.608.9953&rep=rep1&type=pdf

Shildrick, M. and Price, J. (1996) 'Breaking the boundaries of the broken body', *Body & Society*, 2: 93–113.

Shilling, C. (2012) *The Body in Social Theory*, 3rd edn, London: Sage.

Shuttleworth, R. and Meekosha, H. (2013) 'The sociological imaginary and disability enquiry in late modernity', *Critical Sociology*, 39(3): 349–67.

Siebers, T. (2008) *Disability Theory*, Michigan, MI: University of Michigan Press.

Siebers, T. (2017 [2013]) 'Disability, pain, and the politics of minority identity', in Waldschmidt, A., Berressem, H. and Ingwersen, M. (eds) *Culture–Theory–Disability – Encounters between Disability Studies and Cultural Studies*, Bielefeld: Transcript Verlag, pp 111–20.

Silverman, D. (2010) *Doing Qualitative Research*, 3rd edn, London: Sage.

Simcock, P. (2017) 'Ageing with a unique impairment: a systematically conducted review of older deafblind people's experiences', *Ageing and Society*, 37(8): 1703–42.

Slasberg, C. and Beresford, P. (2016) 'The false narrative about personal budgets in England: smoke and mirrors?', *Disability & Society*, 31(8): 1131–7.

Slasberg, C. and Beresford, P. (2020) 'Independent living: the real and present danger', *Disability & Society*, 35(2): 326–31.

Smart, J.F. (2009) 'The power of models of disability', *Journal of Rehabilitation*, 75(2): 3–11.

Snyder, S.L. and Mitchell, D.T. (2001) 'Re-engaging the body: disability studies and the resistance to embodiment', *Public Culture*, 13(3): 367–89.

Snyder, S.L. and Mitchell, D.T. (2006) *Cultural Locations of Disability*, Chicago, IL: University of Chicago Press.

Stillman, T.F. and Baumeister, R.F. (2009) 'Uncertainty, belongingness, and four needs for meaning', *Psychological Inquiry*, 20(4): 249–51.

Stillman, T.F., Baumeister, R.F., Lambert, N.M., Crescioni, W.A., DeWall, N.C. and Fincham, F.D. (2009) 'Alone and without purpose: life loses meaning following social exclusion', *Journal of Experimental Social Psychology*, 45(4): 686–94.

Strauss, A. and Corbin, J. (1998) *Basics of Qualitative Research: Techniques and Procedures for Developing Grounded Theory*, 2nd edn, Thousand Oaks, CA: Sage.

Suddaby, R. (2006) 'From the editors: what grounded theory is not', *Academy of Management Journal*, 49(4): 633–42.

Swain, J. and French, S. (2000) 'Towards an affirmation model of disability', *Disability & Society*, 15(4): 569–82.

Tanner, D. (2010) *Managing the Ageing Experience: Learning from Older People*, Bristol: Policy Press.

Tesch-Römer, C. and Wahl, H.-W. (2017) 'Toward a more comprehensive concept of successful aging: disability and care needs', *Journal of Gerontology: Series B*, 72(2): 310–18.

Thomas, C. (2004) 'How is disability understood? An examination of sociological approaches', *Disability & Society*, 19(6): 569–83.

Thomas, C. (2007) *Sociologies of Disability and Illness: Contested Ideas in Disability Studies and Medical Sociology*, Basingstoke: Palgrave Macmillan.

Thomas, C. (2015) 'Disability and gender: understanding diversity and promoting equality', paper presented at the NNDR conference, Bergen, Norway.

Thomas, C. and Milligan, C. (2018) 'Dementia, disability rights and disablism: understanding the social position of people living with dementia', *Disability & Society*, 33(1): 115–31.

Thompson, N.J., Coker, J., Krause, J.S. and Henry, E. (2003) 'Purpose in life as a mediator of adjustment after spinal cord injury', *Rehabilitation Psychology*, 48(2): 100–8.

Thompson, P. (1992) '"I don't feel old": subjective ageing and the search for meaning in later life', *Ageing and Society*, 12(1): 23–47.

Timonen, V. (2016) *Beyond Successful and Active Ageing: A Theory of Model Ageing*, Bristol: Policy Press.

Timonen, V., Conlon, C., Scharf, T. and Carney, G. (2013) 'Family, state, class and solidarity: re-conceptualising intergenerational solidarity through the grounded theory approach', *European Journal of Ageing*, 10(3): 171–9.

Timonen, V., Foley, G. and Conlon, C. (2018) 'Challenges when using grounded theory: a pragmatic introduction to doing GT research', *International Journal of Qualitative Methods*, 17(1).

Titchkosky, T. (2003) *Disability, Self, and Society*, Toronto: University of Toronto Press.

Titchkosky, T. (2007) *Reading and Writing Disability Differently: The Textured Life of Embodiment*, Toronto: University of Toronto Press.

Titchkosky, T. and Michalko, R. (2009) 'Introduction', in Titchkosky, T. and Michalko, R. (eds) *Rethinking Normalcy: A Disability Studies Reader*, Toronto: Canadian Scholars' Press, pp 1–14.

Tornstam, L. (2005) *Gerotranscendence: A Developmental Theory of Positive Aging*, New York: Springer.

Torres-Gil, F. (2007) 'Translating research into program and policy changes', in Putnam, M. (ed) *Aging and Disability: Crossing Network Lines*, New York: Springer, pp 245–58.

Townsend, P. (1981a) 'Elderly people with disabilities', in Walker, A. and Townsend, P. (eds) *Disability in Britain: A Manifesto of Rights*, Oxford: Martin Robertson, pp 91–118.

Townsend, P. (1981b) 'The structured dependency of the elderly: a creation of social policy in the twentieth century', *Ageing and Society*, 1(1): 5–28.

Townsend, P. (2007) 'Using human rights to defeat ageism: dealing with policy-induced "structured dependency"', in Bernard, M. and Scharf, T. (eds) *Critical Perspectives on Ageing Societies*, Bristol: Policy Press, pp 27–44.

Travaglia, J. and Robertson, H. (2003) 'Diversity and the promotion of disability issues in the Australian health system', *Australian Journal of Communication*, 30(3).

Tregaskis, C. (2002) 'Social model theory: the story so far …', *Disability & Society*, 17(4): 457–70.

Tregaskis, C. (2004) *Constructions of Disability: Researching the Interface between Disabled and Non-disabled People*, London: Routledge.

Tulle, E. and Krekula, C. (2013) 'Ageing embodiment and the search for social change', *International Journal of Ageing and Later Life*, 8(1): 7–10.

Twigg, J. (2004) 'The body, gender, and age: feminist insights in social gerontology', *Journal of Aging Studies*, 18(1): 59–73.

Twigg, J. (2006) *The Body in Health and Social Care*, Basingstoke: Palgrave Macmillan.

Twigg, J. and Martin, W. (2015) 'The field of cultural gerontology: an introduction', in Twigg, J. and Martin, W. (eds) *Routledge Handbook of Cultural Gerontology*, Abingdon: Routledge, pp 1–15.

United Nations (2019) 'Report of the Special Rapporteur on the Rights of Persons with Disabilities', General Assembly 74th session. A/74/186.

United Nations Department of Economic and Social Affairs (2008) *Principles and Recommendations for Population and Housing Censuses, Revision 2, Statistical Papers*, Series M No 67/Rev.2, New York: United Nations.

United Nations General Assembly (2006) 'Final report of the Ad Hoc Committee on a Comprehensive and Integral International Convention on the Protection and Promotion of the Rights and Dignity of Persons with Disabilities', A/61/611.

United Nations Washington Group on Disability Statistics (2008) 'The measurement of disability recommendations for the 2010 round of censuses', United Nations. Available at: www.cdc.gov/nchs/data/washington_group/recommendations_for_disability_measurement.pdf

UPIAS (Union of the Physically Impaired Against Segregation) and The Disability Alliance (1976) Fundamental principles of disability: being a summary of the discussion held on 22nd November 1975. Available at: https://disability-studies.leeds.ac.uk/library/author/upias/

Vamstad, J. (2016) 'Exit, voice and indifference – older people as consumers of Swedish home care services', *Ageing & Society*, 36(10): 2163–81.

Van Campen, C. (2011) *Frail Older Persons in the Netherlands*, The Hague: Netherlands Institute for Social Research.

Van Eenoo, L., Declercq, A., van der Roest, H. and van Hout, H. (on behalf of the IBenC Consortium) (2014) *IBenC Review on the Structure of Community Care of the Six Participating Countries and their Benchmarking Practices*, Amsterdam: IBenC Consortium.

Vehmas, S. and Watson, N. (2014) 'Moral wrongs, disadvantages, and disability: a critique of critical disability studies', *Disability & Society*, 29(4): 638–50.

Vellas, B. (2016) 'Introduction', in Vellas, B., Cesari, M. and Jun, L. (eds) *The White Book on Frailty*, New York: International Association of Gerontology and Geriatrics, Global Aging Research Network.

Verbrugge, L.M. and Jette, A.M. (1994) 'The disablement process', *Social Science & Medicine*, 38(1): 1–14.

Verbrugge, L.M. and Yang, L. (2002) 'Aging with disability and disability with aging', *Journal of Disability Policy Studies*, 12(4): 253–67.

Verbrugge, L.M., Latham, K. and Clarke, P.J. (2017) 'Aging with disability for midlife and older adults', *Research on Aging*, 39(6): 741–77.

Wahl, H.-W. and Weisman, G.D. (2003) 'Environmental gerontology at the beginning of the new millennium: reflections on its historical, empirical, and theoretical development', *The Gerontologist*, 43(5): 616–27.

Wahl, H.-W., Fänge, A., Oswald, F., Gitlin, L.N. and Iwarsson, S. (2009) 'The home environment and disability-related outcomes in aging individuals: what is the empirical evidence?', *The Gerontologist*, 49(3): 355–67.

Wahl, H.-W., Iwarsson, S. and Oswald, F. (2012) 'Aging well and the environment: toward an integrative model and research agenda for the future', *The Gerontologist*, 52(3): 306–16.

Walker, A. (1981a) 'Disability rights and the progress of IYDP (International Year of Disabled People)', in Walker, A. and Townsend, P. (eds) *Disability in Britain: A Manifesto of Rights*, Oxford: Martin Robertson & Company, pp 1–16.

Walker, A. (1981b) 'Towards a political economy of old age', *Ageing and Society*, 1(1): 73–94.

Walker, A. (2002) 'A strategy for active ageing', *International Social Security Review*, 55(1): 121–39.

Walker, A. (2006) 'Active ageing in employment: its meaning and potential', *Asia-Pacific Review*, 13(1): 78–93.

Walker, A. (2014) 'Towards a new science of ageing', in Walker, A. (ed) *The New Science of Ageing*, Bristol: Policy Press, pp 1–23.

Walker, A. and Walker, C. (1998) 'Normalisation and "normal" ageing: the social construction of dependency among older people with learning difficulties', *Disability & Society*, 13(1): 125–42.

Wanka, A., Moulaert, T. and Drilling, M. (2018) 'From environmental stress to spatial expulsion – rethinking concepts of socio-spatial exclusion in later life', *International Journal of Ageing and Later Life*, 12(2): 25–51.

Warmoth, K., Lang, I.A., Phoenix, C., Abraham, C., Andrew, M.K., Hubbard, R.E. and Tarrant, M. (2016) '"Thinking you're old and frail": a qualitative study of frailty in older adults', *Ageing and Society*, 36(7): 1483–500.

Warner, D.F. and Adams, S.A. (2016) 'Physical disability and increased loneliness among married older adults: the role of changing social relations', *Society and Mental Health*, 6: 106–28.

Watson, N. (2002) 'Well, I know this is going to sound very strange to you, but I don't see myself as a disabled person: identity and disability', *Disability & Society*, 17(5): 509–27.

Watson, N. (2003) 'Daily denials: the routinisation of oppression and resistance', in Riddell, S. and Watson, N. (eds) *Disability, Culture and Identity*, Harlow: Pearson Education, pp 34–51.

Weiss, R.S. (1997) 'Adaptation to retirement', in Gotlib, I.H. and Wheaton, B. (eds) *Stress and Adversity over the Life Course*, Cambridge: Cambridge University Press, pp 232–48.

Weiss, R.S. and Bass, S.A. (2002) 'Introduction and epilogue', in Weiss, R.S. and Bass, S.A. (eds) *Challenges of the Third Age: Meaning and Purpose in Later Life*, Oxford: Oxford University Press, pp 3–12, 187–97.

Wendell, S. (1996) *The Rejected Body: Feminist Philosophical Reflections on Disability*, New York: Psychology Press.

Wengraf, T. (2001) *Qualitative Research Interviewing: Biographic Narrative and Semi-structured Methods*, London: Sage.

West, K. and Glynos, J. (2016) ' "Death talk", "loss talk" and identification in the process of ageing', *Ageing and Society*, 36(2): 225–39.

Westwood, S. and Carey, N. (2019) 'Ageing with physical disabilities and/or long-term health conditions', in Westwood, S. (ed) *Ageing, Diversity and Equality: Social Justice Perspectives*, Abingdon: Routledge, pp 225–44.

Wilde, A. (2010) 'Spectacle, performance, and the re-presentation of disability and impairment', *Review of Disability Studies: An International Journal*, 6(3).

Williams, S. (2000) 'Chronic illness as biographical disruption or biographical disruption as chronic illness? Reflections on a core concept', *Sociology of Health & Illness*, 22(1): 40–67.

Woodhouse, K.W., Wynne, H., Bailie, S., James, O.F.W. and Rawlins, M.D. (1988) 'Who are the frail elderly?', *Quarterly Journal of Medicine*, 68(1): 505–6.

Woolham, J., Daly, G., Sparks, T., Ritters, K. and Steils, N. (2017) 'Do direct payments improve outcomes for older people who receive social care? Differences in outcome between people aged 75+ who have a managed personal budget or a direct payment', *Ageing and Society*, 37(5): 961–84.

World Health Organization (2001) *International Classification of Functioning, Disability and Health*, Geneva: World Health Organization.

World Health Organization (2002a) *Active Ageing: a Policy Framework*, Geneva: World Health Organization.

World Health Organization (2002b) *Towards a Common Language for Functioning, Disability and Health. The International Classification of Functioning, Disability and Health*, Geneva: World Health Organization.

World Health Organization (2012) *Good Health Adds Life to Years: Global Brief for World Health Day 2012*, Geneva: World Health Organization.

World Health Organization (2015) *World Report on Aging and Health*, Geneva: World Health Organization.

World Health Organization and World Bank (2011) *World Report on Disability*, Geneva: World Health Organization.

Yoshizaki-Gibbons, H.M. (2019) 'Engaging with ageing: a call for the greying of critical disability studies', in Ellis, K., Garland-Thomson, R., Kent, M. and Robertson, R. (eds) *Manifestos for the Future of Critical Disability Studies*, London: Routledge, pp 179–88.

Yumiko, K., Murphy, C., Savva, G. and Timonen, V. (on Behalf of The Irish Longitudinal Study on Ageing Team) (2012) *Profile of Community-Dwelling Older People with Disability and Their Caregivers in Ireland*, Dublin: The Irish Longitudinal Study on Ageing.

Zarb, G. and Oliver, M. (1993) *Ageing with a Disability: What Do They Expect after All These Years?*, London: University of Greenwich.

Ziegler, F. and Scharf, T. (2014) 'Community-based participatory action research: opportunities and challenges for critical gerontology', in Baars, J., Dohmen, J., Grenier, A. and Phillipson, C. (eds) *Ageing, Meaning and Social Structure: Connecting Critical and Humanistic Gerontology*, Bristol: Policy Press, pp 157–80.

Zola, I.K. (1982) *Missing Pieces: A Chronicle of Living with a Disability*, Philadelphia, PA: Temple University Press.

Zola, I.K. (1989a) 'Aging and disability: toward a unified agenda', *Journal of Rehabilitation*, 55(4): 6–8.

Zola, I.K. (1989b) 'Toward the necessary universalizing of a disability policy', *The Millbank Quarterly*, 67(Supplement 2): 401–8.

Zola, I.K. (1991) 'Bringing our bodies and ourselves back in: reflections on a past, present and future "medical sociology"', *Journal of Health and Social Behavior*, 32: 1–16.

Index

A

Abberley, P., disability levels
  minimised 4, 167
ableism
  'compulsory able-bodiedness' 44–5,
    89, 169–70
  critical studies 43
  definition of 19, 39
  internalised 109, 117
  intersection with ageism 34, 108, 117
  and 'successful' ageing
    approaches 34, 44–5
ableist norms
  normative lifecourse built on 48
  and 'positive' ageing discourses 79, 95
  resistance to 113, 115, 118
'active' ageing approaches 30, 57, 58,
  89–90
activism see disability activism
activities
  loss of 87–9
  day centres addressing 136–8
  meaningful/purposeful 125,
    131, 141–2
activities of daily living (ADLs), as
  measure of disability 22
activity theory 30
AGE Platform Europe 56
ageing policies 57–9
ageing as a social construction see
  critical gerontology
ageism 34
  intersection with ableism 34, 108,
    117, 168
Amundson, R., 'age-frailty' versus
  'disability' 4
anticipated versus disruptive
  chronic illness as 47, 80–1
  disability onset as 75, 147–8
Applebaum, R., Medicaid funding of
  community-based services, US
  states 67
appliances
  access to 101–2
  and others' embarrassment 107–8
  using 112, 113
assistive technology 132
austerity measures, effects of 58–9, 60
Australia 60, 61, 65–6, 68

B

Baars, J., on 'meanings' 37–8, 87, 124,
  126, 172
Baltes, M.M., successful ageing
  model 31
Baltes, P.B., successful ageing model 31
Barnes, C., criticism of the ICF 20
Barnes, M., value of collective
  provision, undermining of 69
Bass, S.A., meaning in life 38
Baumeister, R.F., needs for meaning in
  life 122–3, 138, 139, 158
belonging, basic human need 123
Beresford, P., failure of personal budget
  strategy 60
Berghs, M., intersectionality 44, 169
Bernard, M., critical gerontology 32
Bigby, C., services for intellectually
  disabled older people in
  Australia 66, 68
'biographical disruption' 46–7, 80,
  91, 119
  and discrimination or ableist
    norms 106, 128
  anticipated
    chronic illness as 47, 80–1
    disability onset as 75, 147–8
  expanded version of, Larsson and
    Jeppsson Grassman 47, 81, 86,
    93, 119
  perception of less by people with
    lifelong disability 148–9
biographical narrative method 77,
  78, 177
biomedical definitions of disability in
  older age 22–3, 27
biopsychosocial (interactional)
  models 19–21, 26, 27–8
the body
  critical disability studies 41–2
  disabling bodies 82–95
  and identity 35–6
  material bodies 9, 27, 77, 171
bridging initiatives, disability and
  ageing policy frameworks 66–8,
  70, 174–5
budgets, personalised 59
  age as factor in eligibility criteria 61,
    62, 65
  common problems of service users 69

management of, UK 63
review of 64
Bülow, P., 'fourth age' coming early for some 147
Bury, M.
chronic illness as 'biographical disruption' 46, 80, 85, 86, 91, 93, 119, 122
ways of coping with chronic illness 80, 128–9
Butler, R.N., definition of ageism 34

C

Calasanti, T.M., body central to identity and ageing 35
Campbell, F.K.
ableist ideologies 95
intersectional analysis 43
Canada 55, 65
Carey, G., personalisation agenda in Australia 68
cash-for-care schemes (direct payments) 59, 61
'catastrophic' onset of disability, narratives of 82–5, 93
categories for grounded theory, coding of 78–9, 185–6
Charmaz, K.
grounded theory study 77, 177–8
'loss of self' in chronic illness 80
Chivers, S., older age and disability both constructed as bodily threatening 35, 36
chronic illness 46, 80–1
'chronologised body' 35
coherence (comprehensibility), need for 123, 131, 132, 158
community centres/groups, joining 135–8, 175–6
community living 67, 70
competence(s), need for 122, 123
'compulsory able-bodiedness' 44–5, 89, 169–70
'compulsory youthfulness', Gibbons 45, 108, 168
computers, access to/use of 132
conceptual models of disability 7–8, 17–21
connectedness
need for 123
ways of connecting with others 132–8
control
lack/loss of 56, 69, 82, 85, 86, 164
need for interpretive 85, 87, 123
over personal support 59
personalised budgets 59–60, 63–4

COVID-19 pandemic 2, 173–4
creative pursuits, beginning in later life 134
crip theory, McRuer 43–4
critical disability studies 19, 39–40
bodies 41–3
cultural representations 40
identity and multidimensionality 43–4
and intersectionality 44–5
relational issues 40–1
critical gerontology 32–3, 168, 170–1, 173
the body and identity 35–6
cultural representations 33–5
intersectionality 36
meaning in life 37–8
cultural disability studies see critical disability studies
cultural distancing 40–1
cultural representations of disability 32–3

D

Da Roit, B., cash-for-care schemes 59, 61
daily activities, meaningfulness of 132–3
data analysis 185–6
Davis, L.J.
challenging ideas of normalcy 43
identity politics 98
older people's (re)definition of disability 45, 52
day centres 112–13, 135–8, 140, 142
decline
cultural representations 33
and disablist exclusion 117
perception of 82–5
and 'positive' ageing 90, 94, 118, 164
decline ideology 88, 94–5, 109
dementia
and access to services 65
as 'disability' 8, 45, 71, 168–9
demographic change 5, 55, 70, 76
demographics of study participants 78, 182–5
dependency 44
fear of greater 85
negative imagery of 6–7
Derkx, P., 'needs for meaning' 123–4, 126, 139
direct payments 59, 61, 63, 64
disability activism 6–7
and disability identity 98, 157
and personalisation 59–60, 174
of study participants 111, 113–15, 118–19

disability definitions
  general approaches 17–21
  in older age 22–6
disability identity 43, 97–8
  and disability activism 6–7, 111, 114,
    118–19
  and meaning of experiences 156–7
  and non-identification related to
    policy schism 119
  study participants 111–15
  versus ageing identity 155–6
disability models 7–8, 17–21
  biopsychosocial 19–21, 26, 27–8
  social 7, 17–19, 39
disability prevalence 54–5
disability studies 38–9
  critical or cultural 39–40, 44–5
    bodies 41–3
    cultural representations 40
    identity 43
    multidimensionality 43–4
    relational issues 40–1
disability terminology 12
disablement process 11, 75, 76
  coping with 121
  experienced as 'a disruptive force' 92
  gradual experiences 83–4, 88–9
  integrating 141
disablism 40
  decline ideology buffering
    self-concept 109
  experiences of 117
  resistance to 11, 112, 113–14,
    115, 118
disengagement theory 30
disruption see biographical disruption
'double jeopardy' 84, 93, 145, 146, 156
driving, discontinuing, experienced as
    loss of freedom 87–8
Dannefer, D., formulation of human
    needs and interests 122

E

Edmondson, R., meaning in later
    life 37, 122, 124
efficacy, sense of, need for 123, 129,
    133, 135
Elder, G.H., Jr., lifecourse
    perspective 47, 49, 51, 99
eligibility issues 61, 63, 65, 68
embodied experiences 35, 42, 90–1,
    149–50, 170–1
environmental/external barriers 105–
    106, 114, 116, 150, 153–4
  experienced as social exclusion 106
environmental gerontology 25–6
ethical issues, research study 186

European Network on Independent
    Living 56, 61
everyday activities, investing with new
    meaning 132–3
everyday interactions, sociocultural
    meanings 107, 154–7
  exclusion, disability with ageing
    group 107–9
  inclusion, ageing with disability
    group 109–11
excitement, need for 123, 130
exclusion experiences
  caused by relational issues 40
  disability with ageing group 107–9
  due to physical environment 106,
    153, 175
external physical environments, barriers
    creating disability 105–6, 150

F

familial factors 151
  exclusion experiences 107–8
  lack of intimates increasing
    disability 100–1
  support from spouse reducing
    perception of disability 99–100
fear of death (non-disabled people)
  leading to cultural distancing 40–1
  projected onto disabled 40
fears of greater dependency 85–6,
    93, 129
Featherstone, M., 'mask of ageing' 35
Feely, M., critical disability studies 42
feminist scholarship 35, 169
  feminist care ethics 44, 59
  feminist disability theory 41–2
    and feminist gerontology field 36,
      42, 169
  intersectionality 43, 44
financial resources
  impact of low 105, 151–2
  minimising disability
    experiences 101–2, 105
Fine, M., 'care' and 'dependency'
    conflicts 44
finitude, awareness/sense of 82, 84,
    85–7, 88, 124
'fourth age' 8–9, 24–5, 37, 140–1
  challenges of, similar to 'third
    age' 132
  coming early to disabled people 147
  and continued wish to engage 90–
    1, 132
  and disablism 117
  see also decline
frailty 22–3
  critique of the concept of 23

experienced as both disruptive and
anticipated 93
fourth age often linked to 24
subjective accounts of 23
versus 'disability' 23
Fried, L.P., disability as possible
outcome of frailty 23
future goals/orientations 139–40

G

Gadsby, E.W., review of personal
budgets 64
Garland-Thomson, R
critical disability studies, inclusions
and exclusions 10
disability identity 6
universal engagement with disability
issues across the lifespan 45
gerontology
environmental 26
social 36, 47, 48, 49
see also critical gerontology
Gibbons, H.M.
'compulsory youthfulness'
concept 168
feminist disability studies versus
feminist gerontology 42
'successful' ageing approaches
ableist and ageist 45
limited intersectionality critiques 44
Gilleard, C.
call to document suffering by older
people 92
'social imaginary' 24
third age versus fourth date 24, 33
Glendinning, C., 'care' and
'dependency' conflicts 44
Goodley, D.
critique of ICF 20
disability and life values 51
disabled people driving theory 45
Grenier, A.
acknowledgement of fragility and
limitations 34, 172
challenge to lifecourse
perspective 49, 169
on 'fourth age' definition 52
on frailty 23
impairment as 'permanent state of
uncertainty' 147
transitions
to impairment 37
between models of health
and decline 6
to older age 3, 5
grounded theory 177–8

Grue, J., wide interests of disability
studies 46
Gubrium, J.F., lifecourse 48–9, 79
Gullette, M.M.
'decline ideology' 88, 94–5, 109
social attitudes to the appearance
of ageing 9

H

Hahn, H., minority group model,
US 19
health as a measure of success, focus
on 126–7
'healthy' ageing 30, 57
hearing impairment/loss
and environmental barriers 106
impact on social activities 84
lip-reading classes 114
Heikkinen, R.L., bodily changes
thwarting ability to find meaning
in life 132
Hepworth, M., 'mask of ageing' 35
heterogeneous experiences of ageing
with disability 91–2, 144–5
Higgs, P.
'social imaginary' 24
third age versus fourth date 24, 33
Holstein, J.A., lifecourse 48–9, 79
Holstein, M.B.
chronic illness and self-value 79–80
failure to notice 'real bodies' of older
people 36, 92
and meaning in life 37, 122
home care, marketisation of 58
home help 103, 104
homes, experienced as enabling or
disabling 104–5, 116, 153
Hosking, D.L., ICF consistent with
critical disability theory 20
human rights 7, 21, 42, 45, 56, 71
human vulnerability, fears of 94,
167, 172
humanist perspectives, meaning in
life 123, 165, 173

I

ICF (International Classification of
Functioning, Disability and Health),
WHO 20, 26
identity/identities
the body as central to 35
changes in self-identity and
biographical disruption 79–81
positive old age/ageing 36, 79
see also disability identity
impairment
definitions 12–13, 20

of chronic illness 80
double jeopardy of worsening 146–7
embodiment focus 42
and exclusion experiences 108
and the 'fourth age' 24–5
hearing 84, 106, 114
minimally experienced 149–50
paradox 94, 163
subjective 'improvement' with
age 110
types and severity 182–5
and UK social model of disability 18
visual 88–9, 100, 130–1, 132
impairment–disability
dichotomy 18, 19
inclusion
community centres for older people
and disabled 175–6
experienced by ageing with disability
group 109–11
independent living 56, 59, 61
examples 102, 152
'individualisation', policies on
ageing 57–9
individualised budgets/funding, disabled
people 59, 61, 63, 65, 68–9
inequalities
intersectional issues 36, 161, 169
in services and human rights 56–7
intensive interviewing 178
interactional (biopsychosocial)
models 19–21, 26, 27–8
interdependence 34, 44, 60, 123
international policy approaches 55–7
ageing policies 57–9
disability policies 59–60
interpretive approaches to
lifecourse 48–9
interpretive control 85, 87, 123
intersectionality 36, 43, 44, 169
interviews, research study 77, 78,
178, 181
intimates, effects of losing 100–
1, 127–8
Ireland 21, 62, 65

J

Jeppsson Grassman, E., expanded
version of biographical
'disruption' 47, 81, 86, 93, 119
Jönson, H., ableism in approaches to
ageing 34, 62

K

Kafer, A.
anxiety about ageing and compulsory
able-bodiedness 44–5, 169
group most difficult to include
in disability scholarship/
activism 6, 50
illness and disability are part of what
makes us human 41, 91
unrecognised value of disability
futures 41, 50, 91, 169–70
Kahana, J.S. and Kahana, E.
lifecourse approaches that validate
people living with illness and
disability 49, 169
meaning in older age 37
older people, need for a social model
of support 71
understandings of disability in older
age 8, 50
Kahn, R.L., 'successful' ageing
definition 31
Kelley-Moore, J.A.
frailty's social origins 23
social construction of disability 32
Kelly, C., disability activism 60, 69,
174

L

Laceulle, H., self-realisation and search
for meaning in life 33, 141, 222
Lamb, E.G. need for links between
ageing and disability fields 4,
45, 167
Larsson, A.T., expanded version of
biographical 'disruption' 47, 81,
86, 93, 119
Laslett, P., third age versus fourth
age 24
Lawton, M.P., influence of
environment on optimal level of
functioning 25
Le Bihan, B., cash-for-care
schemes 59, 61
lifecourse perspective 47–50, 51
chronic illness viewed from 80–1
limitations of study 186–7
Lin, J., formulation of human needs and
interests 122
Lloyd, A., frailty 81, 93
Lloyd, L.
'fourth age' identity and debate 25,
52, 79, 141
'moral pressure' of active ageing
approaches 58
personalisation agenda
limiting costs of ageing
population 60
questionable assumptions
underlying 59

M

Mahoney, K., Medicaid funding of community-based services, US states 67
marketisation of home care, Sweden 58
Marshall, B.L., ableism in 'successful ageing' 34, 170
material bodies 9, 27, 77, 171
materialism/materialist perspective social model of disability 39
McGrath. C.
  critical disability theory 34
  'successful' ageing inadvertently reinforcing stigma 31
McRuer, R., crip theory 43–4
meaning in life 122
  challenges to 127–9, 140
    responding to 129–35
  critical gerontology 37–8, 124–5
  and current study 126–7
  and disability experiences 125–6
  versus meaning 'of' life 122
  and needs for meaning 122–4, 139
medical model
  applied to ageing 5, 6, 8, 50
  critiques of 9
  of disability 18, 20, 25
medical sociology 46–7
medicalised approaches 22–3
Mercer, G., criticism of the ICF 20
methodology 77–8, 177–8
Minkler, M., failure to notice 'real bodies' of older people 36, 92
Mitchell, D.T., disability representations 40
mobility issues 105, 179, 182–3
  rollators/walkers 108–109, 112–13, 134, 153
  wheelchair use 103–4, 106, 108–9, 114, 148, 149–50, 153
mobility scooters 105, 113, 114
moral economy perspective 32–3
moral worth/self-worth 123, 124, 129, 135, 158
Morell, C.M., the 'rejected body' 36, 169
Morris, J., relational issues 40
multidimensionality concept, critical disability theory 43

N

Nagi, S.Z., North America, 'disability' as failure to accommodate disability 19
Nahemow, L., influence of environment on optimal level of functioning 25

needs and meaning in life 122–4, 139
Nordic relational model 19
normal crisis, chronic illness viewed as 80–1
normalcy, rejection of exclusive, Davis 43, 115, 157
'normalisation' 109, 137, 155, 156
normative lifecourse 48, 159–60, 165–6
North American minority identity model of disability 19

O

Oliver, M.
  medical model as, 'the personal tragedy theory of disability' 18
  three elements to a disability identity 97–8
oppression experienced by disabled people
  relational issues causing 40
  shared experiences of 98, 119
  shared resistance to 43
  social model of disability 18, 19, 39, 106, 116, 153
    criticism of, Bury 46
'othering' of disabled people 40, 112–13
  and the 'fourth age' 24–5
  within families 107–8

P

paradoxes 3–5, 163
participation opportunities 133–5
  community groups 135–8
  exclusion from 116–17
  loss of 87–9, 127–8, 129, 130
perception
  of being 'othered' or excluded 107–8
  of 'decline' or 'catastrophe' 82–5
  of disability, others reducing 99–100
personal assistance
  ability to purchase 102
  eligibility criteria 61, 62
  inconsistencies in access to 102
  lack of 103–4
personalisation
  disabled people 59–60
  older people 58–9, 63–4
Phillipson, C. 32
  ageing and needs for meaning 124
  austerity cuts, effects on older people 58–9
  neoliberalism and alternatives to 70–1
physical environments
  environmental gerontology 25–6

experiencing as enabling or
disabling 104–6
political economy approach 32
political movements 6–7
population ageing 54, 55, 60, 62, 176
'positive' ageing discourses
disability and age no bar to identifying
with 89–91, 94
policies 57–8
see also 'successful' ageing
postmodernist thinking 35, 43, 98
post-structuralist perspectives 18,
35, 43
prevalence of disability 54–5
Priestley, M.
cultural distancing of older and
disabled people 40–1
lifecourse perspective,
disability 47, 169
public policies 5–6, 53–4
ageing policies 57–9
bridging ageing and disability
policies 66–8, 174–5
disability policies 59–60
and disability prevalence 54–5
human rights 21, 56, 71
international approaches 55–60
'personalisation' issues 64, 68–9
separate policy frameworks, issues
arising from 60–6
public services, experiences of care and
support 101–4, 151–3
public transport, barriers to
accessing 105, 106, 114, 116
purpose, sense of, need for 122–3, 124,
139–40
Putnam, M.
high priority of bridging
research 70, 175
lack of integration between ageing
and disability fields 57
problems of separate policy
frameworks 61
professional perceptions and policy
regulations 67

Q

queer and disability studies, merging
of 43–4

R

'real bodies' of older people, failure to
notice 36, 92
recruitment criteria, study
participants 78, 179–82
'rejected body', Wendell 36, 41, 169
relatedness *see* connectedness

Rembis, M., need for 'new theories of
disability oppression' 42
research questions of study 11, 76
grounded theory addressing 177–8
resistance to disablism 11, 112, 113–14,
115, 118
Riddell, S., disabled people as
'ordinary people' despite cultural
representations 125
rollators
associated with embarrassment
108–9, 112–13
environmental barriers to
using 134, 153
Rowe, J.W., definition of 'successful'
ageing 31

S

Sandberg, L.J., ableism in 'successful
ageing' 34, 170
Scharf, T., critical gerontology 32
'second-class citizens', disabled people
treated as 114, 116
self-advocacy movement, Sweden 56
self-development goals 121, 138, 140,
159, 161
self-identity, changes in 79–81
self-imposed restrictions, disabled
people 154–5
self-realisation aspirations 33, 37, 91,
94, 121, 124, 141
self-worth 123, 129, 132, 134,
135, 158
separate policies on ageing and
disability 3–4, 5, 50, 53, 55–7
consequences of
for people ageing with
disability 64–6
for people experiencing disability
with ageing 61–4
services/support, access to 58, 61, 102,
105, 132
Shakespeare, T.
bodies *and* society disable
people 28, 76
critical realist perspective 51
dementia as disability 45, 71
embodiment research, need
for 42, 170
experiences of 'disruption' and
structural issues 119
on the ICF 20–1
impairment experienced by everyone
across the lifespan 42, 170
Siebers, T.
able-bodiedness is a 'temporary
identity' 4, 45

ableism 89, 167
  disability identity based on shared
    experiences 43, 98, 119, 157
  ideology of ability 79, 89
  notion of 'complex embodiment' 77
  people's fear of disabled body 42
Slasberg, C., failure of personal budget
    strategy 60
Slevin, K.F., body 'central to identity
    and to aging' 35
Snyder, S.L., representations of
    disability 40
social care model, advocacy 56
social care resources, cuts in 58–9, 60,
    70, 71
social construction
  of ageing, critical gerontology 32–8
  of disability 38–45
social exclusion see
    exclusion experiences
social gerontology, lifecourse
    perspective 47–50
social interactions
  community groups allowing 135–8
  and exclusion experiences 117
  need for connectedness 123, 129
  participation opportunities 133–5
social models of disability 7, 17–19, 39
social networks, reduction of 87, 101,
    116, 158, 175
social theories of ageing 29–30
  activity theory 30
  ageing as a social construction 32–3
  cultural representations of ageing 33
  disengagement theory 30
  'successful' ageing 31
sociocultural meanings in everyday
    interactions 107–11, 154–7
socio-economic status (SES) of study
    participants 185
spouses
  loss of 127, 129
  support from, reducing perception of
    disability 99–100
stigmatisation
  of disabled people 40
  negative stereotypes of oldness 31
  and 'successful' ageing ideals 33
subjectivity of researcher, grounded
    theory 177
'successful' ageing 31
  and ableism 34, 44–5
  critiques of 33, 57–8, 170
  factors considered important for 31
  goals promoted by 138

support
  differing experiences of public 151–2
  experience of as enabling or
    disabling 101–4
  from spouses, reducing perception of
    disability 99–100
supported-living accommodation 102–3
Svensson, T., earlier 'fourth age' 147
Sweden 56, 58, 62

T

technology, use of 132
terminology 12–13
terror management theory, ageism 34
Tesch-Römer, C., 'successful'
    ageing 31
theoretical approaches 8–10
  ageing: social theories 29–38
  background to the study 79–81
  disability scholarship 38–45
  lifecourse perspective 47–9
  meaning in life 37–8, 122–7
'third age'
  versus 'fourth age' 8–9, 131–2
  and meaning in life 38, 125
  and positive ageing discourses 33, 90
  and transition to 'fourth' age 24
Thomas, C.
  dementia diagnosis linking ageism and
    disablism 169
  social relational approach to
    disability 18, 27, 40, 77
  psycho-emotional disablism 40,
    107, 154
Thompson, P.
  greatest threat to meaning faced in
    older age 125
  loss of intimates as significant
    challenge in later life 127
Timonen, V., and 'positive ageing 90
Tornstam, L., gerotranscendence 37
transcendence
  as needs for moral worth,
    connectedness and
    excitement 123–4
  older age as a time of 37
transitions 3, 48
  ageing with disability 160
  impairment in later life 49, 50
  retirement 3, 48, 49, 150
  widowhood 30, 49
Twigg, J.
  modern secular culture's silence on
    death 50
  older bodies 9, 35, 41

U

UK
  disability activists 59
  managed/personal budgets 63, 64
    failure of 60
  resource and service cuts 60
  social model 17–18
    and disability in older age 39
    impairment–disability
      distinction 19, 150
    materialism 39
UN Convention on the Rights of
    Persons with Disabilities 13, 21,
    71, 76, 172
UN Special Rapporteur on the Rights
    of Persons with Disabilities
    56–7, 71
uncertainty, increasing sense of 85–6
USA
  disability activists 59–60
  independent living movement 56
  nursing home care versus community-
    based support 66–7
  prevalence of disability 55
  social model of disability 19

V

Vamstad, J., marketisation of home care,
    Sweden 58
Vehmas, S., impairments 42
Verbrugge, L.M., persistent disability
    over time 146
visual impairment
  effect on activities 88–9, 130–1,
    132, 149
  and reliance on help of spouse 100

W

Wahl, H.- W., 'successful' ageing 31
Walker, A. and Walker, C., ageist
    orientation of care services 62–3
Watson, N.
  disabling social relations creating
    disablism 40

experiences of 'disruption' and
    structural issues 119
impairment as universal experience of
    humanity 42
meaning and cultural representations
    of disability 125
Weiss, R.S., meaning in life 38, 125
Wendell, S.
  disabling effects of impairment 18
  the 'rejected body' 36, 41, 169
West, K. and Glynos, J.
  consideration of death and dying 168
  negative evaluations of 'fourth age' 25
  third age fear projected onto 'fourth
    age' 34–5
wheelchair use 103–4, 106, 108–9,
    148, 149–50
  environmental barriers to
    using 114, 153
White Book on Frailty (Vellas) 23
WHO (World Health Organization)
  biopsychosocial definition of
    disability, the ICF 19–20
  World Report on Disability 20, 21, 54
Williams, S., chronic illness as
    biographically anticipated 47,
    80–1, 149
worth, self- or moral, need for 123,
    129, 134, 135, 139, 158

Y

Yoshizaki-Gibbons, H.M., call for
    critical disability and ageing studies
    to engage 45, 167

Z

Zola, I.K.
  activism leading to reinterpretation of
    bodily experiences 95
  denial deprives society of knowledge
    of disability 3
  unified agenda on disability and
    ageing 10